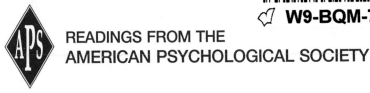

READINGS FROM THE
AMERICAN PSYCHOLOGICAL SOCIETY

Current
Directions
in
DEVELOPMENTAL
PSYCHOLOGY

EDITED BY
Jacqueline Lerner and Amy E. Alberts

PEARSON

Prentice
Hall

Upper Saddle River, New Jersey 07458

ISBN 0-13-189581-8

Printed in the United States of America

Contents

Biology:
Genetics and Neuroscience

In the various fields of scientific psychology, there has been a significant amount of attention paid to recent advances in biology, neuroscience and genetics. More specifically, modern science has allowed for a more in-depth examination of the role of genes and brain structure and function in behavioral development. For example, results of studies using gene mapping have led to the widespread acceptance that nearly all behavioral variation reflects some genetic influence. In addition, advances in neuroscience have increased our understanding of the relations between the brain and cognitive, emotional and behavioral development.

The articles in this section represent some of the most recent findings from biology, neuroscience, and genetics, and together show that the combined influences of both biology and environment on behavior and development are complex. In the article by Danielle Dick and Richard Rose, we see how new research designs are allowing for the exploration of the developmental changes in the nature and magnitude of genetic and environmental effects. These new approaches can also help to shed light on the extent to which different behaviors are influenced by common genes, as well as different forms of gene-environment correlation and interaction. The authors also present their view of how the integration of behavioral and molecular genetics will enhance our knowledge of behavioral variation in the future.

In the article by Brian Kolb, Robin Gibb and Terry Robinson, a new view of the organization of the brain is presented. While we have been aware that the brain shows plasticity (changing constantly as a function of experience), recent research shows that both brain plasticity and behavior can be influenced by a variety of both prenatal and postnatal factors. Drugs, hormones, diet, stress and aging are only some of the factors that can influence brain organization and lead to changes in behavior and development. This new research will not only provide a deeper understanding of development, but will also inform prevention and treatment efforts.

In the article by John Columbo, we are introduced to the recent changes in the study of attention in infancy. Attention has been regarded as a major tool for studying the development of cognitive skills in infancy and early childhood, and had been guided by comparator theory (i.e. simple encoding). However, more recent integrations of the theory and methods involved in the study of attention with models in the field of cognitive neuroscience have led to important implications for this area. Researchers in cognitive neuroscience use both behavioral and cardiac indices of attention or adapt tasks that have been shown with adults to be associated with the brain pathways that control or mediate attention.

Using a similar approach, Columbo and his colleagues were able to better understand variations in infant attention (more specifically, infant looking) as being linked to the maturation of lower-order visual pathways. Columbo asserts that much of the extant research may need to be interpreted within a new framework that relies on a cognitive neuroscience approach.

In the last article by Linda Patia Spear, the link between adolescent characteristics and brain changes is discussed. Some typical behaviors of the adolescent period (increased risk-taking, for example) have been thought to be influenced by the hormonal changes of puberty. New brain research is emerging that elucidates the link between the alterations in the prefrontal cortex during adolescence and behavior. Specifically, the adolescent brain undergoes a transformation in the limbic brain areas and their dopamine input—systems that are sensitive to stressors. These systems also form part of the neural circuitry that modulates the motivational value of drugs and other reinforcing stimuli. This research has led to a recognition that the brain of the adolescent is markedly different from the younger or adult brain, and therefore the behaviors that are specific to adolescents are not surprising. This avenue of research can lead to important insights into the factors that precipitate and maintain both adolescent and adult drug and alcohol use. Overall, multidisciplinary research efforts need to be undertaken in controlled settings for a true understanding of the brain/behavior link.

Taken together, these articles make it clear that the fields of biology, genetics and neuroscience are critical in informing scientists and should be integrated into future research in developmental psychology.

Behavior Genetics: What's New? What's Next?

Danielle M. Dick and Richard J. Rose[1]

Department of Psychology, Indiana University, Bloomington, Indiana

Abstract

What's new in behavior genetics? With widespread acceptance that nearly all behavioral variation reflects some genetic influence, current studies are investigating developmental changes in the nature and magnitude of genetic and environmental effects, the extent to which different behaviors are influenced by common genes, and different forms of gene-environment correlation and interaction. New designs, focused on assessment of unrelated children in the same households or neighborhood environments, and use of measured environmental variables within genetically informative designs, are yielding more incisive evidence of common environmental effects on behavior. What will be next? Behavior genetic techniques and analyses will be used to inform efforts to find genes altering susceptibility for disorder and dispositional genes affecting behavioral variation. The developing integration of behavioral and molecular genetics will identify genes influencing specific behavioral variation and enhance understanding of how they do so. Psychologists will play a pivotal role in communicating that understanding to the public and in facilitating consideration of the inevitable ethical issues then to be confronted.

Keywords

behavior genetics; molecular genetics; development; gene-environment interaction

Through most of its brief history, behavior genetics had a single and simple goal: to demonstrate that some of the variation in behavior is attributable to genetic variance. Now, a diverse array of behaviors has been investigated with twin and adoption designs, yielding evidence that genetic variation contributes to individual differences in virtually all behavioral domains (McGuffin, Riley, & Plomin, 2001). Is behavior genetics, then, a thing of the past, a field whose success makes it obsolete? Not at all: Never has behavior genetic research held more promise. Investigators now possess analytic tools to move from estimating latent, unmeasured sources of variance to specifying the genes and environments involved in behavioral development, and the ways in which they interact. Our modest aim in this essay is to describe the questions now asked by behavior geneticists and to sketch the role that the field will assume in the merging era of behavioral genomics.

A DEVELOPMENTAL PERSPECTIVE

Traditional behavior genetic analyses divide observed behavioral variance into three unobserved (latent) sources: variance attributable to genetic effects, that due to environmental influences shared by siblings (e.g., family structure and status), and that arising in unshared environmental experience that makes siblings differ from one another. Estimates of the magnitude of these genetic and environmental effects are usually obtained from statistical path models that compare identical twins, who share all their genes, with fraternal twins, who like ordinary siblings, on average, share one half their genes. Behavior genetic research now identifies developmental changes in the importance of genetic dispositions and environmental contexts in accounting for individual differences in behavior. Such changes can be dramatic and rapid. For example, we assessed substance use in a sample of adolescent Finnish twins on three occasions from ages 16 to 18 1/2; we found that genetic contributions to individual differences in drinking frequency increased over time, accounting for only a third of the variation at age 16, but half of it just 30 months later (Rose, Dick, Viken, & Kaprio, 2001). Concurrently, the effects of sharing a common environment decreased in importance. Interestingly, parallel analyses of smoking found little change in the importance of genetic and environmental effects, illustrating the trait-specificity of gene-environment dynamics: Some effects are stable across a developmental period; others change.

DIFFERENT BEHAVIORS, SAME GENES?

It is well known that certain behaviors tend to co-occur, as do certain disorders, but the causes of such covariance are much less understood. Behavior genetic models assess the degree to which covariation of different disorders or behaviors is due to common genetic influences, common environmental influences, or both. An example can be found in the significant, albeit modest, correlations observed between perceptual speed (the minimum time required to make a perceptual discrimination, as assessed with computer display methods) and standard IQ test scores (Posthuma, de Geus, & Boomsma, in press); those correlations were found to be due entirely to a common genetic factor, hypothesized to reflect genetic influences on neural transmission. Another example is found in our study of behavioral covariance between smoking and drinking during adolescence. Genes contributing to the age when teens started smoking and drinking correlated nearly 1.0 (suggesting that the same genes influence an adolescent's decision to begin smoking and to begin drinking), but once smoking or drinking was initiated, genes influencing the frequency with which an adolescent smoked or drank were quite substance-specific, correlating only about .25.

GENE-ENVIRONMENT INTERACTION AND CORRELATION

The interaction of genes and environments has been difficult to demonstrate in human behavioral data, despite consensus that interaction must be ubiquitous. New behavior genetic methods are demonstrating what was long assumed. These methods use information from twins who vary in specified environmental exposure to test directly for the differential expression of genes across different environments. For example, genetic effects played a larger role in the use of alcohol among twin women who had been reared in nonreligious households than among those who had been reared in religious households (Koopmans, Slutske, van Baal, & Boomsma, 1999). Similarly, we found greater genetic effects on adolescent alcohol use among Finnish twins living in urban environments than among those living in rural environments (Rose, Dick, et al., 2001).

These demonstrations of gene-environment interaction used simple dichotomies of environmental measures. But subsequently, we explored underlying processes in the interaction effect of urban versus rural environments by employing new statistical techniques to accommodate more continuous measures of the characteristics of the municipalities in which the Finnish twins resided. We hypothesized that communities spending relatively more money on alcohol allow for greater access to it, and communities with proportionately more young adults offer more role models for adolescent twins, and that either kind of community enhances expression of individual differences in genetic predispositions. And that is what we found: up to a 5-fold difference in the importance of genetic effects among twins residing in communities at these environmental extremes (Dick, Rose, Viken, Kaprio, & Koskenvuo, 2001), suggesting that the influence of genetic dispositions can be altered dramatically by environmental variation across communities.

Analysis of gene-environment interaction is complemented by tests of gene-environment correlation. Individuals' genomes interact with the environmental contexts in which the individuals live their lives, but this process is not a passive one, for genetic dispositions lead a person to select, and indeed create, his or her environments. Perhaps the most salient environment for an adolescent is found in the adolescent's peer relationships. In a study of 1,150 sixth-grade Finnish twins, we (Rose, in press) obtained evidence that they actively selected their friends from among their classmates. This result is consistent with the inference that people's genetic dispositions play some role in their selection of friends. People like other people who are like themselves, and genetically identical co-twins make highly similar friendship selections among their classmates.

MEASURING EFFECTS OF THE ENVIRONMENT IN GENETICALLY INFORMATIVE DESIGNS

In traditional behavior genetic designs, environmental influences were modeled, but not measured. Environmental effects were inferred from latent models fit to data. Such designs understandably received much criticism. Now behavior geneticists can incorporate specific environmental measures into genetically informative designs and, by doing so, are demonstrating environmental effects that latent models failed to detect. Thus, we have studied effects of parental monitoring and home atmosphere on behavior problems in 11- to 12-year-old Finnish twins; both parental monitoring and home atmosphere contributed significantly to the development of the children's behavior problems, accounting for 2 to 5% of the total variation, and as much as 15% of the total common environmental effect. Recent research in the United Kingdom found neighborhood deprivation influenced behavior problems, too, accounting for about 5% of the effect of shared environment. Incorporation of specific, measured environments into genetically informative designs offers a powerful technique to study and specify environmental effects.

In other work, new research designs have been used to directly assess environmental effects in studies of unrelated children reared in a common neighborhood or within the same home. We have investigated neighborhood environmental effects on behavior in a large sample of 11- to 12-year-old same-sex Finnish twins. For each twin, we included a control classmate of the same gender and similar age, thus enabling us to compare three kinds of dyads: co-twins, each twin and his or her control classmate, and the two control classmates for each pair of co-twins. These twin-classmate dyads were sampled from more than 500 classrooms throughout Finland. The members of each dyad shared the same neighborhood, school, and classroom, but only the co-twin dyads shared genes and common household experience. For some behaviors, including early onset of smoking and drinking, we found significant correlations for both control-twin and control-control dyads; fitting models to the double-dyads formed by twins and their controls documented significant contributions to behavioral variation from nonfamilial environments—schools, neighborhoods, and communities (Rose, Viken, Dick, Pulkkinen, & Kaprio, 2001).

A complementary study examined genetically unrelated siblings who were no more than 9 months apart in age and who had been reared together from infancy in the same household. An IQ correlation of .29 was reported for 50 such dyads, and in another analysis, 40 of these dyads were only slightly less alike than fraternal co-twins on a variety of parent-rated behaviors (Segal, 1999). Clearly, appropriate research designs can demonstrate effects of familial and extrafamilial environmental variation for some behavioral outcomes at specific ages of development.

INTEGRATING BEHAVIOR AND MOLECULAR GENETICS[2]

Where do the statistical path models of behavior geneticists fit into the emerging era of behavioral genomics (the application of molecular genetics to behavior)? In the same way that specific, measured environments can be incorporated into behavior genetic models, specific information about genotypes can be included, as well, to test the importance of individual genes on behavior. Additionally, the kinds of behavior genetic analyses we have described can be informative in designing studies that maximize the power to detect susceptibility genes. Many efforts to replicate studies identifying genes that influence clinically defined diagnoses have failed. Those failures have stimulated the study of alternatives to diagnoses. When several traits are influenced by the same gene (or genes), that information can be used to redefine (or refine) alternatives to study, to enhance gene detection. For example, because heavy smoking and drinking frequently co-occurred in the Collaborative Study of the Genetics of Alcoholism sample, combined smoking and alcohol dependence was studied (Beirut et al., 2000). The combined dependency yielded greater evidence of linkage with a chromosomal region than did either tobacco dependence or alcohol dependence alone.

This approach is not limited to co-occurring behavioral disorders. It applies to normative behavioral differences, as well: A multidisciplinary international collaboration (Wright et al., 2001) has initiated a study of covariation among traditional and experimental measures of cognitive ability and will employ the correlated measures, once found, in subsequent molecular genetic analyses. And in a complementary way, behavior genetic methods can be useful to identify behavioral outcomes that are highly heritable, because these outcomes are most likely informative for genetic studies: When the definition of major depression was broadened, genetic factors assumed a larger role in women's susceptibility to this disorder (Kendler, Gardner, Neale, & Prescott, 2001), and, interestingly, this broader definition of depression suggested that somewhat different genes may influence depression in men and women.

A second strategy to enhance the power of molecular genetic analyses is to more accurately characterize trait-relevant environmental factors and also incorporate them more accurately in the analyses. In searching for genes, traditional genetic research effectively ignored the interplay of genetic and environmental influences in behavioral and psychiatric traits. Now, new analytic methods are being developed to incorporate environmental information better (Mosley, Conti, Elston, & Witte, 2000). But which specific environmental information is pertinent to a particular disorder? And how does a specific risk-relevant environment interact with genetic dispositions? Behavioral scientists trained in the methods of behavior genetics will play a key role in answering these questions.

BEYOND FINDING GENES

The traditional endpoint for geneticists is finding the gene (or genes) involved in a behavior or disorder. At that point, psychologists should become instrumental in using this genetic information. Applying genetic research on complex disorders to clinical practice will be complicated, because gene-behavior correlations will be modest and nonspecific, altering risk, but rarely determining outcome. Genes confer dispositions, not destinies. Research examining how risk and protective factors interact with genetic predispositions is critical for understanding the development of disorders and for providing information to vulnerable individuals and their family members. Far from ousting traditional psychological intervention, advances in genetics offer opportunities to develop interventions tailored to individual risks in the context of individual lifestyles. Enhanced understanding of the interactions between genetic vulnerabilities and environmental variables may dispel public misconceptions about the nature of genetics and correct erroneous beliefs about genetic determinism. Informed psychologists can play a vital role in disseminating the benefits of genetic research to families whose members experience behavioral and psychiatric disorders, and to the public in general.

CONCLUSIONS

Research questions now addressed by behavior geneticists have grown dramatically in scope: The questions have expanded into developmental psychology and sociology, as researchers have employed measures of the home and community, and utilized longitudinal designs. And behavior geneticists now study the effect of measured genotypes, a study traditionally left to geneticists. These developments create new and compelling research questions and raise new challenges. One such challenge is in addressing the complexity of behavioral development despite current reliance on methods that largely assume additive, linear effects. People who appreciate the complex, interactive, and unsystematic effects

7

underlying behavioral development may be skeptical that the genomic era will profoundly advance understanding of behavior. But there is a preliminary illustration that advance will occur, even within the constraints of additive models: the identification of a gene (ApoE) that increases risk for Alzheimer's disease, and the interaction of that gene with head trauma (Mayeux et al., 1995). Further, new analytic techniques are being developed to analyze simultaneously hundreds of genes and environments in attempts to understand how gene-gene and gene-environment interactions contribute to outcome (Moore & Hahn, 2000). These techniques are beginning to capture the systems-theory approach long advocated by many researchers as an alternative to linear additive models.

This is not to deny that unresolved problems remain. For example, we are enthusiastic about including measured environmental information in genetic research designs, but we note, with disappointment, that the magnitude of shared environmental effects detected to date has been modest. Equally disappointing are the results of recent research efforts to specify nonshared environmental effects (Turkheimer & Waldron, 2000). Such findings underscore a problem acutely evident in contemporary behavior genetics: an imperative need for better measures of trait-relevant environments. Now that researchers have tools to search for measured environmental effects, what aspects of the environment should they measure—and with what yardsticks? These are questions that psychologists are uniquely positioned to address.

Another set of challenging questions will arise from the ethical, legal, and social issues to be confronted once genes conferring susceptibility to disorders are identified. How should information about the nature and meaning of susceptibility genes be conveyed to the media, the public, and the courts? How can erroneous beliefs about genetic determinism be dispelled effectively? Such issues will be even more salient once dispositional genes for normal behavioral variation are identified: Ethical issues surrounding prevention of behavioral disorders are undeniably complex, but surely they are less so than the ethical issues surrounding enhancement of selected behavioral traits.

Results from the first phase of behavior genetics research convincingly demonstrated that genes influence behavioral development. In the next phase, that of behavioral genomics, psychologists will begin to identify specific genes that exert such influence, seek understanding of how they do so, and accept the challenge to interpret that understanding to the public.

Recommended Reading

The Human Genome [Special issue]. (2001, February 16), *Science, 291.*
Rutter, M., Pickles, A., Murray, R., & Eaves, L. (2001). Testing hypotheses on specific environmental causal effects on behavior. *Psychological Bulletin, 127,* 291–324.
Turkheimer, E. (1998). Heritability and biological explanation. *Psychological Review, 105,* 782–791.

Acknowledgments—We gratefully acknowledge the contributions of Lea Pulkkinen, Jaakko Kaprio, Markku Koskenvuo, and Rick Viken to FinnTwin research, and support from the National Institute on Alcohol Abuse and Alcoholism (AA00145, AA09203, and

AA08315) awarded to R.J.R. Manuscript preparation was supported by the Indiana Alcohol Research Center (AA07611) and by a National Science Foundation Pre-Doctoral Fellowship awarded to D.M.D.

Notes

1. Address correspondence to Richard Rose, Indiana University, Department of Psychology, 1101 East 10th St., Bloomington, IN 47405.

2. We use the term molecular genetics broadly to include statistical genetic techniques that test for gene-behavior associations.

References

Beirut, L., Rice, J., Goate, A., Foroud, T., Edenberg, H., Crowe, R., Hesselbrock, V., Li, T.K., Nurnberger, J., Porjesz, B., Schuckit, M., Begleiter, H., & Reich, T. (2000). Common and specific factors in the familial transmission of substance dependence. *American Journal of Medical Genetics, 96*, 459.

Dick, D.M., Rose, R.J., Viken, R.J., Kaprio, J., & Koskenvuo, M. (2001). Exploring gene-environment interactions: Socio-regional moderation of alcohol use. *Journal of Abnormal Psychology, 110*, 625–632.

Kendler, K.S., Gardner, C.O., Neale, M.C., & Prescott, C.A. (2001). Genetic risk factors for major depression in men and women: Similar or different heritabilities and same or partly distinct genes? *Psychological Medicine, 31*, 605–616.

Koopmans, J.R., Slutske, W.S., van Baal, G.C.M., & Boomsma, D.I. (1999). The influence of religion on alcohol use initiation: Evidence for genotype x environment interaction. *Behavior Genetics, 29*, 445–453.

Mayeux, R., Ottman, R., Maestre, G., Ngai, C., Tang, M.X., Ginsberg, H., Chun, M., Tycko, B., & Shelanski, M. (1995). Synergistic effects of traumatic head injury and apolipoprotein-E4 in patients with Alzheimer's disease. *Neurology, 45*, 555–557.

McGuffin, P., Riley, B., & Plomin, R. (2001). Toward behavioral genomics. *Science, 291*, 1232–1249.

Moore, J.H., & Hahn, L.W. (2000). A cellular automata approach to identifying gene-gene and gene-environment interactions. *American Journal of Medical Genetics, 96*, 486–487.

Mosley, J., Conti, D.V., Elston, R.C., & Witte, J.S. (2000). Impact of preadjusting a quantitative phenotype prior to sib-pair linkage analysis when gene-environment interaction exists. *Genetic Epidemiology, 21*(Suppl. 1), S837–S842.

Posthuma, D., de Geus, E.J.C., & Boomsma, D.I. (in press). Perceptual speed and IQ are associated through common genetic factors. *Behavior Genetics*.

Rose, R.J. (in press). How do adolescents select their friends? A behavior-genetic perspective. In L. Pulkkinen & A. Caspi (Eds.), *Paths to successful development*. Cambridge, England: Cambridge University Press.

Rose, R.J., Dick, D.M., Viken, R.J., & Kaprio, J. (2001). Gene-environment interaction in patterns of adolescent drinking: Regional residency moderates longitudinal influences on alcohol use. *Alcoholism: Clinical and Experimental Research, 25*, 637–643.

Rose, R.J., Viken, R.J., Dick, D.M., Pulkkinen, L., & Kaprio, J. (2001, July). *Shared environmental effects on behavior: Distinguishing familial from non-familial sources with data from twins and their classmate controls*. Paper presented at the annual meeting of the Behavior Genetics Association, Cambridge, England.

Segal, N.L. (1999). *Entwined lives*. New York: Penguin Putnam.

Turkheimer, E., & Waldron, M. (2000). Nonshared environment: A theoretical, methodological, and quantitative review. *Psychological Bulletin, 126*, 78–108.

Wright, M., de Geus, E., Ando, J. Luciano, M., Posthuma, D., Ono, Y., Hansell, N., Van Baal, C., Hiraishi, K., Hasegawa, T., Smith, G., Geffen, G., Geffen, L., Kanba, S., Miyake, A., Martin, N., & Boomsma, D. (2001). Genetics of cognition: Outline of a collaborative twin study. *Twin Research, 4*, 48–56.

Critical Thinking Questions

1. Are genetic influences on behaviors stable across development? How might contextual factors influence variation in these behaviors?

2. What methods exist to demonstrate the interaction between genetic and contextual influences on behavior?

3. What will be the effect on the field of psychology once dispositional genes for normal behavioral variation are identified?

Brain Plasticity and Behavior

Bryan Kolb,[1] Robbin Gibb, and Terry E. Robinson
Canadian Centre for Behavioural Neuroscience, University of Lethbridge, Lethbridge, Alberta, Canada (B.K., RG.), and Department of Psychology, University of Michigan, Ann Arbor, Michigan (T.E.R.)

Abstract

Although the brain was once seen as a rather static organ it is now clear that the organization of brain circuitry is constantly changing as a function of experience. These changes are referred to as brain plasticity, and they are associated with functional changes that include phenomena such as memory, addiction, and recovery of function. Recent research has shown that brain plasticity and behavior can be influenced by a myriad of factors, including both pre- and postnatal experience, drugs, hormones maturation, aging, diet, disease, and stress. Understanding how these factors influence brain organization and function is important not only for understanding both normal and abnormal behavior, but also for designing treatments for behavioral and psychological disorders ranging from addiction to stroke.

Keywords

addiction; recovery; experience; brain plasticity

One of the most intriguing questions in behavioral neuroscience concerns the manner in which the nervous system can modify its organization and ultimately its function throughout an individual's lifetime, a property that is often referred to as plasticity. The capacity to change is a fundamental characteristic of nervous systems and can be seen in even the simplest of organisms, such as the tiny worm *C. elegans*, whose nervous system has only 302 cells. When the nervous system changes, there is often a correlated change in behavior or psychological function. This behavioral change is known by names such as learning, memory, addiction, maturation, and recovery. Thus, for example, when people learn new motor skills, such as in playing a musical instrument, there are plastic changes in the structure of cells in the nervous system that underlie the motor skills. If the plastic changes are somehow prevented from occurring, the motor learning does not occur. Although psychologists have assumed that the nervous system is especially sensitive to experience during development, it is only recently that they have begun to appreciate the potential for plastic changes in the adult brain. Understanding brain plasticity is obviously of considerable interest both because it provides a window to understanding the development of the brain and behavior and because it allows insight into the causes of normal and abnormal behavior.

THE NATURE OF BRAIN PLASTICITY

The underlying assumption of studies of brain and behavioral plasticity is that if behavior changes, there must be some change in organization or properties of the neural circuitry that produces the behavior. Conversely, if neural networks are changed by experience, there must be some corresponding change in the functions mediated by those networks. For the investigator interested in understanding the factors that can change brain circuits, and ultimately behavior, a major challenge is to find and to quantify the changes. In principle, plastic changes in neuronal circuits are likely to reflect either modifications of existing circuits or the generation of new circuits. But how can researchers measure changes in neural circuitry? Because neural networks are composed of individual neurons, each of which connects with a subset of other neurons to form interconnected networks, the logical place to look for plastic changes is at the junctions between neurons, that is, at synapses. However, it is a daunting task to determine if synapses have been added or lost in a particular region, given that the human brain has something like 100 billion neurons and each neuron makes on average several thousand synapses. It is clearly impractical to scan the brain looking for altered synapses, so a small subset must be identified and examined in detail. But which synapses should be studied? Given that neuroscientists have a pretty good idea of what regions of the brain are involved in particular behaviors, they can narrow their search to the likely areas, but are still left with an extraordinarily complex system to examine. There is, however, a procedure that makes the job easier.

In the late 1800s, Camillo Golgi invented a technique for staining a random subset of neurons (1–5%) so that the cell bodies and the dendritic trees of individual cells can be visualized (Fig. 1). The dendrites of a cell function as the

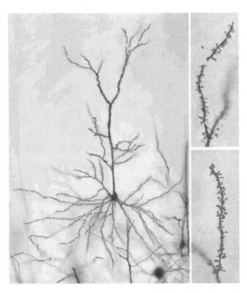

Fig. 1. Photograph of a neuron. In the view on the left, the dendritic field with the extensive dendritic network is visible. On the right are higher-power views of dendritic branches showing the spines, where most synapses are located. If there is an increase in dendritic length, spine density, or both, there are presumed to be more synapses in the neuron.

scaffolding for synapses, much as tree branches provide a location for leaves to grow and be exposed to sunlight. The usefulness of Golgi's technique can be understood by pursuing this arboreal metaphor. There are a number of ways one could estimate how many leaves are on a tree without counting every leaf. Thus, one could measure the total length of the tree's branches as well as the density of the leaves on a representative branch. Then, by simply multiplying branch length by leaf density, one could estimate total leafage. A similar procedure is used to estimate synapse number. About 95% of a cell's synapses are on its dendrites (the neuron's branches). Furthermore, there is a roughly linear relationship between the space available for synapses (dendritic surface) and the number of synapses, so researchers can presume that increases or decreases in dendritic surface reflect changes in synaptic organization.

FACTORS AFFECTING BRAIN PLASTICITY

By using Golgi-staining procedures, various investigators have shown that housing animals in complex versus simple environments produces widespread differences in the number of synapses in specific brain regions. In general, such experiments show that particular experiences embellish circuitry, whereas the absence of those experiences fails to do so (e.g., Greenough & Chang, 1989). Until recently, the impact of these neuropsychological experiments was surprisingly limited, in part because the environmental treatments were perceived as extreme and thus not characteristic of events experienced by the normal brain. It has become clear, however, not only that synaptic organization is changed by experience, but also that the scope of factors that can do this is much more extensive than anyone had anticipated. Factors that are now known to affect neuronal structure and behavior include the following:

- experience (both leading pre- and post-natal)
- psychoactive drugs (e.g., amphetamine, morphine)
- gonadal hormones (e.g., estrogen, testosterone)
- anti-inflammatory agents (e.g., COX-2 inhibitors)
- growth factors (e.g., nerve growth factor)
- dietary factors (e.g., vitamin and mineral supplements)
- genetic factors (e.g., strain differences, genetically modified mice)
- disease (e.g., Parkinson's disease, schizophrenia, epilepsy, stroke)
- stress
- brain injury and leading disease

We discuss two examples to illustrate.

Early Experience

It is generally assumed that experiences early in life have different effects on behavior than similar experiences later in life. The reason for this difference is not understood, however. To investigate this question, we placed animals in complex environments either as juveniles, in adulthood, or in senescence (Kolb, Gibb, & Gorny, 2003). It was our expectation that there would be quantitative

13

differences in the effects of experience on synaptic organization, but to our surprise, we also found *qualitative* differences. Thus, like many investigators before us, we found that the length of dendrites and the density of synapses were increased in neurons in the motor and sensory cortical regions in adult and aged animals housed in a complex environment (relative to a standard lab cage). In contrast, animals placed in the same environment as juveniles showed an increase in dendritic length but a decrease in spine density. In other words the same environmental manipulation had qualitatively different effects on the organization of neuronal circuitry in juveniles than in adults.

To pursue this finding, we later gave infant animals 45 min of daily tactile stimulation with a little paintbrush (15 min three times per day) for the first 3 weeks of life. Our behavioral studies showed that this seemingly benign early experience enhanced motor and cognitive skills in adulthood. The anatomical studies showed, in addition, that in these animals there was a decrease in spine density but no change in dendritic length in cortical neurons—yet another pattern of experience-dependent neuronal change. (Parallel studies have shown other changes, too, including neurochemical changes, but these are beyond the current discussion.) Armed with these findings, we then asked whether prenatal experience might also change the structure of the brain months later in adulthood. Indeed, it does. For example, the offspring of a rat housed in a complex environment during the term of her pregnancy have increased synaptic space on neurons in the cerebral cortex in adulthood. Although we do not know how prenatal experiences alter the brain, it seems likely that some chemical response by the mother, be it hormonal or otherwise, can cross the placental barrier and alter the genetic signals in the developing brain.

Our studies showing that experience can uniquely affect the developing brain led us to wonder if the injured infant brain might be repaired by environmental treatments. We were not surprised to find that postinjury experience, such as tactile stroking, could modify both brain plasticity and behavior because we had come to believe that such experiences were powerful modulators of brain development (Kolb, Gibb, & Gorny, 2000). What was surprising, however, was that prenatal experience, such as housing the pregnant mother in a complex environment, could affect how the brain responded to an injury that it would not receive until after birth. In other words, prenatal experience altered the brain's response to injury later in life. This type of study has profound implications for preemptive treatments of children at risk for a variety of neurological disorders.

Psychoactive Drugs

Many people who take stimulant drugs like nicotine, amphetamine, or cocaine do so for their potent psychoactive effects. The long-term behavioral consequences of abusing such psychoactive drugs are now well documented, but much less is known about how repeated exposure to these drugs alters the nervous system. One experimental demonstration of a very persistent form of drug experience-dependent plasticity is known as behavioral sensitization. For example, if a rat is given a small dose of amphetamine, it initially will show a small increase in motor activity (e.g., locomotion, rearing). When the rat is given the same dose on subsequent occasions, however, the increase in motor activity increases, or sensitizes, and the animal may remain sensitized for weeks, months, or even years, even if drug treatment is discontinued.

Changes in behavior that occur as a consequence of past experience, and can persist for months or years, like memories, are thought to be due to changes in patterns of synaptic organization. The parallels between drug-induced sensitization and memory led us to ask whether the neurons of animals sensitized to drugs of abuse exhibit long-lasting changes similar to those associated with memory (e.g., Robinson & Kolb, 1999). A comparison of the effects of amphetamine and saline treatments on the structure of neurons showed that neurons in amphetamine-treated brains had greater dendritic material, as well as more densely organized spines. These plastic changes were not found throughout the brain, however, but rather were localized to regions such as the prefrontal cortex and nucleus accumbens, both of which are thought to play a role in the rewarding properties of these drugs. Later studies have shown that these drug-induced changes are found not only when animals are given injections by an experimenter, but also when animals are trained to self-administer drugs, leading us to speculate that similar changes in synaptic organization will be found in human drug addicts.

Other Factors

All of the factors we listed earlier have effects that are conceptually similar to the two examples that we just discussed. For instance, brain injury disrupts the synaptic organization of the brain, and when there is functional improvement after the injury, there is a correlated reorganization of neural circuits (e.g., Kolb, 1995). But not all factors act the same way across the brain. For instance, estrogen stimulates synapse formation in some structures but reduces synapse number in other structures (e.g., Kolb, Forgie, Gibb, Gorny, & Rowntree, 1998), a pattern of change that can also be seen with some psychoactive drugs, such as morphine. In sum, it now appears that virtually any manipulation that produces an enduring change in behavior leaves an anatomical footprint in the brain.

CONCLUSIONS AND ISSUES

There are several conclusions to draw from our studies. First, experience alters the brain, and it does so in an age-related manner. Second, both pre- and postnatal experience have such effects, and these effects are long-lasting and can influence not only brain structure but also adult behavior. Third, seemingly similar experiences can alter neuronal circuits in different ways, although each of the alterations is manifest in behavioral change. Fourth, a variety of behavioral conditions, ranging from addiction to neurological and psychiatric disorders, are correlated with localized changes in neural circuits. Finally, therapies that are intended to alter behavior, such as treatment for addiction, stroke, or schizophrenia, are likely to be most effective if they are able to further reorganize relevant brain circuitry. Furthermore, studies of neuronal structure provide a simple method of screening for treatments that are likely to be effective in treating disorders such as dementia. Indeed, our studies show that the new generation of antiarthritic drugs (known as COX-2 inhibitors), which act to reduce inflammation, can reverse age-related synaptic loss and thus ought to be considered as useful treatments for age-related cognitive loss.

Although much is now known about brain plasticity and behavior, many theoretical issues remain. Knowing that a wide variety of experiences and agents can alter synaptic organization and behavior is important, but leads to a new question: How does this happen? This is not an easy question to answer, and it is certain that there is more than one answer. We provide a single example to illustrate.

Neurotrophic factors are a class of chemicals that are known to affect synaptic organization. An example is fibroblast growth factor-2 (FGF-2). The production of FGF-2 is increased by various experiences, such as complex housing and tactile stroking, as well as by drugs such as amphetamine. Thus, it is possible that experience stimulates the production of FGF-2 and this, in turn, increases synapse production. But again, the question is how. One hypothesis is that FGF-2 somehow alters the way different genes are expressed by specific neurons and this, in turn, affects the way synapses are generated or lost. In other words, factors that alter behavior, including experience, can do so by altering gene expression, a result that renders the traditional gene-versus-environment discussions meaningless.

Other issues revolve around the limits and permanence of plastic changes. After all, people encounter and learn new information daily. Is there some limit to how much cells can change? It seems unlikely that cells could continue to enlarge and add synapses indefinitely, but what controls this? We saw in our studies of experience-dependent changes in infants, juveniles, and adults that experience both adds and prunes synapses, but what are the rules governing when one or the other might occur? This question leads to another, which is whether plastic changes in response to different experiences might interact. For example, does exposure to a drug like nicotine affect how the brain changes in learning a motor skill like playing the piano? Consider, too, the issue of the permanence of plastic changes. If a person stops smoking, how long do the nicotine-induced plastic changes persist, and do they affect later changes?

One additional issue surrounds the role of plastic changes in disordered behavior. Thus, although most studies of plasticity imply that remodeling neural circuitry is a good thing, it is reasonable to wonder if plastic changes might also be the basis of pathological behavior. Less is known about this possibility, but it does seem likely. For example, drug addicts often show cognitive deficits, and it seems reasonable to propose that at least some of these deficits could arise from abnormal circuitry, especially in the frontal lobe.

In sum, the structure of the brain is constantly changing in response to an unexpectedly wide range of experiential factors. Understanding how the brain changes and the rules governing these changes is important not only for understanding both normal and abnormal behavior, but also for designing treatments for behavioral and psychological disorders ranging from addiction to stroke.

Recommended Reading

Kolb, B., & Whishaw, I.Q. (1998). Brain plasticity and behavior. *Annual Review of Psychology, 49,* 43–64.

Robinson, T.E., & Berridge, K.C. (in press). Addiction. *Annual Review of Psychology.*
Shaw, C.A., & McEachern, J.C. (2001). *Toward a theory of neuroplasticity.* New York: Taylor and Francis.

Acknowledgments—This research was supported by a Natural Sciences and Engineering Research Council grant to B.K. and a National Institute on Drug Abuse grant to T.E.R.

Note

1. Address correspondence to Bryan Kolb, CCBN, University of Lethbridge, Lethbridge, AB, Canada T1K 3M4.

References

Greenough, W.T., & Chang, F.F. (1989). Plasticity of synapse structure and pattern in the cerebral cortex. In A. Peters & E.G. Jones (Eds.), *Cerebral cortex: Vol. 7* (pp. 391–440). New York: Plenum Press.

Kolb, B. (1995). *Brain plasticity and behavior.* Mahwah, NJ: Erlbaum.

Kolb, B., Forgie, M., Gibb, R., Gorny, G., & Rowntree, S. (1998). Age, experience, and the changing brain. *Neuroscience and Biobehavioral Reviews, 22,* 143–159.

Kolb, B., Gibb, R., & Gorny, G. (2000). Cortical plasticity and the development of behavior after early frontal cortical injury. *Developmental Neuropsychology, 18,* 423–444.

Kolb, B., Gibb, R., & Gorny, G. (2003). Experience-dependent changes in dendritic arbor and spine density in neocortex vary with age and sex. *Neurobiology of Learning and Memory, 79,* 1–10.

Robinson, T.E., & Kolb, B. (1999). Alterations in the morphology of dendrites and dendritic spines in the nucleus accumbens and prefrontal cortex following repeated treatment with amphetamine or cocaine. *European Journal of Neuroscience, 11,* 1598–1604.

Critical Thinking Questions

1. What are the benefits of studying brain plasticity beyond childhood?

2. In what ways will the finding that plastic changes occur in the adult brain alter developmental theory and research?

3. How might one investigate the impact of certain contextual factors on neural circuitry?

Infant Attention Grows Up: The Emergence of a Developmental Cognitive Neuroscience Perspective

John Colombo[1]

Department of Psychology, University of Kansas, Lawrence, Kansas

Abstract

Visual attention has long been regarded as a tool for studying the development of basic cognitive skills in infancy and early childhood. However, over the past decade, the development of attention in early life has emerged as an important topic of research in its own right. This essay describes recent changes in the methods used to study attention in infancy, and in the nature of inferences about the early development of attention, as both research and theory in the area have become progressively integrated with models of attention from cognitive science and neuroscience.

Keywords

infancy; attention; development; individual differences; developmental cognitive neuroscience

The modern investigation of the development of attention in infancy and early childhood evolved from the work of Fantz and Berlyne, who, in the late 1950s, borrowed methods from ethology and comparative psychology in monitoring infants' visual fixations to various visual stimuli. Initially, investigators in the field were content to document infants' selective looking to various visual properties (e.g., color, brightness, visual patterns, contour, "complexity," and stimulus novelty). It was quickly recognized, however, that the presence of systematic visual preferences in infants implied discrimination of the preferred from the nonpreferred stimulus. Furthermore, if one allowed an infant to study a stimulus for some amount of time and then presented a novel one, careful measurement would reveal increased looking to the novel stimulus. This preference for novelty implied the presence of memory and—by logical extension—the occurrence of visual learning in the infant. Investigators readily seized upon these selective-looking techniques to reveal important facts about early sensory function (e.g., visual acuity, detection of color), perceptual processes (e.g., form and pattern perception), and other basic cognitive "products" (e.g., visual discrimination, short- and long-term memory, category formation) during the first years of life. As a result, infant visual attention was for the most part regarded and used as a tool for elucidating the development of various aspects of early cognitive development. The development of attention in infancy and early childhood, however, was largely overlooked as a topic of research in its own right.

ATTENTION AS A PRIMARY FOCUS OF DEVELOPMENTAL RESEARCH

Two trends that emerged in the 1980s led to the consideration of the development of attention as a primary focus of research per se. The first trend was for developmental psychologists to seek an integration of cognitive-developmental phenomena with models of cognitive function that had been developed within the field of cognitive science. As I note later, this represented the origin of inter-disciplinary cross talk that has continued unabated to this day, as work in cognitive development has become increasingly intertwined with both cognitive science and cognitive neuroscience over the past decade. The second trend had its origin in a number of articles published in the early 1980s that reported that various measures of visual attention in infancy were modestly but significantly predictive of cognitive function later in childhood. Both trends suggested that a fundamental understanding of the development of attention in and of itself might be important, useful, and fruitful for many realms in the behavioral and biobehavioral sciences.

Early Theory: Infant Looking as Encoding

Many of the initial studies of selective looking in infants were guided primarily by Sokolov's comparator model, which held that attention is distributed to a stimulus as a function of the match between the stimulus and the internal representation ("engram") of it. According to this model, prolonged looking indicates a mismatch between the two (or a lack of an engram altogether); brief fixations imply that the stimulus has been represented accurately and completely. The comparator model was helpful in explaining why infants show a decline in looking to repetitive stimulus presentations (i.e., visual habituation), although the model itself was directly based on neither attentional theory nor mechanisms proposed in the literature on adult cognition.

In any case, the theoretical bias in initial work on this topic was to interpret individual and developmental changes in looking in terms of visual learning, or encoding. One program of work in our own laboratory at the University of Kansas involved a description of the developmental course of, and the stability of individual differences in, visual attention within the habituation paradigm. These initial studies suggested that the development of attention over the 1st year was primarily manifest in terms of changes in the duration of looking (Colombo & Mitchell, 1990); young infants (e.g., 3- and 4-month-olds) looked for prolonged periods, relative to older infants (e.g., 7- and 8-month-olds). Moreover, although there was wide variability within ages, individual differences in the duration of looking were moderately stable from one testing to another (Colombo, Mitchell, O'Brien, & Horowitz, 1987), at least within age categories.

In the comparator theory framework, the duration of infant looking could be interpreted in terms of how quickly an infant encoded a stimulus. Thus, the developmental course implied that infants got faster or more efficient at encoding as they got older, and the stability of individual differences implied that some individual infants encoded faster or more efficiently than others. This interpretation was supported by subsequent empirical evidence showing that infants with prolonged patterns of looking tended to perform less well than their shorter-looking counterparts on visual recognition tasks in which the amount of time to study stimuli was limited (e.g., Colombo, Mitchell, Coldren, & Freeseman, 1991). As a result, psychologists came to consider prolonged looking in infants as a reflection of slower processing, both across and within ages.

Theoretical Change: Infant Looking and the Cognitive Neuroscience of Attention

Researchers from a more cognitive neuroscience perspective, however, approached the study of attention either by using converging behavioral and cardiac indices of information processing or by adopting the use of tasks that had been shown, at least with adults, to be associated with those brain structures or pathways that control or mediate attention. A major contribution of this work was to demonstrate that infant looking represented a variety of attentional states and components, including orienting and engagement of attention, maintenance of attention, disengagement of attention, and shifting of attention (e.g., Johnson, Posner, & Rothbart, 1991).

This work had two important effects. The first was that it tempered an implicit claim of comparator theory—namely, that the infant is continuously and primarily engaged in active encoding while looking at a visual stimulus. Second, and more important, given that the components of attention identified within looking in human infants were analogous with those identified and documented within the realm of cognitive science and cognitive neuroscience, this research promoted the integration of developmental and contemporary cognitive approaches to visual attention.

In our own research program, we began to look for brain-based mechanisms to explain why prolonged look duration was associated with slower speed or efficiency of encoding, both across and within ages. Normally, adults and children encode visual stimuli efficiently, processing the overall configuration of a stimulus first and the fine detail (i.e., local features) later. However, a number of projects from our laboratory indicated that infants with prolonged look durations were drawn toward, or persevered in, inspecting the smaller local visual features of visual stimuli, rather than the larger patterns or overall configurations (see Colombo & Janowsky, 1998, for a summary of this work). Interestingly, Orlian and Rose (1997) hinted at the possibility that longer looking was associated with better discrimination of visual stimuli that were differentiated by discrepancies in local elements or details. These results could be explained through a number of underlying mechanisms related to maturation of the lower-order visual pathways (see Colombo, 1995). However, they were also consistent with the possibility that infants who showed prolonged looking tended to become "stuck" on certain visual features, and unable to inhibit or disengage their attention to shift it elsewhere (see Hood, 1995). This type of deficit has been linked to mechanisms of visual attention that are mediated by frontal or parietal areas of the brain.

A number of recent studies have lent strong support to this latter interpretation. We (Frick, Colombo, & Saxon, 1999) assessed 3- and 4-month-olds' look duration, and then administered a series of tasks that measured the speed with which infants moved their eyes from a position at midline to a stimulus that appeared unexpectedly in the peripheral visual field. In half of such trials, a stimulus remained illuminated at midline; this forced the infants to disengage attention from the stimulus there in order to make an eye movement to the peripheral one. In the other half of the trials, the stimulus at midline was removed just prior to the appearance of the peripheral stimulus, so that disengagement of attention prior to making the appropriate eye movements was not necessary. The look durations recorded in the pretest, in which infants looked at different slides of visual stimuli, were correlated quite strongly ($r = +.62$) with the time it took for the infants to initiate eye movements when disengagement was necessary, but uncorrelated ($r = +.01$) when disengagement was not necessary. That is, infants' look duration was directly related to their ability to disengage from a visual stimulus. Jankowski and Rose (1997) also found evidence for the association between look duration and the disengagement of attention, as infants showing prolonged looking moved their gaze across regions of visual stimuli far less than their shorter-looking counterparts.

Two recent follow-up studies have approached the issue more directly. My colleagues and I (Colombo, Richman, Shaddy, Greenhoot, & Maikranz, 2001) measured infants' heart rate (HR) while they were looking at stimuli during a recognition memory task. While infants are looking at a visual stimulus, at least some part of that look coincides with a slowing (i.e., deceleration) of HR (see Fig. 1). During this deceleration, infants are less distractible and more engaged in information processing than during other phases of the look, when HR has not yet decelerated (orienting) and after HR has returned

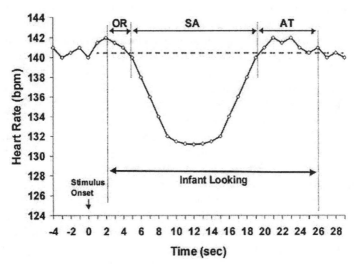

Fig. 1. Three phases of visual attention, as identified using the characteristic heart rate (HR) deceleration that occurs during infants' looking. The period during looking that precedes the attainment of a stable deceleration is called *orienting* (OR), and reflects how quickly the infant begins processing the stimulus. It is most closely identified with the construct of attentional engagement. *Sustained attention* (SA) is defined as the period of HR deceleration that typically occurs during infant looking, and is most closely identified with the encoding, or processing, of the stimulus. *Attention termination* (AT) refers to the period during which the look persists after the characteristic HR deceleration has ended. This phase is most closely identified with the construct of attentional disengagement. Adapted from Richards and Casey (1990); reprinted with permission from Colombo, Richman, Shaddy, Greenhoot, and Maikranz (2001).

to baseline levels (attention termination). Thus, it is possible to use HR data to determine whether infants are actively engaged with a stimulus (Richards & Case, 1990). Of most interest is the period of attention termination, during which infants' looking at the stimulus continues despite the fact that the HR deceleration has ended. Presumably, larger amounts of time spent in this phase should reflect relative difficulty with the disengagement of attention. We suspected that this kind of difficulty might be correlated with prolonged looking, and that it might explain the relationship between prolonged looking and poorer recognition performance; indeed, both suspicions were confirmed. Finally, Jankowski, Rose, and Feldman (2001) recently published an important study in this line of inquiry. They showed that by enticing long-looking infants to shift their fixations among multiple areas of a visual stimulus, they could eliminate the deficits in recognition performance that have often been observed for this group.

Infant Looking: A Broader Developmental View

Overall, then, this research brought about a major change in the way in which individual and developmental differences in infant looking were viewed. At the same time that this evidence was being collected, however, research on the development of attention in primates and toddlers suggested that the development of looking was not accurately represented by a simple linear decline in duration across the entire range of infancy and early childhood. This prompted us to conduct a comprehensive review of the data on the development of look duration over a wider range of infancy than we have typically studied in our research on individual differences in attention (Colombo, Harlan, & Mitchell, 1999). This review yielded evidence for three fairly distinct phases over the 1st year: (a) a period from birth to 8 or 10 weeks during which look duration increases, (b) a period from 3 to 5 or 6 months of age when look duration declines, and (c) a period from 7 months onward during which looking duration plateaus or perhaps even gradually increases (see Fig. 2).

The initial increase is not well understood, although available theory and evidence point to the involvement of arousal and the emergence of alertness, likely mediated by brain pathways that link systems of arousal in the brain stem with higher areas of the cerebral cortex (Colombo, 2001). The decline in looking likely reflects changes in disengagement, although some aspects of object perception may also be involved. The plateau that begins later in the 1st year likely reflects the predominance of endogenous or sustained attention, which is more voluntary and task-driven than the other phases of attention. This latter period has received increased interest over the past several years in studies of distractibility, and the maintenance of attention in problem-solving and competitive contexts. Interest in the emergence of endogenous attention is likely to increase, as it reflects the emergence of components that are more colloquially regarded as attention (e.g., "attention span") by the general population, and that likely underpin the development of a number of cognitive and intellectual skills. It is also likely that research in this area of early attentional development may have clinical relevance.

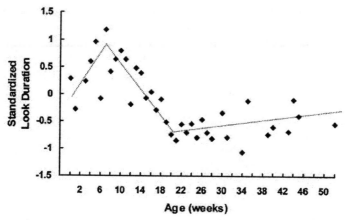

Fig. 2. The developmental course of look duration in infants, as suggested by a statistical review of the literature (Colombo, Harlan, & Mitchell, 1999). Forty-eight studies that included assessments of look duration from at least two ages were surveyed. Durations were standardized (z score) within each study, and a data point for each age was calculated by averaging the standardized scores across all studies that contributed data for that age. The dotted line represents the best-fitting regression line in each of three distinct phases observed during the 1st year (see the text).

CONCLUSIONS AND FUTURE DIRECTIONS

In the past decade, research on the development of attention in infancy has thus moved the field away from a focus based solely on comparator theory (i.e., simple encoding) and toward a perspective that is based on components derived from contemporary cognitive neuroscience models of attention (i.e., engagement, shifting, disengagement, object recognition and perception, and endogenous or sustained attention). Much of the extant research may need to be reinterpreted within this new framework (see Colombo, 2001). However, this change in perspective raises a host of new and critical issues to be addressed by research in this decade and those to follow. For example, differences among models of the development of disengagement in infancy will need to be resolved. Researchers will need to disentangle the relative roles and contributions of the development of the brain pathways that mediate attention to objects and to their locations in the visual field (both of which emerge during the first 6 months). The development of endogenous or sustained forms of attention, which are manifest in measures of distractibility and how attention is controlled under conditions in which multiple stimuli are present, is not particularly well described or well understood. These forms of attention emerge toward the end of the 1st year and are predominant through the preschool years, so studies across this age range are needed.

Among the larger issues to be investigated, however, is how the various components of visual attention, with their distinct and likely independent developmental courses, interact to produce the types of visual behavior seen during infancy. Another issue is how these different components in infancy contribute to the development of higher-order cognitive functions later in life; work on this question will undoubtedly need to delineate how environmental influences interact with (i.e., affect and are affected by) the infant's attentional skills at various points in development. These latter questions truly represent the integration of contemporary cognitive science with developmental psychology, and thus define a field of developmental cognitive neuroscience.

Recommended Reading

Colombo, J. (2001). (See References)
Hood, B.M. (1995). (See References)
Johnson, M. (1997). *Developmental cognitive neuroscience*. Oxford, England: Oxford University Press.
Richards, J.E. (Ed.). (1998). *Cognitive neuroscience of attention: A developmental perspective*. Mahwah, NJ: Erlbaum.
Ruff, H.A., & Rothbart, M.K. (1996). *Attention in early development: Variations and themes*. Hillsdale, NJ: Erlbaum.

Acknowledgements—Preparation of this article was supported by Grant HD35903 from the National Institutes of Health. I am grateful to Wayne Mitchell, Marion O'Brien, Frances Horowitz, and Janet Frick for their past contributions to this research program, and to D. Jill Shaddy, W. Allen Richman, Julie Maikranz, Otilia Blaga, Christa Anderson, and Kathleen Kannass for their contributions to our current program of work.

Note

1. Address correspondence to John Colombo, Department of Psychology, 426 Fraser Hall, 1415 Jayhawk Blvd., University of Kansas, Lawrence, KS 66045-7535; e-mail: colombo@ku.edu.

References

Colombo, J. (1995). On the neural mechanisms underlying developmental and individual differences in infant fixation duration: Two hypotheses. *Developmental Review, 15*, 97–135.

Colombo, J. (2001). The development of visual attention in infancy. *Annual Review of Psychology, 52*, 337–367.

Colombo, J., Harlan, J.E., & Mitchell, D.W. (1999, April). *The development of look duration in infancy: Evidence for a triphasic course*. Poster presented at the annual meeting of the Society for Research in Child Development, Albuquerque, NM. (Available at http://www.people.ku.edu/~ colombo/SRCD99.htm)

Colombo, J., & Janowsky, J.S. (1998). A cognitive neuroscience approach to individual differences in infant cognition. In J.E. Richards (Ed.), *Cognitive neuroscience of attention: A developmental perspective* (pp. 363–392). Mahwah, NJ: Erlbaum.

Colombo, J., & Mitchell, D.W. (1990). Individual and developmental differences in infant visual attention. In J. Colombo & J.W. Fagen (Eds.), *Individual differences in infancy* (pp. 193–227). Hillsdale, NJ: Erlbaum.

Colombo, J., Mitchell, D.W., Coldren, J.T., & Freeseman, L.J. (1991). Individual differences in infant attention: Are short lookers faster processors or feature processors? *Child Development, 62*, 1247–1257.

Colombo, J., Mitchell, D.W., O'Brien, M., & Horowitz, F.D. (1987). Stability of infant visual habituation during the first year. *Child Development, 58*, 474–489.

Colombo, J., Richman, W.A., Shaddy, D.J., Greenhoot, A.F., & Maikranz, J. (2001). HR-defined phases of attention, look duration, and infant performance in the paired-comparison paradigm. *Child Development, 72*, 1605–1616.

Frick, J.E., Colombo, J., & Saxon, T.F. (1999). Individual and developmental differences in disengagement of fixation in early infancy. *Child Development, 70,* 537–548.

Hood, B.M. (1995). Shifts of visual attention in the infant: A neuroscientific approach. In C. Rovee-Collier & L. Lipsitt (Eds.), *Advances in infancy research* (Vol. 9, pp. 163–216). Norwood, NJ: Ablex.

Jankowski, J.J., & Rose, S.A. (1997). The distribution of visual attention in infants. *Journal of Experimental Child Psychology, 65,* 127–140.

Jankowski, J.J., Rose, S.A., & Feldman, J.F. (2001). Modifying the distribution of attention in infants. *Child Development, 72,* 339–351.

Johnson, M.H., Posner, M.I., & Rothbart, M.K. (1991). Components of visual orienting in early infancy: Contingency learning, anticipatory looking, and disengaging. *Journal of Cognitive Neuroscience, 3,* 335–344.

Orlian, E.K., & Rose, S.A. (1997). Speed vs. thoroughness in infant visual information processing. *Infant Behavior and Development, 20,* 371–381.

Richards, J.E., & Casey, B.J. (1990). Development of sustained visual attention in the human infant. In B.A. Campbell, H. Hayne, & R. Richardson (Eds.), *Attention and information processing in infants and adults* (pp. 30–60). Hillsdale, NJ: Erlbaum.

Critical Thinking Questions

1. How does the concept of visual habituation relate to Sokolov's comparator model? How might one inform the other?

2. How might the measurement of infants' heart rates contribute to our understanding of cognitive development?

3. What can be concluded from intra-individual variation in look duration throughout infancy? What are the clinical implications of these conclusions?

Neurobehavioral Changes in Adolescence

Linda Patia Spear[1]

Department of Psychology and Center for Developmental Psychobiology, Binghamton University, Binghamton, New York

Abstract

Adolescents across a variety of species exhibit age-specific behavioral characteristics that may have evolved to help them attain the necessary skills for independence. These adolescent-related characteristics, such as an increase in risk taking, may be promoted less by the hormonal changes of puberty than by developmental events occurring in brain. Among the prominent brain transformations of adolescence are alterations in the prefrontal cortex, limbic brain areas, and their dopamine input, systems that are sensitive to stressors and form part of the neural circuitry modulating the motivational value of drugs and other reinforcing stimuli. Such developmental transformations of the adolescent brain may predispose adolescents to behave in particular ways and make them particularly likely to initiate use of alcohol and other drugs.

Keywords

adolescent; adolescence; brain development; risk taking; drug use

To successfully negotiate the developmental transition from youth to maturity, adolescents of many species must survive the risks and stressors of this disequilibrating passage while acquiring the skills necessary for independence and success in adult life. Although certain attributes of human adolescents are unique and not evident in other species, other characteristic features are expressed by adolescents of diverse species and may be evolutionarily adaptive in helping the adolescent conquer this critical transition. For instance, like their counterparts among human adolescents, rats undergoing the developmental transition of adolescence likewise show a marked developmental increase in the amount of time spent in social investigation and interaction with peers, along with elevations in risk-taking behavior, illustrated by their seeking out novel stimuli and exploring unknown areas more avidly than at younger ages or in adulthood. Although some adolescent-associated increase in risk taking and sensation seeking appears normative across a variety of species, there may be individual differences in the expression of these propensities within species. High levels of risk taking may be maladaptive, leading to excessive use of drugs and alcohol by some human adolescents or their involvement in reckless activities that may be life-threatening for themselves or others.

One of the prominent physiological events occurring at some point within the broad age range of adolescence is a pubertal increase in sex hormones (e.g., estrogen in females and testosterone in males) and the associated emergence of secondary sexual characteristics. Yet, there is surprisingly little evidence that these hormonal alterations are associated in any simple fashion with behavioral change during adolescence (Susman et al., 1987). Instead, striking changes that occur in the adolescent brain may contribute to the behavioral changes characteristic of this age. Brain areas undergoing remodeling during adolescence in a variety of species include stressor-sensitive forebrain regions implicated in novelty seeking and in modulating the motivational value of drugs and other reinforcing stimuli. Given the clear differences between adolescents and adults in functioning of these brain regions, it would be surprising indeed if adolescents did not differ from adults in various aspects of their behavior toward these stimuli.

ADOLESCENT-TYPICAL BEHAVIORS AND RESPONSES TO STRESSORS

Social Interactions and Peer Affiliations

Social interactions, particularly with peers, take on increasing importance during adolescence in many species. Human adolescents spend substantially more time interacting socially with peers than with adults; peer-directed social interactions may help the adolescent develop social skills away from the home environment and hence ease the transition toward independence (Larson & Richards, 1994). In many species, social interactions also help guide choice behavior, such as selection of appropriate food items, and provide the opportunity to practice and model adult-typical behavior patterns (Galef, 1981).

Sensation Seeking and Risk Taking

Adolescents across a variety of species exhibit age-related increases in novelty seeking, sensation seeking, and risk taking (Arnett, 1992; Spear, in press). This may have evolutionary significance in providing the impetus to explore novel and broader areas away from the home, helping to avoid inbreeding via dispersal of male (and sometimes female) offspring to new territories away from the initial social unit before they reproduce. Such increases in risk taking may also provide the opportunity to explore new behaviors and potential rewards, perhaps facilitating the relinquishing of childhood patterns of behavior as well as the acquisition of behaviors essential for successful adult functioning.

The kinds of risks that human adolescents take include not only reckless behavior, school misconduct, and so-called antisocial behaviors (including fighting, stealing, trespassing, and property damage), but also use of alcohol, cigarettes, and illicit drugs. Shedler and Block (1990) have argued that modes amounts of risk taking may represent "developmentally appropriate experimentation," noting that, for instance, adolescents engaging in moderate extents of risk taking have been found to be more socially competent in both childhood and adolescence than abstainers as well as frequent risk takers. Thus, although there may be constructive functions of risk taking—at least in an evolutionary sense and arguably also for the individual human adolescent—excess may be disadvantageous, if not life-threatening, for the adolescent or others.

Adolescent Drug Use

As with other types of risk-taking behavior, some amount of exploratory drug use is normative in human adolescents. According to the 1996 survey results from the Monitoring the Future Study, sponsored by the National Institute of Drug Abuse, by the time that adolescents reach their senior year in high school, approximately 50% have used marijuana or hashish, 65% have smoked cigarettes, and 82% have drunk alcohol (Johnston, O'Malley, & Bachman, 1998). This drug use begins relatively early in adolescence, with 26% of 8th graders reporting use of alcohol and 15% reporting use of illicit drugs in the prior month. Some of this use is excessive. For instance, 10% of 8th graders, 21% of 10th graders, and 31% of 12th graders reported getting drunk one or more times during the past month. Clearly, many adolescents engage in at least some exploratory drug use, with evidence of excessive use emerging in some individuals.

Consequences of such use may be long-lasting. Early onset of drug and alcohol use is one of the strongest predictors of later abuse of alcohol and other drugs (Grant & Dawson, 1997). It remains to be determined whether early drug use serves merely as a marker of later abuse or whether such drug exposure is causal, influencing ongoing brain development to induce long-term alterations in neural function that increase later propensity for drug abuse.

Stress and Adolescence

Studies examining adolescents of a variety of species have shown that adolescents may be more disrupted by stressors than adults are. Although most human adolescents traverse this developmental period without significant psychological problems, the incidence of depressed mood is greater during adolescence than at younger or older ages (Petersen et al., 1993). Adolescents may generally respond with greater negative affect to circumstances in their environment than do children and adults; even when referring to the same activities, adolescents often find them less pleasurable than their parents (Larson & Richards, 1994).

Physiologically as well, adolescents may show an increased responsivity to stressors. Human adolescents exhibit greater increases in blood pressure and in blood flow through the heart in response to various laboratory test procedures than do children (Allen & Matthews, 1997). Similarly, in other species, adolescents often exhibit elevated stress-induced increases in the stress-related hormone corticosterone relative to younger organisms and prolonged increases in corticosterone relative to adults (Spear, in press). Such elevated stress responsivity of adolescents may contribute to their propensity to initiate drug and alcohol use, given that stressors have been shown to enhance alcohol consumption and to facilitate the onset of drug use.

THE ADOLESCENT BRAIN

More dramatic than the often-striking changes occurring in the physical appearance of adolescents are the transformations that are occurring in their brains. This remodeling of the brain is seen in adolescents of a variety of species and entails not only brain growth, including the formation of additional connections between nerve cells, but also a prominent loss (or pruning) of such connections in particular neural regions. Among the brain areas prominently remodeled during adolescence is the prefrontal cortex, a brain region thought to be involved in various goal-directed behaviors (including rule learning, working memory, and spatial learning) and in emotional processing, particularly of aversive stimuli.

Along with a decline in the relative size of the prefrontal cortex during adolescence, there is substantial remodeling of connections between neurons—with some connections lost and others added.

As can be seen in Figure 1, the amount of input received from two key chemicals (neurotransmitters) involved in brain-cell communication—the excitatory neurotransmitter glutamate and the inhibitory neurotransmitter gamma-amino-butyric acid (GABA)—is reduced in prefontral cortex during adolescence, while input from another neurotransmitter, dopamine, peaks in prefrontal cortex during adolescence (Lewis, 1997). Developmental adjustments in dopamine activity are evident not only in prefrontal cortex, but also in limbic brain regions (Andersen, Dumont, & Teicher, 1997). A variety of other adolescent-associated neural alterations are seen across species in various limbic brain regions. For example, Yurgelun-Todd, at the McLean Hospital in Belmont, Massachusetts, has found an age-related shift in activation of the human amygdala, a limbic structure that, among other things, is thought to be involved in emotional reactivity and in coordinating responses to stressful stimuli.

The adolescent-associated changes in dopamine input to prefrontal cortex and limbic brain regions may be of considerable consequence for adolescent

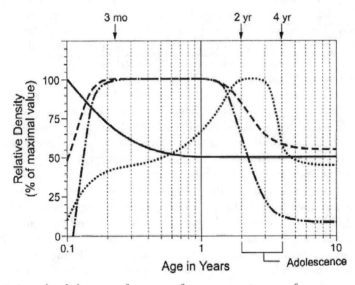

Fig. 1. Age-related changes in four types of input to a major type of output neuron (layer III pyramidal cells) of the primate prefrontal cortex. The x-axis refers to the age of the animals, and the y-axis represents the percentage of the maximal value reached at any point in the life span for each measure. The broken line illustrates excitatory glutaminergic input into this cortical region, the broken line with dots shows gamma-aminobutyric acid (GABA) inhibitory input, and the dotted line illustrates dopamine input; the solid line demonstrates levels of another neurotransmitter (cholecystokinin) in this brain region. Reprinted by permission of Elsevier Science from "Development of the Prefrontal Cortex During Adolescence: Insights Into Vulnerable Neural Circuits in Schizophrenia," by D.A. Lewis, 1997, *Neuropsychopharmacology, 16*, p. 392. Copyright 1997 by American College of Neuropsychopharmacology.

behavior and psychological functioning. This stress-sensitive dopamine system appears to play a role in novelty seeking (Dellu, Piazza, Mayo, Le Moal, & Simon, 1996) and to be part of the neural circuitry involved in assessing the motivational value of stimuli, including potentially reinforcing drugs, and translating this assessment into action (Kalivas, Churchill, & Klitenick, 1993). To the extent that adolescence is associated with developmental alterations in prefrontal cortex, limbic brain areas, and the dopamine input to these regions, concomitant developmental alterations in various motivated behaviors might also be expected. Alterations in the incentive value attributed to stimuli could underlie many of the behavioral alterations seen in adolescents, increasing the importance of social reinforcement derived from peers and provoking the pursuit of new potentially rewarding stimuli, a quest that may lead to increases in drug use and other risk-taking behaviors. Given the differences between adolescents and adults in functioning in these brain regions, it would be astonishing indeed if adolescents did *not* differ from adults in various aspects of their motivated behavior.

FINAL THOUGHTS

Over the past several decades, research in developmental psychology has placed surprisingly little emphasis on the adolescent brain in the quest for determinants of adolescents' typical behavioral propensities. But the focus of research is gradually changing, with the recognition that the brain of the adolescent differs markedly from the younger or adult brain, and that some of these differences are found in neural regions implicated in the typical behavioral characteristics of the adolescent. Yet, much remains to be done.

Additional research is needed to examine normal brain function in adolescence. The rather piecemeal observations of the adolescent brain to date need to be integrated within a broader characterization of adolescent brain function. Then, the relationship of these neural alterations to adolescent-typical behavior patterns needs to be substantiated using experimental approaches.

Neural mechanisms underlying initiation of drug use during adolescence are a particularly important area for study. Given the clear differences between adolescents and adults in brain regions implicated in drug seeking and other motivated behaviors, the factors that serve to precipitate and maintain adolescent drug and alcohol rise may well vary from the factors that underlie such use in adulthood. Yet, study of psychobiological determinants of drug initiation has been almost exclusively conducted in adult organisms, so the findings are of questionable relevance to the typical initiation of alcohol and drug use during adolescence.

The question also remains as to whether early exposure to drugs or alcohol actually increases the propensity for later abuse, or whether early use is just a marker for a later abuse disorder. This issue is clearly germane to current prevention efforts directed toward postponing first use ("just say later").

Multiple research approaches and study populations will be needed in this work. Although some aspects of adolescence can be properly and productively modeled in laboratory animals, others clearly cannot and will require studies in human adolescents. Advances in brain-imaging techniques (Thatcher, Lyon,

Rumsey, & Krasnegor, 1996) have made the brain of the human adolescent more accessible for study, yet many questions about the adolescent brain and its relationship to age-related behavioral characteristics will require experimental manipulations involving laboratory animals. Multidisciplinary studies conducted in species ranging from human and nonhuman primates to rodents and using levels of analysis ranging from gene expression to behavior will help illuminate the dramatic transformations of the adolescent brain and their association with behavioral function during this unique maturational phase.

Recommended Reading

Lewis, D.A. (1997). (See References)
Spear, L.P. (in press). (See References)
Susman, E.J., Inoff-Germain, G., Nottelmann, E.D., Loriaux, D.L., Cutler, G.B., Jr., & Chrousos, G.P. (1987). (See References)
Witt, E.D. (1994). Mechanisms of alcohol abuse and alcoholism in adolescents: A case for developing animal models. *Behavioral and Neural Biology, 62,* 168–177.

Note

1. Address correspondence to Linda Spear, Department of Psychology, Box 6000, Binghamton University, Binghamton, NY 13902-6000; e-mail: lspear@binghamton.edu.

References

Allen, M.T., & Mathews, K.A. (1997). Demodynamic responses to laboratory stressors in children and adolescents. The influences of age, race, and gender. *Psychophysiology, 34,* 329–339.

Andersen, S.L., Dumont, N.L., & Teicher, M.H. (1997). Developmental differences in dopamine synthesis inhibition by (±)-7-OH-DPAT. *Naunyn-Schmiedeberg's Archives of Pharmacology, 356,* 173–181.

Arnett, J. (1992). Reckless behavior in adolescence: A developmental perspective. *Developmental Review, 12,* 339–373.

Dellu, F., Piazza, P.V., Mayo, W., Le Moal, M., & Simon, H. (1996). Novelty-seeking in rats—Biobehavioral characteristics and possible relationship with the sensation-seeking trait in man. *Neuropsychobiology, 34,* 136–145.

Galef, B.G., Jr. (1981). The ecology of weaning: Parasitism and the achievement of independence by altricial mammals. In D.J. Gubernick & P.H. Klopfer (Eds.), *Parental care in mammals* (pp. 211–241). New York: Plenum Press.

Grant, B.F., & Dawson, D.A. (1997). Age at onset of alcohol use and its association with DSM-IV alcohol abuse and dependence: Results from the National Longitudinal Alcohol Epidemiologic Survey. *Journal of Substance Abuse, 9,* 103–110.

Johnston, L.D., O'Malley, P.M., & Bachman, J.G. (1998). *National survey results on drug use from the Monitoring the Future study, 1975–1997: Vol. I. Secondary school students* (NIH Publication No. 98-4345). Rockville, MD: National Institute on Drug Abuse.

Kalivas, P.W., Churchill, L., & Klitenick, M.A. (1993). The circuitry mediating the translation of motivational stimuli into adaptive motor responses. In P.W. Kalivas & C.D. Barnes (Eds.), *Limbic motor circuits and neuropsychiatry* (pp. 237–287). Boca Raton, FL: CRC Press.

Larson, R., & Richards, M.H. (1994). *Divergent realities: The emotional lives of mothers, fathers, and adolescents.* New York: Basic Books.

Lewis, D.A. (1997). Development of the prefrontal cortex during adolescence: Insights into vulnerable neural circuits in schizophrenia. *Neuropsychopharmacology, 16,* 385–398.

Petersen, A.C., Compas, B.E., Brooks-Gunn, J., Stemmler, M., Ey, S., & Grant, K.E. (1993). Depression in adolescence. *American Psychologist, 48,* 155–168.

Shedler, J., & Block, J. (1990). Adolescent drug use and psychological health: A longitudinal inquiry. *American Psychologist, 45,* 612–630.

Spear, L.P. (in press). The adolescent brain and age-related behavioral manifestations. *Neuroscience and Biobehavioral Reviews*.

Susman, E.J., Inoff-Germain, G., Nottelmann, E.D., Loriaux, D.L., Cutler, G.B., Jr., & Chrousos, G.P. (1987). Hormones, emotional disposition, and aggressive attributes in young adolescents. *Child Development, 58*, 1114–1134.

Thatcher, R.W., Lyon, G.R., Rumsey, J., & Krasnegor, N. (Eds.). (1996). *Developmental neuroimaging: Mapping the development of brain and behavior.* San Diego: Academic Press.

Critical Thinking Questions

1. What might be the adaptive function of neural transformations that predispose adolescents to engage in sensation seeking and risk-taking behavior?

2. Are adolescent-associated neural alterations the consequence of contextual factors, invariant maturational unfolding, or a combination of both?

3. How will programs and practice aimed at reducing adolescent risk-taking behavior be affected by research implicating neural transformations in the stereotypic behavior of adolescents?

Cognition

Research in cognitive development has burgeoned with new theoretical perspectives as well as new methodologies. One of the outcomes of the last decade of research is that very young infants have knowledge of physical laws concerning continuity and solidity. In her article, Rachel Keen presents a paradox that has emerged with these findings. Studies of older children at about the age of two or three reveal a lack of such knowledge about the physical properties of objects. The scientific community has questioned whether these differences in abilities reflect discontinuities, or regressions in children's concepts of the physical world, or whether they reflect differences in task requirements or methodology. Elucidating the answer to this paradox is of vital importance to cognitive developmental theorists and scientists. In fact, the nature of cognitive tasks in assessing developmental level has been scrutinized for many years. Through a variety of task manipulations, experiments revealed that the task requirements played a role in the performance of the infants and toddlers. Specifically, the task demands placed on toddlers may have been partly responsible for their poor performance. Overall, this research still leaves a theoretical issue unresolved—that is, the results reveal that toddlers and infants both have knowledge of the physical world, but the contents of such knowledge is unclear.

In the next article, Nora Newcombe and her colleagues review recent research about people's memories for their early childhood, and whether childhood amnesia is a real phenomenon. Overall, they argue that indeed, there is a real phenomenon called childhood amnesia. In addition, people seem to recall parts of their experiences from ages 2 to 5, but their recall is more limited than it is for other periods. In addition, they find that young children are unable to encode or retrieve the linked aspects of events that lend to their autobiographical character. The authors argue that there is a brain structure-memory relationship and that the maturation of the prefrontal cortex may be an important link to the development of episodic memories.

The role of culture in all aspects of development cannot be underestimated. In his article, Michael Tomasello reports on the impact of culture in cognitive development. From comparative research with primates, we learn that humans are better adapted for culture, that is, they show higher levels of social learning skills than their nearest primate relatives. As early as one year of age, human infants engage in joint attentional interactions with others. These interactions help infants to understand others as intentional agents and enable them to learn from others the wisdom of their culture through language and symbols.

Deanna Kuhn presents an overview of *metacognition*—the cognition that reflects on, monitors, or regulates first-order cognition. She notes that John Flavell characterized *metacognition* in 1979 as a promising new area of investigation. Since then, the study of *metacognition* has been central to our understanding intellectual performance. In this article, Kuhn discusses two questions—Where does *metacognition* come from and what kinds of it are there? Throughout this article, you will learn that *metacognition* itself is a developmental construct, and with age becomes more explicit, more powerful, and more effective. Kuhn also notes that many adults do not master the complex metacognitive capabilities that emerge with development and acknowledges that educators and developmentalists should have as a goal the enhancement of metacognitive awareness and control of the application of strategies. Taken together, these articles all enhance our understanding of cognitive development and further support the need to examine multiple influences on such development.

Representation of Objects and Events: Why Do Infants Look So Smart and Toddlers Look So Dumb?

Rachel Keen[1]

Department of Psychology, University of Massachusetts, Amherst, Massachusetts

Abstract

Research has demonstrated that very young infants can discriminate between visual events that are physically impossible versus possible. These findings suggest that infants have knowledge of physical laws concerning solidity and continuity. However, research with 2-year-olds has shown that they cannot solve simple problems involving search for a hidden object, even though these problems require the same knowledge. These apparently inconsistent findings raise questions about the interpretation of both data sets. This discrepancy may be resolved by examining differences in task demands.

Keywords

infant cognition; development; search tasks

A paradox has emerged in the developmental literature. On the one hand, a wealth of research from more than a decade of exciting studies shows that very young infants have knowledge of physical laws concerning continuity and solidity (Baillargeon, Graber, DeVos, & Black, 1990; Spelke, Breinlinger, Macomber, & Jacobson, 1992). On the other hand, recent work has revealed a surprising lack of such knowledge in children between 2 and 3 years of age (Berthier, DeBlois, Poirier, Novak, & Clifton, 2000; Hood, Carey, & Prasada, 2000). The question is raised: Are there true discontinuities, even regressions, in children's concepts of the physical world? Or can the discrepancies between the infant and the toddler data sets be resolved by pointing to differences in task requirements? Or perhaps the explanation lies in differences in methodology. For example, in the infant studies the dependent measure is looking, and in the toddler studies it is active search. Whatever the explanation, this paradox must be resolved before a comprehensive theory of early cognitive development can be constructed.

Beginning with the seminal article by Baillargeon, Spelke, and Wasserman (1985), the emerging picture of infants has been that 3- to 4-month-olds show a stunning sophistication in their perception of the physical world. The typical paradigm in this line of research entails the presentation of an event (e.g., a rotating screen in Baillargeon et al., 1985; a rolling ball in Spelke et al., 1992) during repeated trials (referred to as *habituation* trials). Test trials consist of equal numbers of "possible" (*consistent*) events, which accord with the natural laws of physics, and "impossible" (*inconsistent*) events, which break those laws. The assumption is that if infants look longer at inconsistent than at consistent events, they have detected an incongruence with the physical law.

INFANT STUDIES ABOUT OBJECT AND EVENT REPRESENTATION

The procedure in the infancy studies can be clarified by considering an example from Experiment 3 in Spelke et al. (1992). During habituation trials, 3-month-old infants saw a ball roll from the left and disappear behind a screen. A bright blue wall protruded above the screen. When the screen was lifted, the ball could be seen resting against the wall on the right side of the display. Following these trials, an obstacle was placed on the track to the left of the wall, with the topmost part of the obstacle, as well as the blue wall, showing above the screen. On test trials, the ball was again rolled from left to right. For the inconsistent event, when the screen was raised the ball was resting in the old place by the wall, so that it seemed to have violated rules of solidity (i.e., two solid objects cannot occupy the same space at the same time) and continuity (objects exist continuously and move on connected paths over space and time). By appearing at the far wall, the ball seemed to have moved through the solid obstacle or discontinuously jumped over it. For the consistent event, when the screen was raised the ball was resting against the obstacle, a novel position but one that conformed to physical laws. The infants looked significantly longer at the inconsistent event than at the consistent event. A control group saw the ball in the same positions when the screen was raised, but the ball's movement had not violated any physical laws. This group looked at the ball equally in the old and novel locations, thus indicating that they had no intrinsic preference for either display and no preference for the original position. From this and other experiments, investigators have drawn the conclusion that very young infants reason about objects and events by drawing on some form of knowledge about solidity and continuity (Baillargeon, 1993; Spelke et al., 1992).

SURPRISING RESULTS FROM TODDLERS

The discordant results from toddlers come from experiments presenting the same type of physical event—a rolling ball that goes behind a screen and stops—but in this case the child's task is to actually find the ball (Berthier et al., 2000). The apparatus (see Fig. 1) features a wooden screen with four doors that hides the progress of the ball down the track. The ball is always stopped by a barrier, which can be positioned at any of the four doors. The cue to the ball's location is the top of the barrier protruding several centimeters above the screen. If the child understands physical laws of solidity and continuity, he or she should open the door by the barrier. Test trials consist of the experimenter placing the barrier on the track and lowering the screen to conceal the track. Then the experimenter draws the child's attention to the ball and releases it at the top of the track. Finally, the child is invited to open a door to find the ball.

In Figure 2, the columns labeled "opaque" show individual performance on this task in the study by Berthier et al. (2000). Children under 3 years old performed no better than would be expected if they were simply guessing at the ball's location. Of 16 children in each age group, no 2-year-old and only three 2.5-year-olds performed above chance levels; 13 of the 3-year-olds did so, however. (Note:

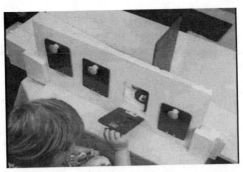

Fig. 1. View of the apparatus used for the toddler task. The child is opening the third door, and the ball, resting against the wall, is visible through the door. From "Where's the Ball? Two- and Three-Year-Olds Reason About Unseen Events," by N.E. Berthier, S. DeBlois, C.R. Poirier, J.A. Novak, and R.K. Clifton, 2000, *Developmental Psychology, 36,* p. 395. Copyright by the American Psychological Association. Reprinted with permission of the author.

Data for 3-year-olds are not displayed in Fig. 2.) The almost total lack of success for children under 3 years of age was quite surprising, and in a series of studies my colleagues and I have sought to understand why their performance is so poor.

Offering more visual information about the ball's trajectory seemed like a reasonable way to help the toddlers (Butler, Berthier, & Clifton, 2002). We

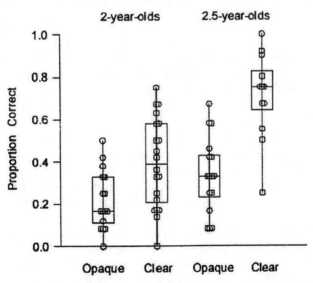

Fig. 2. Proportion of trials correct on the first reach for 2- and 2.5-year olds. Results are shown separately for trials with an opaque screen and a transparent screen. Each circle represents one child's performance. The boxes enclose the second and third quartiles of the distributions, and the horizontal lines in the boxes are the medians. From "Two-Year-Olds' Search Strategies and Visual Tracking in a Hidden Displacement Task," by S.C. Butler, N.E. Berthier, and R.K. Clifton, 2002, *Development Psychology, 38,* p. 588. Copyright by the American Psychological Association. Reprinted with permission of the author.

replaced the opaque wooden screen with a transparent one of tinted Plexiglas, leaving four opaque doors to hide the bottom of the wall and the ball's final resting position. Otherwise we kept the procedure and the rest of the apparatus the same. Now children had a view of the ball as it passed between doors, with the additional cue of no emergence beyond the wall. Despite this substantial increase in visual information about the ball's whereabouts, 2-year-old children still had great difficulty in searching accurately: Only 6 out of 20 children performed above chance. Of the 12 children tested at 2.5 years of age, 10 were above chance, so this age group benefited notably from the additional information (see data in Fig. 2 labeled "clear").

We also recorded eye gaze, monitored from a digital video camera trained on the child's face. Children at both ages were highly attentive as the ball was released, and they tracked its movement down the ramp on 84% of trials. Two aspects of their tracking behavior predicted their response: the point where they stopped tracking the ball and whether they broke their gaze before choosing a door. For older children, tracking the ball to its disappearance was the most typical pattern, and this virtually guaranteed they would open the correct door. A different story emerged for the 2-year-olds. Like 2.5-year-olds, they typically tracked the ball to its final location, but this did not ensure success. If they looked away after correctly tracking the ball, they made errors, although this was not the case for 2.5-year-olds (Butler et al., 2002).

IS THE PROBLEM KEEPING TRACK OF HIDDEN MOVEMENT?

A second visual manipulation was tried (Mash, Keen, & Berthier, in press). We hypothesized that if the children were given a full view of the ball's trajectory until it came to rest against a wall, they would be able to search correctly. In effect, we reversed the sequence of events that concealed the ball: In our previous studies (Berthier et al., 2000; Butler et al., 2002), the screen was first positioned in front of the ramp, hiding most of it from view, and then the ball was released at the top of the ramp, going out of sight while still moving. In this new study, the ball rolled down the ramp and came to a stop by a wall, then the screen was lowered to conceal both the ramp and the ball. At that point, the child's task was the same as in previous studies—open a door to find the ball. Note, however, that in this case the child did not have to reason about solidity and continuity in order to find the ball. Keeping track of its position behind the screen was all that was required.

Allowing complete access to the ball's movements benefited the older children somewhat, but the great majority of 2-year-olds still had enormous problems. Only two out of eighteen 2-year-olds tested performed above chance, whereas seven out of eighteen 2.5-year-olds did. As when we used the clear screen, gaze offered clues as to why children failed. If children looked at the ball as the screen was lowered and maintained this orientation until opening a door, they were correct about 90% of the time. Most children, however, broke their gaze, which resulted in errors. Merely watching as the screen was lowered over the ramp and ball did not aid search; only a continuous fixation up to the point of choosing the door led to success.

WHAT ABOUT TASK DIFFERENCES

In the infant task, 3- to 4-month-old infants looked longer at physically impossible events than at possible events (Baillargeon et al., 1990; Spelke et al., 1992). No prediction was required on the infants' part, as they simply reacted to a visual array of an object in the wrong place or the right place. In contrast, the search task used with toddlers involved prediction and planning within a more complex apparatus. In order to make the infant and toddler tasks more comparable, we designed a looking-time task in which the same door apparatus was used, but the children never opened a door (Mash, Clifton, & Berthier, 2002). Instead, they observed the same events as before, but a puppet, Ricky the raccoon, opened the door.

Most of the time, Ricky opened the correct door and removed the ball. But on test trials, Ricky opened an incorrect door (no ball found, a physically possible, or consistent, event) or opened the correct door but found no ball (a physically impossible, or inconsistent, event). After the door was opened and no ball was found, the experimenter raised the screen to reveal the ball resting against the wall (consistent event) or beyond the wall (inconsistent event). This visual array is highly similar to what infants saw on the test trials of Experiment 3 in Spelke et al. (1992), described earlier. Like the infants, the toddlers looked longer at the inconsistent placement of the ball than at the consistent placement. This result was independently corroborated by a looking-time study with toddlers that used a similar apparatus but a different procedure in which the experimenter opened the doors while the child watched (Hood, Cole-Davies, & Dias, 2003).

CONCLUSIONS

To interpret the results of these studies, first consider what can be ruled out as an explanation of toddlers' poor performance in this search task. The results from the original study using an opaque screen (Berthier et al., 2000; and from Hood et al., 2000, as well) suggested that toddlers have no knowledge of continuity or solidity. In the clear-screen study (Butler et al., 2002), 2-year-olds again failed to recognize the barrier's role in stopping the ball. Maintaining gaze on the spot where the ball disappeared was the behavior most predictive of correct door choice—more evidence that toddlers did not reason about this physical event. But unexpectedly, taking away the reasoning requirement did not lead to success. Observing the disappearance of a stationary ball should have enabled the children to select the correct door if the problem were either hidden movement or the necessity to reason about the barrier's role (Mash et al., in press). The fact that performance remained poor in this condition rules out these explanations of toddlers' poor search performance. The puppet study, which used looking as the response rather than reaching, found that 2-year-olds, like infants, looked longer at the inconsistent event (Mash et al., 2002). This study rules out the disconcerting possibility that infants are endowed with knowledge about physical events that gets lost during development, and is regained around 3 years of age. Finally, although infants and toddlers both fail in search tasks that require a reaching response, previous work not discussed here demonstrated that 6-month-olds will reach for objects hidden by darkness (Clifton,

Rochat, Litovsky, & Perris, 1991). Thus, it is not the response of reaching, in contrast to looking, that is the cause of infants' and toddlers' failure, but rather a problem of knowing where to search.

What could be the toddlers' problem in the search task? A distinct possibility, already mentioned, is the requirement of prediction. In order to plan and execute a successful search, toddlers had to know the ball's location in advance. Moreover, they had to coordinate this knowledge with appropriate action. Further research is needed to determine if either or both of these aspects are critical. One means of exploring this possibility is to devise new tasks that require location prediction but have fewer spatial elements to be integrated than the ball-barrier-door task and require simpler action plans.

A second prime issue needing further investigation is the relation between gaze behavior and search. Choice of the correct door was associated with continuous gaze at the hiding event; gaze breaks before searching were fatal to success. These data imply that children did not use sight of the barrier's top as a cue for the correct door. Likewise, adults faced with an array of 20 identical doors with no further marker might well use unbroken gaze at the point of disappearance as a strategy. If confusion among identical doors is the children's problem, then making the doors distinct should help. This manipulation coupled with careful analysis of gaze could determine whether the toddlers' problem is simply spatial confusion among identical doors. If so, the interesting question remains as to why the barrier's top does not cue location.

Finally, a theoretical issue is unresolved. The results for the looking-time task indicate that toddlers, and even infants, have some knowledge about the ball's expected location, but the contents of their knowledge is unclear. According to Spelke (Spelke et al., 1992), the principles of continuity and solidity are part of a constant core of physical knowledge that infants are endowed with. Infants of 3 to 4 months in age mentally represent hidden objects and can reason about an object's motion being constrained by continuity and solidity. Spelke et al. (1992) did not claim, however, that the infants in their study could predict the ball's location, and the toddler data suggest that infants' and even 2-year-olds' reasoning may be limited to recognizing after-the-fact incongruent events. If so, perceptual recognition of implausible event outcomes seems like a valuable building block on which to construct further knowledge, and eventually prediction, about the physical world.

Recommended Reading

Bertenthal, B.I. (1996). Origins and early development of perception, action, and representation. *Annual Review of Psychology, 47*, 431–459.

Bremner, J.G. (1997). From perception to cognition. In G. Bremner, A. Slater, & G. Butterworth (Eds.), *Infant development: Recent advances* (pp. 55–74). Hove, England: Psychology Press.

Spelke, E.S. (1991). Physical knowledge in infancy: Reflections on Piaget's theory. In S. Carey & R. Gelman (Eds.), *The epigenesis of mind: Essays on biology and cognition* (pp. 133–169). Hillsdale, NJ: Erlbaum.

Willatts, P. (1997). Beyond the "Couch Potato" infant. How infants use their knowledge to regulate action, solve problems, and achieve goals. In G. Bremner, A. Slater, & G. Butterworth (Eds.), *Infant development: Recent advances* (pp. 109–135). Hove, England: Psychology Press.

Acknowledgments—This research was supported by Grant HD27714 from the National Institutes of Health and Research Scientist Award MH00332 from the National Institute of Mental Health to Rachel K. Clifton (now Rachel Keen). I am grateful to Neil Berthier, my collaborator in all of these studies, and to the other collaborators who contributed to various phases of this work.

Note

1. Address correspondence to Rachel Keen, Department of Psychology, Tobin Hall, University of Massachusetts, Amherst, MA 01003.

References

Baillargeon, R. (1993). The object concept revisited: New directions in the investigation of infants' physical knowledge In C.E. Granrud (Ed.), *Visual perception and cognition in infancy* (pp. 265–315). Hillsdale, NJ: Erlbaum.

Baillargeon, R., Graber, M., DeVos, J., & Black, J. (1990). Why do young infants fail to search for hidden objects? *Cognition, 36,* 225–284.

Baillargeon, R., Spelke, E., & Wasserman, S. (1985). Object permanence in five-month-old infants. *Cognition, 20,* 191–208.

Berthier, N.E., DeBlois, S., Poirier, C.R., Novak, J.A., & Clifton, R.K. (2000). Where's the ball? Two- and three-year-olds reason about unseen events. *Developmental Psychology, 36,* 394–401.

Butler, S.C., Berthier, N.E., & Clifton, R.K. (2002). Two-year-olds' search strategies and visual tracking in a hidden displacement task. *Developmental Psychology, 38,* 581–590.

Clifton, R., Rochat, P., Litovsky, R., & Perris, E. (1991). Object representation guides infants' reaching in the dark. *Journal of Experimental Psychology: Human Perception and Performance, 17,* 323–329,

Hood, B., Carey, S., & Prasada, S. (2000). Predicting the outcomes of physical events: Two-year-olds fail to reveal knowledge of solidity and support. *Child Development, 71,* 1540–1554.

Hood, B., Cole-Davies, V., & Dias, M. (2003). Looking and search measures of object knowledge in pre-school children. *Developmental Psychology, 39,* 61–70.

Mash, C., Clifton, R.K., & Berthier, N.E. (2002, April). Two-year-olds' event reasoning and object search. In L. Santos (Chair), *Interpreting dissociations between infant looking and reaching: A comparative approach.* Symposium conducted at the meeting of the International Society on Infant Studies, Toronto, Ontario, Canada.

Mash, C., Keen, R., & Berthier, N.E. (in press). Visual access and attention in two-year-olds' event reasoning and object search. *Infancy.*

Spelke, E.S., Breinlinger, K., Macomber, J., & Jacobson, K. (1992). Origins of knowledge. *Psychological Review, 99,* 605–632.

Critical Thinking Questions

1. Do discontinuities exist across early development in children's knowledge of physical laws such as continuity and solidity? Or are discrepancies between infant and toddler data sets a result of methodological inconsistencies or misinterpretation of data?

2. Do psychological constructs associated with cognitive development possess different age-related manifestations? If differences indeed exist, how might they inhibit drawing developmental conclusions? What are the methodological challenges?

3. How does one know beyond a reasonable doubt that two different measures designed for two different age groups are measuring the same aspect of cognitive development?

Remembering Early Childhood: How Much, How, and Why (or Why Not)

Nora S. Newcombe,[1] Anna Bullock Drummey,

Nathan A. Fox, Eunhui Lie, and Wendy Ottinger-Alberts

Department of Psychology, Temple University, Philadelphia, Pennsylvania (N.S.N., A.B.D., W.O.-A.); College of Human Development, University of Maryland, College Park, Maryland (N.A.F.); and Temple University School of Medicine, Philadelphia, Pennsylvania (E.L.)

Abstract

In this article, we consider recent research on three questions about people's memories for their early childhood: whether childhood amnesia is a real phenomenon, whether implicit memories survive when explicit memories do not, and why early episodic memories are sketchy. The research leads us to form three conclusions. First, we argue that childhood amnesia is a real phenomenon, as long as the term is defined clearly. Specifically, people are able to recall parts of their lives from the period between ages 2 and 5 years, but they recall less from that period than from other periods. Second, we conclude that implicit memories from early childhood may be evident even when explicit memories are not, a finding that suggests early experience may affect behavior in ways that people do not consciously recognize. Third, we argue that although young children are well known to be wonderfully efficient learners of semantic information, they have difficulty in either encoding or retrieving the interlinked aspects of events that lend them their autobiographical character. Although more evidence is needed, the relative lack of episodic memories of early childhood may be linked to maturation of prefrontal cortex.

Keywords

memory; development; amnesia; frontal lobes

Do you remember your third birthday party? When your younger brother was born? What happened on your first day at preschool? For most people, the answer to these questions is "no." However, most people *can* remember their high school prom, the birth of their children, or their arrival at college. This intuitive contrast between memory for early childhood and memory for middle childhood and beyond has led to the idea that there is a phenomenon called childhood amnesia, and researchers have searched to understand its dimensions and explain it. In this article, we consider three questions about childhood amnesia. First, is the intuitive phenomenon real? Some investigators have suggested that memory is essentially at adult levels at least by age 2, whereas others have thought that childhood amnesia extends for variable periods, up to age 5 or 6. Second, if there is such a phenomenon, an interesting question is whether, as in "real" amnesia (the kind arising from some kinds of brain damage), early experience might affect behavior in ways that people would not consciously recognize. Third, there is the issue of why memories for early childhood seem to be lacking. Children learn much before the age of 5 years, including most of the language they will ever need to know and a host of facts about the world; why should these voracious learners lack the ability to remember some of the basic elements of their own daily lives during this period?

IS CHILDHOOD AMNESIA A REAL PHENOMENON?

Salient events occurring in children's lives when they are as young as 2 years, such as the birth of a younger sibling, can sometimes be recalled even in adulthood (e.g., Eacott & Crawley, 1998). Furthermore, controlled studies have shown that when children only a year or so old are shown certain actions by an adult, they can remember those actions when they are 2 or so, as indicated by their production of the actions when shown the context again (Bauer & Wewerka, 1995). In the face of data such as these, showing startling evidence of the existence of early memory, some investigators have doubted whether there is a real phenomenon of childhood amnesia at all.

It is important to remember, however, that verbal recall of early events in these studies is usually sketchy. Memories are more likely to occur and are likely to be more detailed as the age when the event occurred increases. This phenomenon does not appear to be explained simply by the fact that older memories necessarily involve longer delays. Our research has shown that not only is verbal recall for childhood events sketchy, but visual memories of familiar faces from childhood are sketchy as well. For example, we showed 10-year-olds pictures of their preschool classmates, mixed with pictures of other preschool children. The children correctly recognized just over 20% of their preschool classmates, a level of performance that is better than would be expected by chance but unimpressive compared with how well adults recognize photos from their high school yearbooks (Newcombe & Fox, 1994). Even after almost five decades, adults can pick out their high school classmates with better than 70% accuracy (Bahrick, Bahrick, & Wittlinger, 1975). In another relevant study (Lie & Newcombe, 1999), about 3 years after leaving preschool, children were much poorer at recognizing their former classmates than were their preschool teachers.

The phenomenon shown in these studies is not an absolute one. Although virtually nothing can usually be recalled from before the age of 2 years, stimuli children encounter when they are 2, 3, and 4 years old are often remembered with above-chance accuracy. However, the fact that memory at these ages is substantially lower than comparable memories formed by older individuals suggests a phenomenon appropriately called childhood amnesia, even though the amnesia is not profound or absolute. Indeed, the amnesia induced by brain damage is often not absolute either.

DO IMPLICIT MEMORIES SURVIVE IN CHILDHOOD AMNESIA?

One of the most fascinating discoveries in recent research on memory has been the finding that people suffering from brain damage causing amnesia can still show evidence of being affected by prior experience. For instance, they can learn motor skills, exhibit classical conditioning, and show evidence of what is called priming (i.e., increased swiftness and accuracy in processing previously encountered stimuli). Such research gives rise to the question of whether similar phenomena can be seen in childhood amnesia. Do children who show failure to recall or even recognize things from their preschool years show evidence that this information is nevertheless preserved in some fashion?

In one study (Newcombe & Fox, 1994), we used small changes in the skin's electrical conductance as a measure of implicit (i.e., nonconscious) memory for preschool classmates' faces. Even children who had no apparent explicit (i.e., consciously stateable) memory of the faces exhibited skin conductance responses that discriminated between classmates and unknown children. This discrimination was equivalent to that shown by children who did have some ability to recognize their former classmates. In another study (Lie & Newcombe, 1999), we used instead a behavioral test of implicit memory, asking children to judge whether pictures of two faces, taken from different angles, showed the same person or not. The children were better able to make these judgments if the faces were pictures of a former classmate rather than pictures of a stranger. (Explicit memory in this case was not low enough to examine the issue of whether the facilitation existed even when explicit memory was lacking.)

Studies of memory for faces encountered in natural social settings are interesting, but they are difficult to control for various important variables, such as length of exposure to the faces. For this reason, in yet another study of implicit memory (Drummey & Newcombe, 1995), we showed storybook pictures to 3-year-olds, 5-year-olds, and adults. Three months later, they were asked to name the pictures, in a situation in which the pictures were initially out of focus and became progressively sharper. Being able to recognize pictures that are not in good focus is a measure of perceptual priming, a type of implicit memory. After 3 months, 3-year-old children's recognition memory for the pictures was at chance (i.e., the children demonstrated no explicit memory for the pictures), but they still showed perceptual priming for those pictures. Five-year-olds and adults did better on recognition memory than 3-year-olds, but no consistent age differences were seen in perceptual priming.

These data are consistent with the general conclusion, derived from many studies, that implicit memory is formed at an earlier age than explicit memory and shows little developmental improvement. Taken together, the findings suggest that much that people forget about their early childhood influences their responses later in life. In this sense, there may truly be an unconscious—not the kind of unconscious postulated by Freud, in which material is repressed because it is unacceptable, but rather a source of feelings and facilities that the conscious mind does not fully understand.

WHY ARE EARLY MEMORIES SKETCHY?

Observations of the survival of implicit memories of early childhood do not explain (in some sense, they deepen) the mystery of why early explicit memory is lacking. An additional element in the mystery is that young children do form certain kinds of explicit memories easily—the kinds of memories that fall into the category of what is called semantic memory. For instance, they learn large numbers of words. What they seem not to do as well is to encode and retain what are called episodic memories, that is, memories for particular events, or particular stimuli occurring in particular contexts. An important factor in explaining the dramatic changes in episodic memory occurring during the preschool years can be derived from the source-monitoring framework developed by Johnson, Hashtroudi, and Lindsay (1993). Johnson et al. suggested that the ability to bind together specific combinations of memory characteristics, including perceptual, contextual, and affective information, underlies the ability to show explicit episodic memory. In their view, access to such perceptual, contextual, and affective memory characteristics allows people to determine the source of information, for instance, whether an event was imagined or real (e.g., "Did I really take my pill or just think about doing it?"). A memory for a real event would include more perceptual information (e.g., color), more spatial-temporal information, and more meaningful details than a memory for an imagined event. In addition, knowing that an event is real—and having access to particular information about details, spatial-temporal context, and so on—is critical for having memories that seem to be part of the personal past.

Consider memories for an event, such as a trip to the beach. If one remembers vivid and interlinked details about the trip to the beach, such as the hot weather, wearing a polka-dot bathing suit, and eating a pistachio ice-cream cone under the shade of the palm tree, the event will both be considered real rather than imagined and have an episodic (i.e., autobiographical) quality. A memory for a more isolated aspect of the experience, such as the weather taken alone, may be thought to be merely imagined, or to be simply a semantic memory (i.e., knowledge of the fact that people usually go to the beach when the weather is hot).

Previous work on the development of children's ability to recall the source of facts (source monitoring) suggests that source monitoring is relatively mature by the time children are 6 years old. However, there is evidence of rapid development between the ages of 3 and 5 years. For instance, Gopnik and Graf (1988) found that 3-year-olds performed only slightly better than would be expected by chance when asked how they knew what was in a drawer (i.e., whether they had been shown, had been told, or had been given a clue). More recently, we adapted a source-monitoring paradigm previously used to study elderly people and people with brain damage for use with young children (Drummey & Newcombe, 1999). We taught children of various ages a set of novel facts (e.g., that the Nile is the longest river in the world) and later asked the children questions about these facts. The 4-year-olds later recalled, or at least recognized, more than 70% of these facts, but were strikingly unable to remember where they learned the information, succeeding in only 21% of the cases. Most of the errors involved saying that the information was learned in a situation outside the experiment, for example, from a parent, a teacher, or the media. The 6- and 8-year-olds in this study rarely made such errors.

However, children's failure to remember a source could be due to factors not relevant to their difficulties with episodic recall. For instance, children might perform poorly because of a lack of interest in such information (i.e., young children may not realize how important it is to discriminate real from imagined events). Finding a similar developmental improvement in the preschool years for other kinds of information about simple events, such as perceptual, contextual, and affective information, would bolster the case for a source-monitoring approach toward explaining why early episodic memory is lacking. We found such evidence in a study with children 4, 6, and 8 years old (Ottinger-Alberts & Newcombe, 1999). The children either experienced or imagined scenarios (e.g., planting a flower, unpacking a picnic basket), guided by a taped script. One week later, they were asked whether the events had been experienced or imagined, and answered a number of questions concerning perceptual, spatial-temporal, and semantic aspects of the events. For example, in the case of unpacking a picnic basket, they were asked what color the napkin was, what shape the basket was, and what kind of utensil was in the basket. Recall for aspects of real events increased markedly between the ages of 4 and 6, but relatively little between the ages of 6 and 8, despite the fact that recall levels for older children were quite far from perfect. In addition, 4-year-olds performed quite poorly in distinguishing experienced from imagined events, whereas 6- and 8-year-olds did very well. When 4-year-olds were tested on the same day the events took place, their memories were much better than after a 1-week delay, and they were easily able to make source-monitoring judgments. Thus, the difficulty after the 1-week delay was likely due to the fact that the younger children's memories for the real events, although more vivid than their memories for the imagined events, were still too impoverished to support a judgment that an event had actually taken place.

Development of contextualized memories may be linked to development of function of prefrontal cortex, a process known to be ongoing at this age. Prefrontal cortex is the area of cortex at the front of the brain that has been linked to working memory, inhibition, decision making, and executive control of behavior. The hypothesis of a linkage to prefrontal development is suggested by several findings. First, people with damage to this area perform poorly on tests of source memory. Second, poor source memory can also be seen in the elderly, and their scores on tests of prefrontal functioning are often correlated with their scores for source memory. Third, in normal adults, neuroimaging studies have shown that the prefrontal cortex is activated during encoding and retrieval of episodic (autobiographical) memories.

The results of two studies we recently conducted are in line with this hypothesis. In one study (Drummey & Newcombe, 1999), source memory was correlated with measures of prefrontal functioning. In the second study (Ottinger-Alberts & Newcombe, 1999), 4-year-olds' recall scores for real events were significantly predicted from another measure of prefrontal functioning. The relations held true even in analyses controlling for age, IQ, and, in the latter study, size of vocabulary.

NEW DIRECTIONS

One reason for the difficulty people have recalling events and stimuli from the preschool period may be that either the encoding or the retrieval, or both, of episodic memory depends on effortful use of the prefrontal lobes to coordinate and interlink the aspects of events that give them their particular and autobiographical quality. These areas of the brain may not yet be mature enough at this age to easily or efficiently support such activity. This hypothesis needs further assessment, however. A promising tactic is to use electrophysiological methods to examine the relation between prefrontal activation at encoding and retrieval in young children and the probability of successful recall or recognition. In addition, we need to understand how social and biological factors interact in memory development. For instance, children's growing appreciation of the importance of memory to other people (e.g., parents want to know what happened at preschool) might depend on brain maturation. Alternatively, social factors leading to such appreciation might recruit and shape prefrontal cortex in the service of this socially valued function.

Recommended Reading

Fivush, R., & Hammond, N.R. (1990). Autobiographical memory across the preschool years: Toward reconceptualizing childhood amnesia. In R. Fivush & L.A. Hudson (Eds.), *Knowing and remembering in young children* (pp. 223–248). New York: Cambridge University Press.

Howe, M.L., & Courage, M.L. (1993). On resolving the enigma of infantile amnesia. *Psychological Bulletin, 113*, 305–326.

Johnson, M.K., Hashtroudi, S., & Lindsay, D.S. (1993). (See References)

Nelson, K. (1992). Emergence of autobiographical memory at age 4. *Human Development, 35*, 172–177.

Perner, J., & Ruffman, T. (1995). Episodic memory and autonoetic consciousness: Developmental evidence and a theory of childhood amnesia. *Journal of Experimental Child Psychology, 59*, 516–548.

Note

1. Address correspondence to Nora S. Newcombe, 565 Weiss Hall, Temple University, 1701 North 13th St., Philadelphia, PA 19122-6085; e-mail: newcombe@astro.temple.edu.

References

Bahrick, H.P., Bahrick, P.O., & Wittlinger, R.P. (1975). Fifty years of memory for names and faces: A cross-sectional approach. *Journal of Experimental Psychology: General, 104*, 54–75.

Bauer, P.J., & Wewerka, S. (1995). One- to two-year olds' recall of events: The more expressed, the more impressed. *Journal of Experimental Child Psychology, 59*, 475–496.

Drummey, A.B., & Newcombe, N. (1995). Remembering versus knowing the past: Children's explicit and implicit memories for pictures. *Journal of Experimental Child Psychology, 59*, 540–565.

Drummey, A.B., & Newcombe, N. (1999). *Prefrontal cortex development and changes in episodic memory.* Manuscript submitted for publication.

Eacott, M.J., & Crawley, R.A. (1998). The offset of childhood amnesia: Memory for events that occurred before age 3. *Journal of Experimental Psychology: General, 127*, 22–33.

Gopnik, A., & Graf, P. (1988). Knowing how you know: Young children's ability to identify and remember the source of their beliefs. *Child Development, 59*, 1366–1371.

Johnson, M.K., Hashtroudi, S., & Lindsay, D.S. (1993). Source monitoring. *Psychological Bulletin, 114*, 3–28.

Lie, E., & Newcombe, N. (1999). Elementary school children's explicit and implicit memory for faces of preschool classmates. *Developmental Psychology, 35*, 102–112.

Newcombe, N., & Fox, N. (1994). Infantile amnesia: Through a glass darkly. *Child Development,* *65,* 31–40.

Ottinger-Alberts, W., & Newcombe, N. (1999, April). *Retrieval effort, source monitoring, and childhood amnesia: A new look at an old problem.* Paper presented at the annual meeting of the Society for Research in Child Development, Albuquerque, NM.

Critical Thinking Questions

1. What does the phenomenon of childhood amnesia mean to the notion of critical periods in development?

2. How do implicit memories in early childhood influence later development?

3. What kinds of explicit memories are formed during early childhood? What kinds are not?

Culture and Cognitive Development

Michael Tomasello[1]

Max Planck Institute for Evolutionary Anthropology, Leipzig, Germany

Abstract

Human beings are biologically adapted for culture in ways that other primates are not. The difference can be clearly seen when the social learning skills of humans and their nearest primate relatives are systematically compared. The human adaptation for culture begins to make itself manifest in human ontogeny at around 1 year of age as human infants come to understand other persons as intentional agents like the self and so engage in joint attentional interactions with them. This understanding then enables young children (a) to employ some uniquely powerful forms of cultural learning to acquire the accumulated wisdom of their cultures, especially as embodied in language, and also (b) to comprehend their worlds in some uniquely powerful ways involving perspectively based symbolic representations.

Keywords

culture; cognition; human evolution; language; joint attention

Until fairly recently, the study of children's cognitive development was dominated by the theory of Jean Piaget. Piaget's theory was detailed, elaborate, comprehensive, and, in many important respects, wrong. In attempting to fill the theoretical vacuum created by Piaget's demise, developmental psychologists have sorted themselves into two main groups. In the first group are those theorists who emphasize biology. These neonativists believe that organic evolution has provided human beings with some specific domains of knowledge of the world and its workings arid that this knowledge is best characterized as "innate." Such domains include, for example, mathematics, language, biology, and psychology.

In the other group are theorists who have focused on the cultural dimension of human cognitive development. These cultural psychologists begin with the fact that human children grow into cognitively competent adults in the context of a structured social world full of material and symbolic artifacts such as tools and language, structured social interactions such as rituals and games, and cultural institutions such as families and religions. The claim is that the cultural context is not just a facilitator or motivator for cognitive development, but rather a unique "ontogenetic niche" (i.e., a unique context for development) that actually structures human cognition in fundamental ways.

There are many thoughtful scientists in each of these theoretical camps. This suggests the possibility that each has identified some aspects of the overall theory that will be needed to go beyond Piaget and incorporate adequately both the cultural and the biological dimensions of human cognitive development. What is needed to achieve this aim, in my opinion, is (a) an evolutionary approach to the human capacity for culture and (b) an ontogenetic approach to human cognitive development in the context of culture.

CHIMPANZEE AND HUMAN CULTURE

It is widely agreed among behavioral biologists that the best examples of animal culture come from chimpanzees. For example, different chimpanzee communities have been documented to have different tool-use traditions, such as termite-fishing, ant-fishing, ant-dipping, nut-cracking, and leaf-sponging (Tomasello & Call, 1997). Some of these community differences are due to the different local ecologies of different groups of chimpanzees. The individuals of each group learn to solve the problems presented by their local environment using the resources available in that environment.

But experimental studies have shown that there is more to it than this; chimpanzees can learn things from observing others using tools. What they learn, however, is less than might be expected. They learn the effects on the environment that can be produced with a particular tool; they do not actually learn to copy another chimpanzee's behavioral strategies. For example, in one study, chimpanzees were presented with a rakelike tool and an out-of-reach object. The tool could be used in either of two ways to obtain the object. One group of chimpanzees observed one way of using the tool, and another group observed the other way. However, the demonstration observed had no effect on which method or methods the chimpanzees used to obtain the object. This kind of learning is called emulation learning. In contrast, when human children were given this same task, they much more often imitatively learned the precise technique demonstrated for them (see Tomasello, 1996, for a review). Studies of chimpanzee gestural communication have found similar results. Young chimpanzees ritualize signals with group mates over repeated encounters in which they essentially shape one another's behavior. They do not learn the signals of group mates via imitation (Tomasello et al., 1997).

Chimpanzees and other nonhuman animals may thus engage in some forms of cultural transmission, defined very broadly as the nongenetic transfer of information, but they do not do this by means of imitative learning if this is defined more narrowly as the reproduction of another individual's actual behavioral strategy toward. a goal. In contrast, human beings learn from conspecifics by perceiving their goals and then attempting to reproduce the strategies the other persons use in attempting to achieve those goals—truly cultural learning, as opposed to merely social learning (Tomasello, Kruger, & Ratner, 1993).

This small difference in learning process leads to a huge difference in cultural evolution; specifically, only cultural learning leads to cumulative cultural evolution in which the culture produces artifacts—both material artifacts, such as tools, and symbolic artifacts, such as language and Arabic numerals—that accumulate modifications over historical time. Thus, one person invents something, other persons learn it and then modify and improve it, and then this new and improved version is learned by a new generation—and so on across generations. Imitative learning is a key to this process because it enables individuals to acquire the uses of artifacts and other practices of their social groups relatively faithfully, and this relatively exact learning then serves as a kind of ratchet—keeping the practice in place in the social group (perhaps for many generations) until some creative innovation comes along. Each human child, in using these artifacts to mediate its interactions with the world, thus grows up in the context of something like the accumulated wisdom of its entire social group, past and present.

HUMAN CULTURAL LEARNING

The human adaptation for cultural learning is best seen ontogenetically and in the context of infants' other social and cognitive activities. The key transition occurs at 9 to 12 months of age, as infants begin to engage in interactions that are triadic in the sense that they involve the referential triangle of child, adult, and some outside entity to which they are both attending. Thus, infants at this age begin to flexibly and reliably look where adults are looking (gaze following), use adults as emotional reference points (social referencing), and act on objects in the way adults are acting on them (imitative learning)—in short, 1-year-olds begin to "tune in" to the attention and behavior of adults toward outside entities. At this same age, infants also begin to use communicative gestures to direct adult attention and behavior to outside entities in which *they* are interested—in short, to get the adult to "tune in" to them. Most often, the term joint attention has been used to characterize this whole complex of triadic social skills and interactions, and it represents a revolution in the way infants understand other persons. There is evidence that infants can begin to engage in joint attentional interactions only when they understand other persons as intentional agents like themselves, that is, as persons who have behavioral and perceptual goals and make active choices among the means for attaining those goals (Carpenter, Nagell, & Tomasello, 1998). (I understand attention to be intentional focusing on one aspect of experience to the exclusion of others.)

This social-cognitive revolution at 1 year of age sets the stage for the 2nd year of life, in which infants begin to imitatively learn the use of all kinds of tools, artifacts, and symbols. For example, in a study by Meltzoff (1988), 14-month-old children observed an adult bend at the waist and touch his head to a panel, thus turning on a light. They followed suit. Infants engaged in this unusual and awkward behavior even though it would have been easier and more natural for them simply to push the panel with their hand. One interpretation of this behavior is that the infants understood that (a) the adult had the goal of illuminating the light and then chose one means for doing so, from among other possible means, and (b) if they had the same goal, they could choose the same means. Cultural learning of this type thus relies fundamentally on infants' tendency to identify with adults, and on their ability to distinguish in the actions of others the underlying goal and the different means that might be used to achieve it. This interpretation is supported by Meltzoff's (1995) more recent finding that 18-month-old children also imitatively learn actions that an adult intends to perform, even if she is unsuccessful in doing so. Similarly, my colleagues and I (Carpenter, Akhtar, & Tomasello, 1998) found that 16-month-old infants imitatively learned from a complex behavioral sequence only those behaviors that appeared intentional, ignoring those that appeared accidental. Young children do not just mimic the limb movements of other persons; rather, they attempt to reproduce other persons' intended, goal-directed actions in the world.

Although it is not obvious at first glance, something like this same imitative learning process must happen if children are to learn the symbolic conventions of their native language. In some recent experiments, we have found that children learn words in situations in which they must work fairly hard to discern the adult's communicative intentions. For example, one study involved an adult playing a "finding game" with children. The adult bid each child find four different objects in four different hiding places, one of which was a very distinctive toy barn. Once the child had learned which objects went with which places, the adult announced her intention to "find the gazzer." She then went to the toy barn, but it turned out to be "locked." She then frowned at the barn and proceeded to extract other objects from the other hiding places. Later, the children demonstrated that they had learned "gazzer" as the name of the object locked in the barn. What is significant about this finding is that the children knew which one was the gazzer even though they never saw the target object after they heard the new word; they had to infer from the adult's behavior (trying to get into the barn and frowning when it was impossible) which object she wanted, without even seeing the object (see Tomasello, in press, for a review).

This kind of learning can be referred to as cultural learning because the child is not just learning things *from* other persons but is learning things *through* them—in the sense that he or she must know something of the adult's perspective on a situation in order to learn the same intentionally communicative act (Tomasello et al., 1993). The adult in the study just described is not just moving and picking up objects randomly, she is searching for an object, and the child must know this in order to make enough sense of her behavior to connect the new word to its intended referent. An organism can engage in cultural learning of this type only when it understands others as intentional agents like the self who have a perspective on the world that can be entered into, directed, and shared. Indeed, a strong argument can be made that children can understand a symbolic convention in the first place only if they understand their communicative partner as an intentional agent with whom one may share attention— because a linguistic symbol is nothing other than a marker for an intersubjectively shared understanding of a situation (Tomasello, in press). Thus, children with autism do not understand other persons as intentional agents, or they do so to only an imperfect degree, and so (a) they are very poor at the imitative learning of intentional actions in general, (b) only half of them ever learn any language at all, and (c) those who do learn some language are very poor in word-learning situations such as those just described (Hobson, 1993).

It is important to emphasize as well that when children learn linguistic symbols, what they are learning is a whole panoply of ways to manipulate the attention of other persons, sometimes on a single entity, on the basis of such things as

- generality (*thing, furniture, chair, desk chair*),
- perspective (*chase-flee, buy-sell, come-go, borrow-lend*), and
- function (*father, lawyer, man, American; coast, shore, beach*).

And there are many other perspectives that arise in grammatical combinations of various sorts (*She smashed the vase* vs. *The vase was smashed*). Consequently, as children internalize a linguistic symbol—as they learn the human perspective embodied in that symbol—they not only cognitively represent the perceptual or motoric aspects of a situation, but also cognitively represent one way, among other ways of which they are also aware, that the current situation may be attentionally construed by "us," the users of the symbol. The perspectival nature of linguistic symbols thus represents a clear break with straightforward perceptual or sensory-motor cognitive representations, and indeed this perspectivity is what gives linguistic symbols their awesome cognitive power (Tomasello, 1999). It even allows children to learn linguistic means for conceptualizing objects as actions (*He porched the newspaper*), actions as objects (*Skiing is fun*), and many other metaphorical construals (*Love is a journey*).

CULTURAL COGNITION

The biological origin of human culture is an adaptation that occurred at some point in human evolution—probably quite recently, in the past 150,000 years, with the rise of modern humans. It was not an everyday adaptation, however, because it did not just change one relatively isolated characteristic, it changed the process of human evolution. It did this most immediately by changing the nature of human social cognition, which in turn changed the nature of human cultural transmission, which in turn led to a series of cascading sociological and psychological events in historical and ontogenetic time. The new form of social cognition that started the entire process was the understanding of other persons as intentional agents like the self, and the new process of cultural transmission was the various forms of cultural learning, the first and most important of which was imitative learning (the others are instructed learning and collaborative learning). These new forms of cultural learning created the possibility of a kind of ratchet effect in which human beings not only pooled their cognitive resources contemporaneously, but also built on one another's cognitive inventions over time. This new form of cultural evolution thus created artifacts and social practices with a "history." The most important artifact in this connection is language, the acquisition of which leads to some new forms of perspectivally based (i.e., symbolic) cognitive representation. Modern human cognition is thus a result not just of processes of biological evolution, but also of cultural processes that human biological evolution made possible in both cultural-historical time and ontogenetic time.

Recommended Reading

Boesch, C., & Tomasello, M. (1998). Chimpanzee and human culture. *Current Anthropology, 39*, 591–604.
Carpenter, M., Nagell, K., & Tomasello, M. (1998). (See References)
Tomasello, M. (1999). (See References)
Tomasello, M., & Call, J. (1997). (See References)
Tomasello, M., Kruger, A., & Ratner, H. (1993). (See References)

Note

1. Address correspondence to Michael Tomasello, Max Planck Institute for Evolutionary Anthropology, Inselstrasse 22, D-04103 Leipzig, Germany; e-mail: tomas@eva.mpg.de.

References

Carpenter, M., Akhtar, N., & Tomasello, M. (1998). 14- through 18-month-old infants differentially imitate intentional and accidental actions. *Infant Behavior and Development, 21*, 315–330.

Carpenter, M., Nagell, K., & Tomasello, M. (1998). Social cognition, joint attention, and communicative competence from 9 to 15 months of age. *Monographs of the Society for Research in Child Development, 63*(4, Serial No. 255).

Hobson, P. (1993). *Autism and the development of mind.* Hillsdale, NJ: Erlbaum.

Meltzoff, A. (1988). Infant imitation and memory: Nine-month olds in immediate and deferred tests. *Child Development, 59*, 217–225.

Meltzoff, A. (1995). Understanding the intentions of others: Re-enactment of intended acts by 18-month-old children. *Developmental Psychology, 31*, 838–850.

Tomasello, M. (1996). Do apes ape? In J. Galef & C. Heyes (Eds.), *Social learning in animals: The roots of culture* (pp. 319–346). New York: Academic Press.

Tomasello, M. (1999). *The cultural origins of human cognition.* Cambridge, MA: Harvard University Press.

Tomasello, M. (in press). Perceiving intentions and learning words in the second year of life. In M. Bowerman & S. Levinson (Eds.), *Language acquisition and conceptual development.* New York: Cambridge University Press.

Tomasello, M., & Call, J. (1997). *Primate cognition.* New York: Oxford University Press.

Tomasello, M., Call, J., Warren, J., Frost, T., Carpenter, M., & Nagell, K. (1997). The ontogeny of chimpanzee gestural signals: A comparison across groups and generations. *Evolution of Communication, 1*, 223–253.

Tomasello, M., Kruger, A., & Ratner, H. (1993). Cultural learning. *Behavioral and Brain Sciences, 16*, 495–552.

Critical Thinking Questions

1. How might the notion that human beings are biologically adapted for culture exemplify the nature/nurture debate?

2. What is the function of *joint attention* in human cultural learning?

3. Is all learning embedded in human perspectives? Is there such a thing as "objective", aperspectival learning?

Metacognitive Development

Deanna Kuhn[1]

Teachers College, Columbia University, New York, New York

Abstract

Traditional developmental research in memory and reasoning, as well as current investigations in such disparate areas as theory of mind, epistemological understanding,
knowledge acquisition, and problem solving, share the need to invoke a meta-level of
cognition in explaining their respective phenomenon The increasingly influential construct of metacognition can be conceptualized in a developmental framework. Young
children's dawning awareness of mental functions lies at one end of a developmental
progression that eventuates in complex metaknowing capabilities that many adults do
not master. During its extended developmental course, metacognition becomes more
explicit, powerful, and effective, as it comes to operate increasingly under the individual's conscious control. Enhancing (a) metacognitive awareness of what one believes
and how one knows and (b) metastrategic control in application of the strategies that
process new information is an important developmental and educational goal.

Keywords

metacognition; development; knowledge acquisition

Metacognition—that is, cognition that reflects on, monitors, or regulates first-
order cognition—was characterized by Flavell in 1979 as a "promising new area
of investigations (p. 906). He appears to have been on the right track. The claim
that metacognition is "where the action is" in understanding intellectual performance would meet with approval in many (though not all) circles today. If so,
what do we need to know about this construct? The answer is, a great many
things, but here I focus on two fundamental questions that have lacked clear
answers: Where does metacognition come from and what kinds of it are there?
In addition, I examine the relation between metacognition and cognition. Do
they work together closely, or is the relation a more distant and formal one, akin
to that between metaphysics and physics?

The answer I propose to the first question is that metacognition develops.
It does not appear abruptly from nowhere as an epiphenomenon in relation to
first-order cognition. Instead, metacognition emerges early in life, in forms that
are no more than suggestive of what is to come, and follows an extended developmental course during which it becomes more explicit, more powerful, and
hence more effective, as it comes to operate increasingly under the individual's
conscious control. Placing metacognition in this developmental framework helps
to clarify its nature and significance.

DEVELOPMENTAL ORIGINS OF METACOGNITION IN THEORY OF MIND

Over the past decade, the wave of research on children's understanding of the
mind has been valuable in highlighting the earliest forms of metacognition. By

age 3, children have acquired some awareness of themselves and others as know-ers. They distinguish thinking about an object from actually perceiving it, and begin to refer to their own knowledge states, using verbs such as *think* and *know* (Flavell, 1999). By age 4, they understand that others' behavior is guided by beliefs and desires and that such beliefs may not match their own and could be incorrect. This so-called false belief understanding is a developmental milestone because it connects assertions to their generative source in human knowers. These early years are also a period of rapidly developing awareness of how one has come to know that what one claims is so—that is, awareness of the sources of one's knowledge.

These early metacognitive achievements serve as foundations for much of the higher-order thinking that appears later. Understanding knowledge as the product of human knowing is a critical first step in the development of episte-mological thinking, which is metacognitive in the sense of constituting in implicit theory of how things are known and increasingly is becoming recognized as influ-ential in higher-order thinking (Hofer & Pintrich, 1997). Scientific thinking is another form of higher-order thinking whose roots lie in early metacognitive achievements (Kuhn & Pearsall, 2000). Awareness of the sources of one's knowl-edge is critical to understanding evidence as distinct from and bearing on the-ories—an understanding that lies at the heart of scientific thinking. In skilled scientific thinking, existing understandings are coordinated with new evidence, and new knowledge is thereby acquired, in a highly deliberate, rule-governed, and therefore metacognitively controlled process.

DEVELOPMENTAL ORIGINS OF METASTRATEGIC AWARENESS AND CONTROL

Are there different kinds of metacognition? A long-standing distinction in cog-nitive psychology is that between declarative (knowing that) and procedural (knowing how) knowing. If these two kinds of knowing are fundamentally dif-ferent, perhaps meta-level operations on them also differ. Specifically, I propose, we would expect meta-level operations to have their greatest influence on pro-cedural knowing. Meta-level awareness of strategies for comprehending a chap-ter in a textbook, for example, may influence comprehension efforts, whereas explicit meta-level awareness of the declarative knowledge gained from the chap-ter ("knowing that I know") has less obvious effects on the knowledge itself.

I have proposed *metastrategic knowing* as a separate term to refer to meta-knowing about procedural knowing, reserving *metacognitive knowing* (addressed in the preceding section) to refer to metaknowing about declarative knowing. Metastrategic knowledge can be further divided into *metatask* knowledge about task goals and *metastrategic* knowledge about the strategies one has available to address these goals (Kuhn & Pearsall, 1998).

How and when does metastrategic cognition originate? Central to Vygotsky's (1962) view of cognitive development is the child's acquisition of voluntary con-trol in initiating or inhibiting actions, with Vygotsky attributing a major role to meta-level awareness in this achievement. More recently, Zelazo and his associ-ates have investigated early origins of what they call executive control in the execution of a simple object-sorting task. To perform the task, an executive function is called on to select which of two previously learned rules (sort by shape or by color) to apply. Three-year-olds, these researchers have found, have difficulty selecting the called-for rule, even though they can easily execute either rule. The requisite executive control of cognitive functions, it is proposed, is acquired gradually and undergoes multiple developmental transitions (Zelazo & Frye, 1998).

META-LEVEL CONSTRUCTS IN THE STUDY
OF DEVELOPMENTAL PROCESS

Why do metastrategic and metacognitive functions warrant our attention? One reason is that they help to explain how and why cognitive development both occurs and fails to occur (Kuhn, in press). Developmentalists have long been criticized for failing to address the core question of how change occurs. The picture has changed with the advent of microgenetic methods in which the process of change is observed directly as individuals engage in the same task repeatedly. The consistent finding of microgenetic studies is that people possess a repertory of multiple strategies of varying adequacy that they apply variably to the same problem. Development, then, rather than constituting a single transition from one way of being to another, entail a shifting distribution in the frequencies with which more or less adequate strategies are applied, with the inhibition of inferior strategies as important an achievement as the acquisition of superior ones (Kuhn, 1995; Siegler, 1996).

This revised conception of the developmental process has important implications in the present context because it suggests a critical role for meta-level processes. If shifts in strategy usage cannot be satisfactorily explained at the level of performance (e.g., frequency of prior use dictates the probability of a strategy's appearance), the explanatory burden shifts from the performance level to a meta-level that dictates which strategies are selected for use on a given occasion. The meta-level directs the application of strategies, but feedback from this application is directed back to the meta-level. This feedback leads to enhanced meta-level awareness of the goal and the extent to which it is being met by different strategies, as well as enhanced awareness and understanding of the strategies themselves, including their power and limitations. These enhancements at the meta-level lead to revised strategy selection. These changes in strategy usage in turn feed back to further enhance understanding at the meta-level, in a continuous cycle in which the meta-level both directs and is modified by the performance level.

Such a model privileges the meta-level as the locus of developmental change. Developmentally, then, increasing meta-level awareness and control may be the most important dimension in terms of which we see change (Kuhn, in press). In addition, the model makes it clear why efforts to induce change directly at the performance level have only limited success, indicated by failures of a newly acquired strategy to transfer to new materials or contexts. Strategy training may appear successful, but if nothing has been done to influence the meta-level, the new behavior will quickly disappear once the instructional context is withdrawn and individuals resume meta-level management of their own behavior.

EXTENDING THE SCOPE OF METACOGNITION RESEARCH

A second reason that metacognition warrants our attention has to do with the phenomena to which it is applied. In the era in which Flavell wrote his 1979 article, almost all the research on metacognitive development was confined to metamemory—the study of what children and adults know about how to remember and about their own memory functions and how such knowledge relates to memory performance. Today, metacognition is conceptualized and studied in a much broader context. Metacognitive and metastrategic functions are being investigated within domains of text comprehension, problem solving, and reasoning, as well as memory. Metacognition in the year 2000, then, is "about" more than it was in 1979.

It thus becomes more feasible to construct and evaluate alternative theories of the role that meta-level processes play in regulating and advancing cognitive development (Crowley, Shrager, & Siegler, 1997; Kuhn, in press). It is a reasonable hypothesis that the nature of strategy-metastrategy relations shows some generality across different kinds of cognition, specifically in the ways in which meta-level processes operate to select and regulate performance strategies. Studies of these phenomena across different kinds of cognitive strategies stand to inform one another.

ENDPOINTS OF METACOGNITIVE DEVELOPMENT

A third reason that metacognition warrants attention has to do with the later rather than early portions of its developmental course. Despite the centrality of knowledge acquisition as a topic of theoretical and practical significance, we lack sufficient research observing individuals engaged in the process of acquiring new knowledge. Microgenetic methods allow us to study this process of "knowledge building" (Chan, Burtis, & Bereiter, 1997) during which existing understandings are modified in the course of their interaction with new information. In addition, we can examine how knowledge-acquisition strategies are themselves transformed in the course of their continuing application. Such studies point to the critical role of metacognitive and metastrategic processes in regulating knowledge-acquisition processes.

Adults show more skill in these respects than do children (Kuhn, Garcia-Mila, Zohar, & Andersen, 1995), but the performance of adults is far from optimum. Their beliefs are frequently modified by the new information they encounter, to be sure, and they may become more certain of these beliefs over time, but they often lack awareness of why they are certain (i.e., of the process of theory-evidence coordination that has transpired), and they apply knowledge-acquisition and inference strategies in a selective way to protect their own, often erroneous, beliefs. Enhancing (a) metacognitive awareness of what one believes and how one knows and (b) metastrategic consistency in application of the strategies that select and interpret evidence is thus both a developmental and an educational (Olson & Astington, 1993) goal.

SUPPORTING METACOGNITIVE DEVELOPMENT

In sum, competence in metaknowing warrants attention as a critical endpoint and goal of childhood and adolescent cognitive development. Young children's dawning awareness of their own and others' mental functions lies at one end of a developmental progression that eventuates in complex metaknowing capabilities not realized before adulthood, if they are realized at all. Linking these diverse attainments within a developmental framework makes it possible to investigate ways in which earlier attainments prepare the way for later ones.

As I suggested in the introduction, much remains to be learned about metacognition. We need to know more about how it develops and how it comes to regulate first-order cognition, or, very often, fails to do so. The fact that such failure is a common occurrence raises what is perhaps the most consequential question in need of more investigation: How can metacognitive development be facilitated?

Flavell (1979) expressed a broad vision in this respect:

It is at least conceivable that the ideas currently brewing in this area could someday be parlayed into a method teaching children (and adults) to make wise and thoughtful life decisions as well as to comprehend and learn better in formal educational settings. (p. 910)

Although it has yet to be realized, this vision conveys the potential significance of achieving metalevel control of one's knowing processes. A promising approach to fostering metacognitive development focuses on the idea of exercising, at an external, social level, the cognitive forms we would hope to become operative as well at the individual level. One of a number of researchers who have pursued this approach is Brown (1997), whose "community of learners" curriculum relies on

the development of a discourse genre in which constructive discussion, questioning, querying, and criticism are the mode rather than the exception. In time, these reflective activities become internalized as self-reflective practices. (p. 406)

There would seem few more important accomplishments than people becoming aware of and reflective about their own thinking and able to monitor and manage the ways in which it is influenced by external sources, in both academic, work, and personal life settings. Metacognitive development is a construct that helps to frame this goal.

Recommended Reading

Crowley, K., Shrager, J., & Siegler, R. (1997), (See References)
Hofer, B., & Pintrich, P. (1997), (See References)
Kuhn, D. (1999). A developmental model of critical thinking. *Educational Researcher,* 28, 16–25.
Kuhn, D. (1999). Metacognitive development. In L. Balter & C. Tamis-LeMonda (Eds.), *Child psychology: A handbook of contemporary issues* (pp. 259–286). Philadelphia: Psychology Press.

Kuhn, D. (in press). How do people know? *Psychological Science.*
Olson, D., & Astington, J. (1993). (See References)

Note

1. Address correspondence to Deanna Kuhn, Box 119, Teachers College, Columbia University, New York, NY 10027.

References

Brown, A. (1997). Transforming schools into communities of thinking and learning about serious matters. *American Psychologist, 52,* 399–413.

Chan, C., Burtis, J., & Bereiter, C. (1997). Knowledge-building as a mediator of conflict in conceptual change. *Cognition and Instruction, 15,* 1–40.

Crowley, K., Shrager, J., & Siegler, R. (1997). Strategy discovery as a competitive negotiation between metacognitive and associative mechanisms. *Developmental Review, 17,* 462–489.

Flavell, J. (1979). Metacognition and cognitive monitoring: A new area of cognitive-developmental inquiry. *American Psychologist, 34,* 906–911.

Flavell, J. (1999). Cognitive development: Children's knowledge about the mind. *Annual Review of Psychology, 50,* 21–45.

Hofer, B., & Pintrich, P. (1997). The development of epistemological theories: Beliefs about knowledge and knowing and their relation to learning. *Review of Educational Research, 67,* 88–140.

Kuhn, D. (1995). Microgenetic study of change: What has it told us? *Psychological Science, 6,* 133–139.

Kuhn, D. (in press). Why development does (and doesn't) occur: Evidence from the domain of inductive reasoning. In R. Siegler & J. McClelland (Eds.), *Mechanisms of cognitive development: Neural and behavioral perspectives.* Mahwah, NJ: Erlbaum.

Kuhn, D., Garcia-Mila, M., Zohar, A., & Andersen, C. (1995). Strategies of knowledge acquisition. *Society for Research in Child Development Monographs, 60*(4, Serial No. 245).

Kuhn, D., & Pearsall, S. (1998). Relations between metastrategic knowledge and strategic performance. *Cognitive Development, 13,* 227–247.

Kuhn, D., & Pearsall, S. (2000). Developmental origins of scientific thinking. *Journal of Cognition and Development, 1,* 113–129.

Olson, D., & Astington, J. (1993). Thinking about thinking: Learning how to take statements and hold beliefs. *Educational Psychologist, 28,* 7–23.

Siegler, R. (1996). *Emerging minds: The process of change in children's thinking.* New York: Oxford University Press.

Vygotsky, L.S. (1962). *Thought and language.* Cambridge, MA: MIT Press.

Zelazo, P., & Frye, D. (1998). Cognitive complexity and control: II. The development of executive function in childhood. *Current Directions in Psychological Science, 7,* 121–125.

Critical Thinking Questions

1. What forms of higher-order thinking are rooted in early metacognitive achievements?

2. How might metacognition and metastrategies inform our understanding of intra-individual development of first-order cognition? What are the applied implications?

3. If the meta-level is the locus of developmental change, how might one go about inducing change at the performance level?

Parents and Family

The family context is the most proximal setting that influences child development. In this section, several articles illuminate some of the complexities of parent and family influences. Frank Fincham addresses the topic of marital conflict, and asserts that research has revealed that marital conflict has negative effects on mental, physical, and family health. However, decades of research have not really addressed the complexities of such conflict, and Fincham notes that other factors need to be evaluated such as the parents background and the broader ecological context.

Lisa Serbin and Jennifer Karp review a recent approach to studying the intergenerational processes that place children and families at risk for social, behavioral and health problems. Through an analysis of studies of two or more generations across several countries, findings point to several interesting processes. For example, it seems that adults learn negative parenting behaviors in part through modeling their own parents behaviors, and that parents who were aggressive in childhood have continuing social, behavioral and health difficulties, and so do their offspring. Positive factors such as cognitive stimulation, warmth and nurturance protect offspring against negative outcomes. An essential protective factor, parental educational attainment, appears to be a powerful buffer against the transfer of risk between generations.

Ann Crouter and Matthew Bumpus address another aspect of family life—the link between parents' work stress and child and adolescent adjustment. As with other research efforts aimed at delineating the relationship between parental and child variables, the findings from this work are complex. Studies are typically characterized by a focus on global assessments of work demands, family dynamics and child adjustment, or by a focus on within-person assessments of family interactions on days characterized by low or high work stress. Overall, there appears to be an indirect link between parental work stress and child adjustment. When parents are stressed from work demands, they show less acceptance of their child and have higher levels of conflict. These processes in turn influence aspects of the child's adjustment. As with other research in this area, Crouter and Bumpus also report that the strength of these findings depends on parent personality and coping styles, and on the work and family circumstances.

Parents not only influence their children's social, emotional, and behavioral adjustment, but they have also been linked to the early development of conscience. In the article by Grazyna Kochanska, we see that some parents establish what she calls a mutually responsive orientation (MRO). A MRO is a relationship that is close, mutually binding, and cooperative and is characterized by positive emotion. These positive characteristics of the mother-child relationship have been found in other research to be related to many aspects of positive child functioning. In this report, Kochanska asserts that the characteristics of mutual responsiveness and shared positive affect also foster the development of conscience in young children. In addition, she emphasizes that this early relationship sets the stage for subsequent moral development.

All of the above articles point to the necessity of understanding the family as a system, embedded in several contexts with multiple influences. Parental characteristics and experiences are part of the system of influences on child development, but there are also dynamic transactions across multiple levels of family systems. Martha Cox and Blair Paley present an overview of the research that has applied principles of general systems theory to the study of the family as an organized system. They assert that from this perspective, the family is seen as a whole that is greater than the sum of its parts, has a hierarchical structure, and is characterized by adaptive self-organization.

This systems framework has been useful in understanding the complexities of influences on child development. As the authors point out in the article, great progress has been made in conceptualizing and measuring processes at the whole family level. Taken together, these articles stress the importance of examining the specific processes involved in parent-child interaction as well as processes that are characteristics of the whole family system.

Marital Conflict: Correlates, Structure, and Context

Frank D. Fincham[1]

Psychology Department, University of Buffalo, Buffalo, New York

Abstract

Marital conflict has deleterious effects on mental, physical, and family health, and three decades of research have yielded a detailed picture of the behaviors that differentiate distressed from nondistressed couples. Review of this work shows that the singular emphasis on conflict in generating marital outcomes has yielded an incomplete picture of its role in marriage. Recently, researchers have tried to paint a more textured picture of marital conflict by studying spouses' backgrounds and characteristics, investigating conflict in the contexts of support giving and affectional expression, and considering the ecological niche of couples in their broader environment.

Keywords

conflict patterns; marital distress; support

Systematic psychological research on marriage emerged largely among clinical psychologists who wanted to better assist couples experiencing marital distress. In the 30 years since this development, marital conflict has assumed a special status in the literature on marriage, as evidenced by three indices. First, many of the most influential theories of marriage tend to reflect the view that "distress results from couples' aversive and ineffectual response to conflict" (Koerner & Jacobson, 1994, p. 208). Second, research on marriage has focused on what spouses do when they disagree with each other, and reviews of marital interaction are dominated by studies of conflict and problem solving (see Weiss & Heyman, 1997). Third, psychological interventions for distressed couples often target conflict-resolution skills (see Baucom, Shoham, Mueser, Daiuto, & Stickle, 1998).

IS MARITAL CONFLICT IMPORTANT?

The attention given marital conflict is understandable when we consider its implications for mental, physical, and family health. Marital conflict has been linked to the onset of depressive symptoms, eating disorders, male alcoholism, episodic drinking, binge drinking, and out-of-home drinking. Although married individuals are healthier on average than the unmarried, marital conflict is associated with poorer health and with specific illnesses such as cancer, cardiac disease, and chronic pain, perhaps because hostile behaviors during conflict are related to alterations in immunological, endocrine, and cardiovascular functioning. Physical aggression occurs in about 30% of married couples in the United States, leading to significant physical injury in about 10% of couples. Marriage is also the most common interpersonal context for homicide, and more women are murdered by their partners than by anyone else. Finally, marital conflict is associated with important family outcomes, including poor parenting, poor adjustment of children increased likelihood of parent-child conflict, and conflict between siblings. Marital conflicts that are frequent, intense, physical, unresolved, and child related have a particularly negative influence on children, as do marital conflicts that spouses attribute to their child's behavior (see Grych & Fincham, 2001).

WHAT ARE MARITAL CONFLICTS ABOUT?

Marital conflicts can be about virtually anything. Couples complain about sources of conflict ranging from verbal and physical abusiveness to personal characteristics and behaviors. Perceived inequity in a couple's division of labor is associated with marital conflict and with a tendency for the male to withdraw in response to conflict. Conflict over power is also strongly related to marital dissatisfaction. Spouses' reports of conflict over extramarital sex, problematic drinking, or drug use predict divorce, as do wives' reports of husbands being jealous and spending money foolishly. Greater problem severity increases the likelihood of divorce. Even though it is often not reported to be a problem by couples, violence among newlyweds is a predictor of divorce, as is psychological aggression (verbal aggression and nonverbal aggressive behaviors that are not directed at the partner's body).

HOW DO SPOUSES BEHAVE DURING CONFLICT?

Stimulated, in part, by the view that "studying what people say about themselves is no substitute for studying how they behave" (Raush, Barry, Hertel, & Swain, 1974, p. 5), psychologists have conducted observational studies, with the underlying hope of identifying dysfunctional behaviors that could be modified in couple therapy. This research has focused on problem-solving discussions in the laboratory and provides detailed information about how maritally distressed and nondistressed couples behave during conflict.

During conflict, distressed couples make more negative statements and fewer positive statements than nondistressed couples. They are also more likely to respond with negative behavior when their partner behaves negatively. Indeed, this negative reciprocity, as it is called, is more consistent across different types of situations than is the amount of negative behavior, making it the most reliable overt signature of marital distress. Negative behavior is both more frequent and more frequently reciprocated in couples that engage in physical aggression than in other couples. Nonverbal behavior, often used as an index of emotion, reflects marital satisfaction better than verbal behavior, and unlike verbal behavior does not change when spouses try to fake good and bad marriages.

Are There Typical Patterns of Conflict Behavior?

The sequences of behavior that occur during conflict are more predictable in distressed than in nondistressed marriages and are often dominated by chains of negative behavior that usually escalate and are difficult for the couple to stop. One of the greatest challenges for couples locked into negative exchanges is to find an adaptive way of exiting from such cycles. This is usually attempted through responses that are designed to repair the interaction (e.g., "You're not listening to me") but are delivered with negative affect (e.g., irritation, sadness). The partners tend to respond to the negative affect, thereby continuing the cycle. This makes their interactions structured and predictable. In contrast, nondistressed couples appear to be more responsive to attempts at repair and are thereby able to exit from negative exchanges early on. For example, a spouse may respond to "Wait, you're not letting me finish" with "Sorry . . . please finish what you were saying." Their interaction therefore appears more random and less predictable.

A second important behavior pattern exhibited by maritally distressed couples is the demand-withdraw pattern, in which one spouse pressures the other with demands, complaints, and criticisms, while the partner withdraws with defensiveness and passive inaction. Specifically, behavior sequences in which the husband withdraws and the wife responds with hostility are more common in distressed than in satisfied couples. This finding is consistent with several studies showing that wives display more negative affect and behavior than husbands, who tend to not respond or to make statements suggestive of withdrawal, such as irrelevant comments. Disengagement or withdrawal is, in turn, related to later decreases in marital satisfaction. However, inferring reliable gender differences in demand-withdraw patterns would be premature, as recent research shows that the partner who withdraws varies according to which partner desires change. So, for example, when a man desires change, the woman is the one who withdraws. Finally, conflict patterns seem to be relatively stable over time (see Karney & Bradbury, 1995).

Is There a Simple Way to Summarize Research Findings on Marital Conflict?

The findings of the extensive literature on marital conflict can be summarized in terms of a simple ratio: The ratio of agreements to disagreements is greater than 1 for happy couples and less than 1 for unhappy couples. Gottman (1993) utilized this ratio to identify couple types. He observed husbands and wives during conversation, recording each spouse's positive and negative behaviors while speaking, and then calculated the cumulative difference between positive and negative behaviors over time for each spouse. Using the patterns in these difference scores, he distinguished regulated couples (increase in positive speaker behaviors relative to negative behaviors for both spouses over the course of conversation) from nonregulated couples (all other patterns). The regulated couples were more satisfied in their marriage than the nonregulated couples, and also less likely to divorce. Regulated couples displayed positive problem-solving behaviors and positive affect approximately 5 times as often as negative problem-solving behaviors and negative affect, whereas the corresponding ratio was approximately 1:1 for nonregulated couples.

Interestingly, Gottman's perspective corresponds with the findings of two early, often overlooked studies on the reported frequency of sexual intercourse and of marital arguments (Howard & Dawes, 1976; Thornton, 1977). Both showed that the ratio of sexual intercourse to arguments, rather than their base rates, predicted marital satisfaction.

Don't Research Findings on Marital Conflict Just Reflect Common Sense?

The findings described in this article may seem like common sense. However, what we have learned about marital interaction contradicts the long-standing belief that satisfied couples are characterized by a *quid pro quo* principle according to which they exchange positive behavior and instead show that it is dissatisfied spouses who reciprocate one another's (negative) behavior. The astute reader may also be wondering whether couples' behavior in the artificial setting of the laboratory is a good reflection of their behavior in the real world outside the lab. It is therefore important to note that couples who participate in such studies themselves report that their interactions in the lab are reminiscent of their typical interactions. Research also shows that conflict behavior in the lab is similar to conflict behavior in the home; however, laboratory conflicts tend to be less severe, suggesting that research findings underestimate differences between distressed and nondistressed couples.

THE SEEDS OF DISCONTENT

By the early 1980s, researchers were attempting to address the limits of a purely behavioral account of marital conflict. Thus, they began to pay attention to subjective factors, such as thoughts and feelings, which might influence behavioral interactions or the relation between behavior and marital satisfaction. For example, it is now well documented that the tendency to explain a partner's negative behavior (e.g., coming home late from work) in a way that promotes conflict (e.g., "he thinks only about himself and his needs"), rather than in less conflictual ways (e.g., "he was probably caught in traffic"), is related to less effective problem solving, more negative communication in problem-solving discussions, more displays of specific negative affects (e.g., anger) during problem solving, and steeper declines in marital satisfaction over time (Fincham, 2001). Explanations that promote conflict are also related to the tendency to reciprocate a partner's negative behavior, regardless of a couple's marital satisfaction. Research on such subjective factors, like observational research on conflict, has continued to the present time. However, it represents an acceptance and expansion of the behavioral approach that accords conflict a central role in understanding marriage.

In contrast, very recently, some investigators have argued that the role of conflict in marriage should be reconsidered. Longitudinal research shows that conflict accounts for a relatively small portion of the variability in later marital outcomes, suggesting that other factors need to be considered in predicting these outcomes (see Karney & Bradbury, 1995). In addition, studies have demonstrated a troubling number of "reversal effects" (showing that greater conflict is a predictor of improved marriage; see Fincham & Beach, 1999). It is difficult to account for such findings in a field that, for much of its existence, has focused on providing descriptive data at the expense of building theory.

Rethinking the role of conflict also reflects recognition of the fact that most of what we know about conflict behavior comes from observation of problem-solving discussions and that couples experience verbal problem-solving situations infrequently; about 80% of couples report having overt disagreements once a month or less. As a result, cross-sectional studies of distressed versus nondistressed marriages and longitudinal studies of conflict are being increasingly complemented by research designs that focus on how happy marriages become unhappy.

Finally, there is evidence that marital conflict varies according to contextual factors. For example, diary studies illustrate that couples have more stressful marital interactions at home on days of high general life stress than on other days, and at times and places where they are experiencing multiple competing demands; arguments at work are related to marital arguments, and the occurrence of stressful life events is associated with more conflictual problem-solving discussions.

NEW BEGINNINGS: CONFLICT IN CONTEXT

Although domains of interaction other than conflict (e.g., support, companionship) have long been discussed in the marital literature, they are only now emerging from the secondary status accorded to them. This is somewhat ironic given the simple summary of research findings on marital conflict offered earlier, which points to the importance of the context in which conflict occurs.

Conflict in the Context of Support Giving and Affectional Expression

Observational laboratory methods have recently been developed to assess supportive behaviors in interactions in which one spouse talks about a personal issue he or she would like to change and the other is asked to respond as she or he normally would. Behaviors exhibited during such support tasks are only weakly related to the conflict behaviors observed during the problem-solving discussions used to study marital conflict. Supportive spouse behavior is associated with greater marital satisfaction and is more important than negative behavior in determining how supportive the partners perceive an interaction to be. In addition, the amount of supportive behavior partners exhibit is a predictor of later marital stress (i.e., more supportive behavior correlates with less future marital stress), independently of conflict behavior, and when support is poor, there is an increased risk that poor skills in dealing with conflict will lead to later marital deterioration. There is also evidence that support obtained by spouses outside the marriage can influence positively how the spouse behaves within the marriage.

In the context of high levels of affectional expression between spouses, the association between spouses' negative behavior and marital satisfaction decreases significantly. High levels of positive behavior in problem-solving discussions also mitigate the effect of withdrawal or disengagement on later marital satisfaction. Finally, when there are high levels of affectional expression between spouses, the demand-withdraw pattern is unrelated to marital satisfaction, but when affectional expression is average or low, the demand-withdraw pattern is associated with marital dissatisfaction.

Conflict in the Context of Spouses' Backgrounds and Characteristics

Focus on interpersonal behavior as the cause of marital outcomes led to the assumption that the characteristics of individual spouses play no role in those outcomes. However, increasing evidence that contradicts this assumption has generated recent interest in studying how spouses' backgrounds and characteristics might enrich our understanding of marital conflict.

The importance of spouses' characteristics is poignantly illustrated in the intergenerational transmission of divorce. Although there is a tendency for individuals whose parents divorced to get divorced themselves, this tendency varies depending on the offspring's behavior. Divorce rates are higher for offspring who behave in hostile, domineering, and critical ways, compared with offspring who do not behave in this manner.

An individual characteristic that is proving to be particularly informative for understanding marriage comes from recent research on attachment, which aims to address questions about how the experience of relationships early in life affects interpersonal functioning in adulthood. For example, spouses who tend to feel secure in relationships tend to compromise and to take into account both their own and their partner's interests during problem-solving interactions; those who tend to feel anxious or ambivalent in relationships show a greater tendency to oblige their partner, and focus on relationship maintenance, than do those who tend to avoid intimacy in relationships. And spouses who are preoccupied with being completely emotionally intimate in relationships show an elevated level of marital conflict after an involuntary, brief separation from the partner.

Of particular interest for understanding negative reciprocity are the findings that greater commitment is associated with more constructive, accommodative responses to a partner's negative behavior and that the dispositional tendency to forgive is a predictor of spouses' responses to their partners' transgressions; spouses having a greater tendency to forgive are less likely to avoid the partner or retaliate in kind following a transgression by the partner. Indeed, spouses themselves acknowledge that the capacity to seek and grant forgiveness is one of the most important factors contributing to marital longevity and satisfaction.

Conflict in the Context of the Broader Environment

The environments in which marriages are situated and the intersection between interior processes and external factors that impinge upon marriage are important to consider in painting a more textured picture of marital conflict. This is because problem-solving skills and conflict may have little impact on a marriage in the absence of external stressors. External stressors also may influence marriages directly. In particular, nonmarital stressors may lead to an increased number of negative interactions, as illustrated by the fact that economic stress is associated with marital conflict. There is a growing need to identify the stressors and life events that are and are not influential for different couples and for different stages of marriage, to investigate how these events influence conflict, and to clarify how individuals and marriages may inadvertently generate stressful events. In fact, Bradbury, Rogge, and Lawrence (2001), in considering the ecological niche of the couple (i.e., their life events, family constellation, socioeconomic standing, and stressful circumstances), have recently argued that it may be "at least as important to examine the struggle that exists between the couple . . . and the environment they inhabit as it is to examine the interpersonal struggles that are the focus of our work [observation of conflict]" (p. 76).

CONCLUSION

The assumption that conflict management is the key to successful marriage and that conflict skills can be modified in couple therapy has proved useful in propelling the study of marriage into the mainstream of psychology. However, it may have outlived its usefulness, and some researchers are now calling for greater attention to other mechanisms (e.g., spousal social support) that might be responsible for marital outcomes. Indeed, controversy over whether conflict has beneficial or detrimental effects on marriage over time is responsible, in part, for the recent upsurge in longitudinal research on marriage. Notwithstanding diverse opinions on just how central conflict is for understanding marriage, current efforts to study conflict in a broader marital context, which is itself seen as situated in a broader ecological niche, bode well for advancing understanding and leading to more powerful preventive and therapeutic interventions.

Recommended Reading

Bradbury, T.N., Fincham, F.D., & Beach, S.R.H. (2000). Research on the nature and determinants of marital satisfaction: A decade in review. *Journal of Marriage and the Family, 62*, 964–980.
Fincham, F.D., & Beach, S.R. (1999). (See References)
Grych, J.H., & Fincham, F.D. (Eds.). (2001). (See References)
Karney, B.R., & Bradbury, T.N. (1995). (See References)

Acknowledgments—This article was written while the author was supported by grants from the Templeton, Margaret L. Wendt, and J.M. McDonald Foundations.

Note

1. Address correspondence to Frank D. Fincham, Department of Psychology, University at Buffalo, Buffalo, NY 14260.

References

Baucom, D.H., Shoham, V., Mueser, K.T., Daiuto, A.D., & Stickle, T.R. (1998). Empirically supported couple and family interventions for marital distress and adult mental health problems. *Journal of Consulting and Clinical Psychology, 66*, 53–88.
Bradbury, T.N., Rogge, R., & Lawrence, E. (2001). Reconsidering the role of conflict in marriage. In A. Booth, A.C. Crouter, & M. Clements (Eds.), *Couples in conflict* (pp. 59–81). Mahwah, NJ: Erlbaum.
Fincham, F.D. (2001). Attributions and close relationships: From balkanization to integration. In G.J. Fletcher & M. Clark (Eds.), *Blackwell handbook of social psychology* (pp. 3–31). Oxford, England: Blackwell.
Fincham, F.D., & Beach, S.R. (1999). Marital conflict: Implications for working with couples. *Annual Review of Psychology, 50*, 47–77.
Gottman, J.M. (1993). The roles of conflict engagement, escalation, and avoidance in marital interaction: A longitudinal view of five types of couples. *Journal of Consulting and Clinical Psychology, 61*, 6–15.
Grych, J.H., & Fincham, F.D. (Eds.). (2001). *Interparental conflict and child development: Theory, research, and applications.* New York: Cambridge University Press.
Howard, J.W., & Dawes, R.M. (1976). Linear prediction of marital happiness. *Personality and Social Psychology Bulletin, 2*, 478–480.

Karney, B.R., & Bradbury, T.N. (1995). The longitudinal course of marital quality and stability: A review of theory, method, and research. *Psychological Bulletin, 118,* 3–34.

Koerner, K., & Jacobson, N.J. (1994). Emotion and behavior in couple therapy. In S.M. Johnson & L.S. Greenberg (Eds.), *The heart of the matter: Perspectives on emotion in marital therapy* (pp. 207–226). New York: Brunner/Mazel.

Raush, H.L., Barry, W.A., Hertel, R.K., & Swain, M.A. (1974). *Communication, conflict, and marriage.* San Francisco: Jossey-Bass.

Thornton, B. (1977). Toward a linear prediction of marital happiness. *Personality and Social Psychology Bulletin, 3,* 674–676.

Weiss, R.L., & Heyman, R.E. (1997). A clinical-research overview of couple interactions. In W.K. Halford & H. Markman (Eds.), *The clinical handbook of marriage and couples interventions* (pp. 13–41). Brisbane, Australia: Wiley.

Critical Thinking Questions

1. Why is it important to consider a couple's ecological niche when assessing marital conflict? How would such a consideration effect therapeutic intervention?

2. How have the findings from this article challenged the long-standing belief that satisfied couples are distinguished by a quid pro quo principle? How might this reshape research and practice concerning marital conflict?

3. Why might observational methods of marital conflict research not be sufficient? How might other methods of data collection contribute to a more comprehensive picture of marital conflict?

Intergenerational Studies of Parenting and the Transfer of Risk From Parent to Child

Lisa Serbin[1] and Jennifer Karp
Centre for Research in Human Development and Department of Psychology, Concordia University, Montreal, Quebec, Canada

Abstract

This review describes a recent approach to studying the intergenerational processes that place families and children at risk for a broad variety of social, behavioral, and health problems. Intergenerational studies typically involve two (or more) generations of participants, observed over time. These projects are utilized to study the origins and early determinants of parenting behavior and of other environmental, health, and social conditions that place young offspring at risk for continuing behavioral, cognitive, and health problems. Convergent findings, across a broad range of research populations in several countries, suggest that problematic parenting develops in part through learning the behavior modeled by one's own parents. In addition, problematic parenting seems to be an extension of an individual's early style of aggressive and problematic social behavior. Parents with a history of childhood aggression, in particular, tend to have continuing social, behavioral, and health difficulties, as do their offspring. Conversely, parental involvement, cognitive stimulation, warmth, and nurturance appear to have important protective effects for offspring. Finally, educational achievement appears to be a powerful buffer against problematic parenting and a wide variety of difficult family circumstances, protecting families against the transfer of risk between generations.

Keywords

intergenerational; risk; longitudinal; parenting psychopathology

Longitudinal studies following the lives of children into adulthood are generally familiar to psychologists. Over the 20th century, such studies have contributed a great deal to our understanding of the course of development. In particular, longitudinal studies that have followed individuals across the life course have provided basic information about the ways in which young children's psychological and behavioral characteristics interact with their environment and experiences, leading to various positive or negative life trajectories. Recently, there has been a new feature introduced into many ongoing and recently initiated longitudinal studies (Serbin & Stack, 1998). As their young participants reach adulthood, many of these projects are being utilized to study the origins and early determinants of parenting behavior. In addition, birth circumstances, pre- and perinatal maternal health, and other aspects of the family environment that may affect the psychological growth of young offspring are being studied within prospective longitudinal designs.

In part, this focus on the developmental origins of parenting and child rearing is a response to renewed interest in the outcomes of atypical patterns of social behavior, such as extreme aggression in girls (Peplar, Madsen, Webster, &

Levene, 2003; Underwood, 2003). Girls' aggression is attracting increasing attention as a risk factor for ongoing social maladjustment, as well as mental and physical health problems. Early aggression may become a stable pattern of social behavior in both males and females, leading to maladaptive family relationships, including violent and dysfunctional behavior toward spouses and children. In other words, there has been considerable recent interest in understanding the long-term consequences of childhood aggression and other problematic patterns of social behavior. Psychologists are particularly interested in examining how these types of behaviors in childhood may affect a person's future family relationships and transfer risk to a new generation of children.

BACKGROUND

Risk Research and Prospective Longitudinal Designs

Current theory, supported by a growing body of empirical research, strongly suggests that genetic and environmental influences combine to produce intergenerational similarities between parents and children. Individual characteristics, learning experiences, environmental context, and the process of development interact to create differing life trajectories and outcomes. These variables and a subject's life outcomes can be observed and measured over time. Despite the overall tendency for similarity and continuity within families, there is always considerable variability in behavior between individuals, even within families identified as at risk or within disadvantaged groups. Studies of the circumstances, environments, and experiences that promote differential outcomes for children and their families are often referred to in the literature as risk research.

Intergenerational Research Designs

Longitudinal research has historically been concerned with understanding the processes of socialization: how one generation transfers patterns of behavior to the next. In a variation of this theme, recent intergenerational studies have often focused on the prediction of parenting behavior and other environmental conditions within the life course of one generation, with a view to identifying the processes that place the offspring of the original subjects at risk for social, behavioral, and health problems across childhood and adulthood. Outcomes studied have included parenting conditions and environmental conditions that place a new generation at risk for a disadvantaged life course, as well as the actual behavior and health of the young offspring. In these studies, a series of steps involving developmental processes that lead to the outcomes of interest is proposed, based on theory. These proposed steps are then statistically tested for their fit with the observed data. If members of both generations (parent and child) are examined at approximately the same ages, researchers can compare parents and children to determine the similarity of their behavior at similar points in development (Cairns, Cairns, Xie, Leung, & Hearne, 1998). At the same time, the impact of parenting behavior and other environmental factors can be examined (Conger, Neppl, Kim, & Scaramella, 2003).

CONCEPTUAL AND RESEARCH ISSUES

Predicting Early Parenthood, Parenting Behavior, and Environmental Rearing Conditions

The most basic design for studying intergenerational risk involves following a sample of children as they mature and become parents themselves. Some such studies focus primarily on a single generation, but many also include the parents of the target participants, and also the target participants' children, the generation born during the course of the study. Intergenerational studies, in this way, often include up to three generations. Outcomes that are relevant to the intergenerational transfer of risk may include the circumstances of the next generation's birth, the parenting behavior of the participants, and the rearing environment that they establish for the next generation.

For example, a number of studies have examined the predictors of teen parenthood within various high-risk populations, including low-income rural families, foster children, inner-city urban children, and racial minority groups (Fagot, Pears, Capaldi, Crosby, & Leve, 1998; Hardy, Astone, Brooks-Gunn, Shapiro, & Miller, 1998; Scaramella, Conger, Simons, & Whitbeck, 1998; Serbin et al., 1998; Serbin, Peters, McAffer, & Schwartzman, 1991). Both behavioral and environmental predictors of teen parenthood have been identified in these longitudinal studies. Such factors include early aggression and other antisocial behavior, risk-taking behavior (such as smoking, or alcohol and drug use), having delinquent friends, failing in school, and dropping out of high school. Protective factors include family income (above poverty level), social support to parents (by extended family, friends, and the community), parental involvement in their child's activities and schoolwork, and high academic abilities and achievement of the child during the elementary and high school years.

Along with teen parenthood, other problematic conditions for offspring have been predicted from parents' earlier patterns of aggressive behavior and low levels of educational achievement. These conditions include obstetric and delivery problems and poor pre- and postnatal infant health. Longitudinal studies with participants drawn from many geographic and cultural regions (including the United Kingdom, United States, Canada, and Scandinavia), and from diverse social and ethnic groups, have yielded a general convergence of findings about risk factors and protective factors for teen parenthood, problematic parenting, and impoverished early environment.

The Intergenerational Transfer of Parenting Behavior

Many ongoing intergenerational studies are examining the similarity of parenting behavior from one generation to the next. Most of these studies have focused on the transfer of harsh and punitive parenting, or on effective versus ineffective transfer of styles of parenting behavior (see also Capaldi, Pears, Patterson, & Owen, 2003; Chen & Kaplan, 2001; Conger et al., 2003; Thornberry Freeman-Gallant, Lizotte, Krohn, & Smith, 2003). General support has been found for the idea that direct modeling of parenting behaviors leads to the transfer of those behaviors from one generation to the next. However, these studies also suggest that there is continuity of an aggressive behavioral style from childhood to parenthood. In other words, adults' style of parenting incorporates both (a) what they learned directly from parenting behavior that was modeled in their child-hood and (b) their own behavioral style, which was already apparent during childhood.

Predicting Outcomes in a Second Generation

Parents' histories are often used to predict a variety of outcomes in the next gen-eration, such as their offsprings' early health, behavior, and development. In studies that include parents and their children, both individual and environ-mental sources of risk may be identified. Predictors of interest often include events that occurred years prior to the birth of the offspring. For example, in sev-eral studies of the offspring of teen parents (e.g., Fagot et al., 1998; Serbin, Peters, & Schwartzman, 1996), parents who had been aggressive and antisocial as children tended to have offspring who had poorer physical health (e.g., asthma, frequent respiratory infections) and made more visits to the emergency room during the first years of life than the offspring of other parents. One vari-able that may be involved in these specific negative outcomes for early health is maternal smoking, as mothers who smoke tend to have a history of childhood aggression, risk taking, and antisocial behavior.

Predicting Diverse Outcomes Within Populations Identified as at Risk

Some intergenerational designs focus on atypical or clinical risk factors, such as specific behavioral problems or having a family member with diagnosed mental illness. For example, a researcher might observe children whose parents have depression or parents who are raising developmentally delayed children. Some intergenerational studies include a range of risk profiles, or include multiple comparison groups, each with a distinct risk profile (see McMahon & Peters, 2002, for a recent collection of studies of the children of dysfunctional, men-tally ill, and at-risk parents).

SUMMARY OF CENTRAL FINDINGS AND CONCLUSIONS TO DATE

Several generally consistent findings deserve emphasis. First, problematic par-enting seems to be the combined outcome of modeling by the individual's own parents and the continuation of a pattern of aggressive and antisocial behavior that can be observed in the individual early in childhood. Second, childhood aggression and antisocial behavior also seem to lead to problematic parenting and negative outcomes for offspring via an indirect pathway from childhood behav-ior patterns to adolescent risk-taking behavior, low educational and occupational attainment, maternal smoking, substance abuse, poverty, and other problematic circumstances of birth and parenthood. Third, parental involvement, warmth, and nurturance during childhood appear to have important protective effects on later family formation and parenting. Finally, educational achievement appears to be a powerful buffer against problematic parenting and the transfer of risk to the next generation, within both normative samples and at-risk populations.

UNRESOLVED ISSUES AND DIRECTIONS FOR FUTURE RESEARCH

The Need for Integrated Theoretical Models and Research Designs

The specific and interrelated pathways linking maladaptive behavior during childhood to future parenting problems need to be examined within comprehensive research models and designs. In particular, history of socialization, the indirect effects of early maladaptive behavior (such as school dropout, substance abuse, ill health, and poverty), and genetic factors affecting behavior and temperament should all be included in both the theoretical models and the empirical designs used in intergenerational research. In many current studies that are focusing on behavior and environment in the absence of genetic information, researchers are studying only a piece of the puzzle of intergenerational transfer of risk. Advances in work with physiological, behavioral, or molecular genetic markers may provide new opportunities to measure the genetic and physiological similarity of parent and child generations. Both projects in the planning stage and ongoing intergenerational research programs may choose to incorporate these new methods into their designs in future phases of data collection.

Statistics and Methodological Limitations

The complexity of intergenerational processes—in particular, the interactive and sequential nature of individuals' life trajectories—presents many challenges for researchers using traditional methods of quantitative and qualitative statistical analysis. Multiple regression and path modeling are widely used in intergenerational research, but these methods have definite and well-known limitations, especially when dealing with interactive, cumulative processes. A variety of new and evolving methods that utilize multiple predictors to project developmental trajectories (i.e., hierarchical linear modeling, growth curve analysis) present some intriguing possibilities for expanding the array of theoretical and empirical issues that can be investigated within intergenerational studies.

Moving Beyond the Limits of Current Correlational Designs

Uncontrolled situations and events are often important conceptually and statistically, representing naturally occurring influences on the life course of individuals. Examining converging results from several studies will help us determine if predictive patterns related to individuals' characteristics and experiences are specific to particular studies, historical periods, or research populations, or occur more generally. In order to confirm whether the predictive effects identified in intergenerational research projects to date are causal, intervention studies using experimental or quasiexperimental designs, including random assignment of participants to intervention and control groups, will be required. In the future, it may be possible to employ experimental designs to examine well-specified research questions, such as the effects of parent training or other prevention programs, within intergenerational research projects.

APPLICATIONS AND IMPLICATIONS FOR SOCIAL POLICY

Issues of intergenerational transfer of risk are central to the field of human development. However, their importance extends further because identifying risk factors provides crucial information that can be used in developing social, educational, and health policy. Policymakers often want to design and implement preventive interventions aimed at improving children's health and well-being. Before such interventions are designed and evaluated, however, it is essential to identify and evaluate specific predictors of risk and protective factors that increase children's resiliency. Because healthy functioning during early childhood is an important predictor of healthy lifelong development, it is important to design preventive strategies that can be implemented during early childhood, pregnancy, and even prior to conception. For example, many intergenerational studies suggest that maternal education is a key protective element for children in high-risk families. Based on these findings, an experimental study could be designed to investigate the effects of providing increased educational and social support to girls who are at risk for dropping out of school. These girls could be followed into adulthood so that we might evaluate the usefulness of such increased support for the future health and development of their children.

The opportunity to study complex, important phenomena with intergenerational designs has been compelling for many developmental researchers in recent years. This trend seems likely to continue and expand.

Recommended Reading

Patterson, G. (1998). Continuities—a search for causal mechanisms: Comment on the Special Section. *Developmental Psychology, 34,* 1263–1268.
Putallaz, M., Costanzo, P.R., Grames, C.L., & Sherman, D.M. (1998). Intergenerational continuities and their influences on children's social development. *Social Development, 7,* 389–427.
Rutter, M. (1998). Some research considerations on inter-generational continuities and discontinuities: Comment on the Special Section. *Developmental Psychology, 34,* 1269–1273.
Serbin, L.A., & Karp, J. (in press). The inter-generational transfer of psycho-social risk: Mediators of vulnerability and resilience. *Annual Review of Psychology.*
Serbin, L.A., & Stack, D.M. (Eds.). (1998). Longitudinal studies of inter-generational continuity and the transfer of psycho-social risk [Special section]. *Developmental Psychology, 34,* 1159–1273.

Note

1. Address correspondence to Lisa Serbin, Centre for Research in Human Development, Concordia University, 7141 Sherbrooke St. West, Montreal, Quebec, Canada, H4B 1R6.

References

Cairns, R.B., Cairns, B.D., Xie, H., Leung, M.C., & Hearne, S. (1998). Paths across generations: Academic competence and aggressive behaviors in young mothers and their children. *Developmental Psychology, 34,* 1162–1174.

Capaldi, D.M., Pears, K.C., Patterson, G.R., & Owen, L.D. (2003). Continuity of parenting practices across generations in an at-risk sample: A prospective comparison of direct and mediated associations. *Journal of Abnormal Child Psychology, 31*, 127–142.

Chen, Z.Y., & Kaplan, H.B. (2001). Intergenerational transmission of constructive parenting. *Journal of Marriage & Family, 63*, 17–31.

Conger, R.D., Neppl, T., Kim, K.J., & Scaramella, L. (2003). Angry and aggressive behavior across three generations: A prospective, longitudinal study of parents and children. *Journal of Abnormal Child Psychology, 31*, 143–160.

Fagot, B.J., Pears, K.C., Capaldi, D.M., Crosby, L., & Leve, C.S. (1998). Becoming an adolescent father: Precursors and parenting. *Developmental Psychology, 34*, 1209–1219.

Hardy, J.B., Astone, N.M., Brooks-Gunn, J., Shapiro, S., & Miller, T.L. (1998). Like mother, like child: Intergenerational patterns of age at first birth and associations with childhood and adolescent characteristics and adult outcomes in the second generation. *Developmental Psychology, 34*, 1220–1232.

McMahon, R.J., & Peters, R.D. (Eds.). (2002). *The effects of parental dysfunction on children.* New York: Kluwer Academic/Plenum Publications.

Peplar, D., Madsen, K., Webster, C., & Levene, K. (Eds.) (2003). *The development and treatment of girlhood aggression.* Hillsdale, NJ: Erlbaum.

Scaramella, L.V., Conger, R.D., Simons, R.L., & Whitbeck, L.B. (1998). Predicting risk for pregnancy by late adolescence: A social contextual perspective. *Developmental Psychology, 34*, 1233–1245.

Serbin, L.A., Cooperman, J.M., Peters, P.L., Lehoux, P.M., Stack, D.M., & Schwartzman, A.E. (1998). Intergenerational transfer of psychosocial risk in women with childhood histories of aggression, withdrawal, or aggression and withdrawal. *Developmental Psychology, 34*, 1246–1262.

Serbin, L.A., Peters, P.L., McAffer, V.J., & Schwartzman, A.E. (1991). Childhood aggression and withdrawal as predictors of adolescent pregnancy, early parenthood, and environmental risk for the next generation. *Canadian Journal of Behavioural Science, 23*, 318–331.

Serbin, L.A., Peters, P.L., & Schwartzman, A.E. (1996). Longitudinal study of early childhood injuries and acute illnesses in the offspring of adolescent mothers who were aggressive, withdrawn, or aggressive/withdrawn in childhood. *Journal of Abnormal Psychology, 105*, 500–507.

Serbin, L.A., & Stack, D.M. (1998). Introduction to the special section: Studying intergenerational continuity and the transfer of risk. *Developmental Psychology, 34*, 1159–1161.

Thornberry, T.P., Freeman-Gallant, A., Lizotte, A.J., Krohn, M.D., & Smith, C.A. (2003). Linked lives: The intergenerational transmission of antisocial behavior. *Journal of Abnormal Child Psychology, 31*, 171–184.

Underwood, M.K. (2003). *Social aggression among girls.* New York: Guilford.

Critical Thinking Questions

1. Given the diversity of pathways linking maladaptive behavior during childhood to future parenting problems, is it impossible to develop a unified theoretical model of intergenerational transmission of risk?

2. What are the unique statistical and methodological challenges of intergenerational research?

3. What is (are) the "entry point(s)" for policymakers and practitioners guided by intergenerational research and concerned with implementing preventive interventions?

Linking Parents' Work Stress to Children's and Adolescents' Psychological Adjustment

Ann C. Crouter[1] and Matthew F. Bumpus

Department of Human Development and Family Studies, Pennsylvania State University, University Park, Pennsylvania

Abstract

Recent research indicates that parental work stress has implications for the quality of family interaction and, in turn, children's and adolescents' adjustment. Studies in two distinct genres are reviewed: investigations relying on global reports of work demands, family dynamics, and child and adolescent adjustment and studies focusing on within-person comparisons of family interaction on days characterized by high and low work stress. The effects of parental work stress on children's and adolescents' adjustment appear to be indirect. Work stress is linked to parents' feelings of overload and strain, which in turn predict lower parent-child acceptance and higher conflict, processes that in turn are related to less positive adjustment of children and adolescents. In the face of high work stress, withdrawing from family involvement may be adaptive in the short run but ultimately problematic. The strength of these associations depends on parents' personality qualities, parents' coping styles, and work and family circumstances.

Keywords

work-family spillover; child adjustment

From the 1930s until well into the 1980s, many developmental researchers were preoccupied with the question of whether having a working mother was problematic for children. The focus on maternal employment status meant that researchers frequently ignored the specific nature of parents' work situations, as well as the fact that there are two sets of work circumstances that may impinge on a family in which both parents work: the mother's and the father's (Perry-Jenkins, Repetti, & Crouter, 2000). About 15 years ago, however, the field underwent a sea change. The growing consensus that maternal employment status per se did not represent a risk factor for children, coupled with increased interest in fathers' family roles, led researchers to pay greater attention to the implications of mothers' and fathers' occupational circumstances for their offspring. One strand of this body of research has focused on parents' experiences of stress on the job. These studies have asked questions such as "Does parents' work stress make a difference for the adjustment of children and adolescents, and, if so, through what processes?"

Within the body of research on the impacts of work stress on families and children, there are two distinct, complementary genres: (a) studies that rely on global assessments of parents' work stress, family dynamics, and children's or adolescents' psychosocial functioning and (b) investigations that focus on the implications of day-to-day variations in individuals' stressful work experiences for family interactions. Studies in the global tradition are our primary focus here because they have considered the linkages between parents' work stress and children's and adolescents' adjustment. Studies of day-to-day variability in work stress are illuminating as well because they offer a window into how work-to-family emotional transmission may operate (Larson & Almeida, 1999). In this review, we describe research findings from both traditions and discuss individual characteristics and contextual conditions that appear to moderate these associations.

GLOBAL ASSESSMENTS OF PARENTAL WORK STRESS

Parental work stress does not appear to exert direct effects on children's psychological functioning. Rather, "parents' work experiences indirectly influence children's behavior through their sequential effects on parents' work-related affect and parenting" (Stewart & Barling, 1996, p. 222). For example, in a study of Canadian two-parent, dual-earner families with adolescent offspring, Galambos, Sears, Almeida, and Kolaric (1995) tested a three-stage model relating work stress to adolescents' adjustment. The first stage involved the link between parents' occupational stress (i.e., working long hours and feeling overloaded) and their generalized feelings of stress. The second stage traced the association between general feelings of stress and relations between parents and their adolescents, including the warmth and conflict evident in these relations. The last stage concerned the connections between parent-adolescent relations and adolescents' problem behavior. For mothers, work overload led to increased overall stress, which in turn predicted lower warmth toward their adolescents; when mothers were less warm and accepting, adolescents, in turn, exhibited higher levels of problem behavior. For fathers, the linkages looked quite similar except that the aspect of parent-adolescent relations that linked paternal stress and adolescents' problem behavior was not acceptance, but father-adolescent conflict.

In a recent study with our colleagues (Crouter, Bumpus, Maguire, & McHale, 1999), we examined a similar set of linkages but analyzed data from mothers and fathers simultaneously. We investigated not only the implications of work pressure for a given parent, but also the implications of one parent's work pressure for the other parent's feelings of being overloaded. There were hints in the literature that wives tend to be responsive to husbands' work stress in ways that are not reciprocated by husbands, a theme echoed in our findings. The linkages between fathers' and mothers' own perceptions of work pressure (measured primarily in terms of work pace and deadlines) and adolescents' psychological adjustment resembled a series of upright dominos; knocking over the first domino set in motion a chain of associations that ultimately knocked over the last metaphorical domino in the row. Work pressure predicted mothers' own feelings of being overloaded; such feelings, in turn, were related to elevated levels of mother-adolescent conflict; and higher mother-adolescent conflict, in turn, predicted lower levels of psychological well-being for adolescents. For fathers, the domino chain was very similar, with one interesting exception. Fathers' work pressure predicted not only their own feelings of role overload but their wives' as well. Thus, fathers' experiences and perceptions of work pressure may be particularly influential in families because they are associated not only with fathers' feelings of role overload but with mothers' as well, whereas mothers' work pressure is linked only to mothers' own feelings of overload.

Why are wives apparently more susceptible to their spouse's work-related stress than husbands are? We ruled out one possible answer to this question, namely, that because husbands tend to work longer hours than their wives, their work-related affect has less chance to be diluted by other experiences; the pattern of results was the same in families in which husbands worked much longer hours than their wives and in families in which spouses invested similar amounts of time at work (Crouter et al., 1999). Another possible explanation stems from the fact that even in families in which wives are employed full-time, husbands often earn more and are seen as the primary economic provider, a status that may give their work circumstances more visibility in the family. Wives, in contrast, often are still responsible for much of the housework and child care and perhaps cannot afford to stay focused on the strains of the workday. Another explanation focuses on physiological differences in how men and women respond to stress. Gottman and Levenson (1986) theorized that "males show a larger autonomic nervous system response to stress, respond more readily, and recover more slowly than females" (p. 45). This tendency may make men more likely than women to carry work stress home, where it can be noticed and reacted to by their wives.

WITHIN-PERSON VARIATIONS IN WORK STRESS

Studies focused on the implications of an individual's variations in daily work stress enable researchers to fine-tune their understanding of work-family processes. In these studies, individuals, couples, or families are followed intensively over multiple days, with an eye to how fluctuations in the daily experience of work stress predict the quality of subsequent family interactions. In these investigations, work stress is usually measured in terms of work overload, tense, conflictual interactions with co-workers or supervisors, or both overload and negative interactions.

A study by Repetti (1989) exemplifies this type of research. Interested in the impact of daily stress, she focused on an occupation renowned for work pressure: air traffic control. She collected two kinds of data on daily work stress—air traffic controllers' reports of how stressful the day had been and objective data on daily air traffic conditions—and then linked these data to daily reports of marital interaction after work. Repetti found that marital interactions were more positive when wives enabled their air traffic controller husbands to withdraw from marital interaction following particularly stressful work days. These data led Repetti to propose that, at least in the short run, withdrawal from family interaction is an adaptive response to high levels of work stress.

Subsequently, Repetti and Wood (1997a) examined the connections between daily work stress and mother-child interaction at the end of the workday. By studying mothers whose children were enrolled in a work-site child-care program and focusing on mother-child reunions at the end of the workday, the researchers reduced the chances that other intervening experiences, such as a long commute, would alter the mothers' mood. Mothers tended to withdraw from both positive and negative interaction with their children on stressful workdays.

It is not always possible, however, to withdraw. Analysis of daily diary data completed on 42 consecutive evenings revealed that, for both husbands and wives, on days when they experienced high levels of both work stress and home stress, parent-adolescent tension escalated, a finding that echoes themes from studies that have employed global assessments of work stress (Almeida & McDonald, 1998).

WHAT MODERATES THESE ASSOCIATIONS?

The extent to which work stressors spill over to influence employees' interactions with family members is likely to depend on a host of moderating conditions (Perry-Jenkins et al., 2000). Studies focused on day-to-day variability in work stress have paid attention to these conditions, but studies in the global tradition generally have not.

One factor that may moderate the linkages between work stress and children's and adolescents' adjustment is the different personality qualities and coping styles that mothers and fathers bring to their work and family lives. Some studies have found exaggerated emotional responses to daily stressors, including work stressors, among individuals with high levels of depression or anxiety. Similarly, there is a higher association between daily work stress and less positive mother-child interactions among women who describe themselves as high on Type A qualities (e.g., aggressive, driven) than among other women (Repetti & Wood, 1997a).

Coping and stress-management styles are also likely to moderate the extent to which men and women transmit work-related stress. A study of single mothers raising adolescents, for example, found that mothers were less likely to transmit anxious feelings to their adolescent offspring if the mothers spent more time alone (Larson & Gillman, 1999). Time alone may give mothers a chance to manage their negative emotions and, in so doing, break the cycle of transmitting negative emotion within the family.

Family and work contexts also play a role in shaping the relative strength of the connections between work stress and subsequent family interactions. Almeida, Wethington, and Chandler (1999) found that the connections between stress at home and at work and mother-child tension were stronger for mothers who were raising adolescents than for mothers bringing up younger children, even though mothers reported higher overall rates of negative interactions with younger children than with adolescents. In addition, the tendency for mothers and fathers to experience tense parent-child interactions on days when they also experienced other stressors was confined to families in which the mothers worked full-time. When mothers worked less than full-time, daily stressors were not associated with mother-child or father-child tension. Almeida et al. speculated that working fewer hours may give mothers more time and energy to manage their own emotions and the emotional undercurrents in their families, with subsequent benefits not only for their own interactions with offspring but for their husbands' interactions as well. Full-time employment is such a normative role for fathers that studies have not asked whether fathers take advantage of working fewer hours to manage their own emotions and the emotional undercurrents in their families, or if this effect is confined to mothers, who are often seen as the emotion-management specialists in families.

NEXT STEPS

The studies reviewed here employed nonexperimental designs, which cannot determine causal relationships between work stress, family dynamics, and children's and adolescents' adjustment. Putting together the two strands of research—the studies relying on global reports and investigations focusing on day-to-day variability in work stress—reveals a plausible picture of how these processes may operate. Work that is highly demanding in terms of time, deadlines, pace, negative interactions with co-workers and supervisors, or some combination of these factors may lead parents to feel distressed or overloaded. Fathers' work stress appears to be associated not only with fathers' own feelings of overload but with their wives' feelings as well. One response of overloaded parents may be to withdraw from family interaction. This may be a satisfactory short-term strategy, but in the long run, a parent who is chronically stressed at work and withdrawn at home may be seen by other family members as inaccessible and disengaged. Repetti and Wood (1997b) predicted that when parents exhibit a chronic pattern of withdrawal, "there will be protests and resistance" (p. 210) as children escalate their bids for attention and as partners push for change. Researchers know little, however, about the dividing line between adaptive and maladaptive patterns of withdrawal in the face of exposure to work stress. The literature relying on global reports of work stress and family processes suggests that some parents may respond to high levels of role overload by becoming less accepting of their children and engaging in more conflict, relationship dynamics that ultimately may erode children's psychological adjustment.

Given widespread concern that work is more time-consuming and demanding than ever, it is imperative to learn more about how parental work stress makes its mark on families, children, and adolescents. There are many exciting avenues for future research. One is to examine work stress in the context of other dimensions of work, including positive dimensions. For example, some stressful jobs entail high levels of autonomy and complexity, occupational characteristics associated with stimulating home environments for children (Parcel & Menaghan, 1994). It is important to learn more about these trade-offs.

Family conflict and withdrawal are the two family processes that have received the most attention, but it is also possible that work stress impinges on other parenting domains, such as the ability to maintain firm and consistent standards for children's behavior or to stay knowledgeable about children's daily experiences, aspects of parenting that have implications for children's psychosocial functioning. Work stress may also be confounded in important ways with parents' characteristics (e.g., motivation to achieve) or with children's exposure to settings outside the family (e.g., overreliance on after-school care), factors that exert their own effects on children.

In addition, more research is needed on how parents cope with work stress. Larson and Gillman (1999), for example, found that mothers heading single-parent households were less likely to transmit anxiety to their adolescent offspring if the mothers spent more time alone, but, interestingly, anxiety transmission was not moderated by social support. Identifying the conditions that impede the transmission of negative affect would pave the way for prevention-oriented studies.

Finally, little is known about the role of individual differences in children and adolescents. Are children who are particularly challenging (e.g., children who are highly demanding, very active, or very emotionally labile) at increased risk of experiencing negative family fallout when their parents experience job stress? Is it helpful to children and adolescents if they are able to attribute their parents' negative mood or irritable behavior to a bad day at work, rather than, for example, to something they themselves did or said?

As knowledge accumulates, a goal should be to create intervention programs for parents, particularly those employed in stressful occupations. These programs should help parents recognize how they respond emotionally to work stress and give them effective strategies for minimizing the possible corrosive effects of those negative emotions on family interaction.

Recommended Reading

Crouter, A.C., Bumpus, M.F., Maguire, M.C., & McHale, S.M. (1999). (See References)
Larson, R.W., & Almeida, D.M. (1999). (See References)
Perry-Jenkins, M., Repetti, R.L., & Crouter, A.C. (2000). (See References)

Note

1. Address correspondence to Ann C. Crouter, Department of Human Development and Family Studies, 105 White Building, Pennsylvania State University, University Park, PA 16802; e-mail: acl@psu.edu.

References

Almeida, D.M., & McDonald, D. (1998). Weekly rhythms of parents' work stress, home stress, and parent adolescent tension. In A.C. Crouter & R. Larson (Eds.), *Temporal rhythms in adolescence: Clocks, calendars, and the coordination of daily life* (New Directions in Child and Adolescent Development No. 82, pp. 53–67). San Francisco: Jossey Bass.
Almeida, D.M., Wethington, E., & Chandler, A.L. (1999). Daily transmission of tensions between marital dyads and parent-child dyads. *Journal of Marriage and the Family, 61*, 49–61.
Crouter, A.C., Bumpus, M.F., Maguire, M.C., & McHale, S.M. (1999). Linking parents' work pressure and adolescents' well-being: Insights into dynamics in dual-earner families. *Developmental Psychology, 35*, 1453–1461.
Galambos, N.L., Sears, H.A., Almeida, D.M., & Kolaric, G.C. (1995). Parents' work overload and problem behavior in young adolescents. *Journal of Research on Adolescence, 5*, 201–223.
Gottman, J.M., & Levenson, R.W. (1986). Assessing the role of emotion in marriage. *Behavioral Assessment, 8*, 31–48.
Larson, R.W., & Almeida, D.M. (1999). Emotional transmission in the daily lives of families: A new paradigm for studying family process. *Journal of Marriage and the Family, 61*, 5–20.
Larson, R.W., & Gillman, S. (1999). Transmission of emotions in the daily interactions of single-mother families. *Journal of Marriage and the Family, 61*, 21–37.
Parcel, T.L., & Menaghan, E.G. (1994). *Parents' jobs and children's lives*. Hawthorne, NY: Aldine de Gruyter.
Perry-Jenkins, M., Repetti, R.L., & Crouter, A.C. (2000). Work and family in the 1990s. *Journal of Marriage and the Family, 62*, 981–998.
Repetti, R. (1989). Effects of daily workload on subsequent behavior during marital interaction: The roles of social withdrawal and spouse support. *Journal of Personality and Social Psychology, 57*, 651–659.
Repetti, R.L., & Wood, J. (1997a). The effects of daily stress at work on mothers' interactions with preschoolers. *Journal of Family Psychology, 11*, 90–108.

Repetti, R.L., & Wood, J. (1997b). Families accommodating to chronic stress: Unintended and unnoticed processes. In B.H. Gottlieb (Ed.), *Coping with chronic stress* (pp. 191–220). New York: Plenum Press.

Stewart, W., & Barling, J. (1996). Fathers' work experiences affect children's behaviors via job-related affect and parenting behaviors. *Journal of Organizational Behavior, 17*, 221–232.

Critical Thinking Questions

1. How might Bronfenbrenner's Ecological Systems Theory of development inform research and theory on parental work stress and children's and adolescents' psychological adjustment?

2. Why might withdrawal from family interactions after stressful workdays be adaptive?

3. What moderates associations between parental work stress and subsequent family interactions? Could strategies for stopping the transmission of negative emotions between work and family address these moderators? Why?

Mutually Responsive Orientation Between Mothers and Their Young Children: A Context for the Early Development of Conscience

Grazyna Kochanska[1]

Department of Psychology, University of Iowa, Iowa City, Iowa

Abstract

Some parent-child dyads establish a mutually responsive orientation (MRO), a relationship that is close, mutually binding, cooperative, and affectively positive. Such relationships have two main characteristics—mutual responsiveness and shared positive affect—and they foster the development of conscience in young children. Children growing up with parents who are responsive to their needs and whose interactions are infused with happy emotions adopt a willing, responsive stance toward parental influence and become eager to embrace parental values and standards for behavior. The concurrent and longitudinal beneficial effects of MRO for early development of conscience have been replicated across studies, for a broad range of developmental periods from infancy through early school age, and using a wide variety of behavioral, emotional, and cognitive measures of conscience in the laboratory, at home, and in school. These findings highlight the importance of the early parent-child relationship for subsequent moral development.

Keywords

relationships; mutuality; conscience

How do young children become aware of rules, values, and standards of behavior accepted within their families and cultures? How do they gradually come to internalize those values and make them their own? Why do some children adopt societal norms wholeheartedly and with ease, and become conscientious citizens, whereas others do not?

The emergence of an individual conscience, a reliable internal guidance system that regulates conduct without the need for external control, is the endpoint of the process of integrating a child into a broader network of values. How this process works continues to be debated as one of the perennial and central issues in human socialization (Grusec, 1997).

Research on conscience was once dominated by a cognitive approach, focused on children's abstract understanding of societal rules, measured by their ability to reason about hypothetical moral dilemmas. Moral development was seen as a product of cognitive maturation, aided by peer interactions, but fundamentally unrelated to parental influence. In contrast, other theories acknowledged parental contributions. Parents and other socializing agents were seen as critical in several versions of learning theory. Those approaches emphasized the importance of parental discipline and modeling as instruments that modify and shape children's behavior. Somewhat later, attributional theories underscored the importance of children's perceptions of parental discipline, and revealed surprising, often paradoxical effects of salient parental rewards and punishments.

More recently, many scholars have come to appreciate an approach grounded in psychoanalytic and neo-psychoanalytic theories. Although Freud's views or the early development of conscience as linked to the Oedipus or Electra complex have long been discarded, his general emphasis on the role of early emotions and early relationships in emerging morality has proven insightful. That approach has been strongly reinvigorated and modernized by John Bowlby and the burgeoning research on attachment. From that perspective, moral emotions, moral conduct, and moral thought are all components of an internal guidance system, or conscience, whose foundations are established in early childhood in the context of socialization in the family. The early parent-child relationship, which encompasses but is not limited to control and discipline, can substantially foster or undermine that process (Emde, Biringen, Clyman, & Oppenheim, 1991).

THE RELATIONSHIP PERSPECTIVE: MUTUALLY RESPONSIVE ORIENTATION

In 1951, Robert Sears argued for a shift in psychological research from studying individuals to studying dyads. Over the past two or three decades, the science of relationships has blossomed in personality, social, and developmental psychology (Collins & Laursen, 1999; Reis, Collins, & Berscheid, 2000). Several scholars have proposed that when relationship partners—whether two adults or a parent and a child—are responsive and attuned to each other, are mutually supportive, and enjoy being together, they form an internal model of their relationship as a cooperative enterprise, and develop an eager, receptive stance toward each other's influence and a compelling sense of obligation to willingly comply with the other. For example, Clark (1984) referred to "communal relationships" in adults as contexts in which the partners are invested in each other's well-being, are empathic and responsive to each other, and experience an internal sense of mutual obligation.

In developmental research, those resurging perspectives afford a productive vantage point for exploring social development. Socialization is seen as a process jointly constructed by parents and children over time (Collins & Laursen, 1999; Collins, Maccoby, Steinberg, Hetherington, & Bornstein, 2000; Maccoby, 1999; Reis et al., 2000). Maccoby (1999) referred to parent-child mutuality as a positive socialization force that engenders a spirit of cooperation in the child. Attachment scholars believe that children raised in a loving, responsive manner become eager to cooperate with their caregivers and to embrace their values.

To describe such relationships between parents and children, my colleagues and I have proposed a construct of *mutually responsive orientation (MRO)*. MRO is a positive, close, mutually binding, and cooperative relationship, which encompasses two components: *responsiveness* and *shared positive affect*. Responsiveness refers to the parent's and the child's willing, sensitive, supportive, and developmentally appropriate response to one another's signals of distress, unhappiness, needs, bids for attention, or attempts to exert influence. Shared positive affect refers to the "good times" shared by the parent and the child—pleasurable, harmonious, smoothly flowing interactions infused with positive emotions experienced by both.

We further proposed that children who grow up in mutually responsive dyads, compared with those who do not, become more eager to embrace their parents' values and more likely to develop a strong conscience. Their eager stance to embrace parental values reflects an internal sense of obligation to respond positively to parental influence, and emerges from a history of mutually gratifying, mutually accommodating experiences. A child who has developed a mutually responsive relationship with the parent comes to trust the parent and to expect that the parent will be responsive and supportive; at the same time, the child comes to feel motivated to cooperate willingly with the parent, to embrace the parent's values, and to adopt parental standards for behavior and make them his or her own. In this view, the parent-child relationship influences the child's conscience mainly through a gradually evolving shared working model of the relationship as a mutually cooperative enterprise rather than through the cumulative history of parental discipline as the instrument of behavior modification.

MOTHER-CHILD MRO AND CHILDREN'S CONSCIENCE: EMPIRICAL EVIDENCE

In two large studies, we measured the qualities of the mother-child relationship and the child's emerging conscience for more than 200 mother-child dyads. To assess the strength of MRO for the individual dyads, we observed the mothers and children interacting in multiple lengthy, naturalistic yet carefully scripted contexts at home and in the laboratory. The situations we observed included care-giving routines, preparing and eating meals, playing, relaxing, and doing household chores. We coded each mother's responsiveness to her child's numerous signals of needs, signs of physical or emotional distress or discomfort, bids for attention, and social overtures. We also assessed shared positive affect by coding the flow of emotion expression for both the mother and the child over the course of each interaction, focusing particularly on the times when they both displayed positive emotion. We obtained these measures repeatedly, following the same families over a period of several years.

In the individual dyads, the degree of MRO was significantly consistent across separate sessions close in time, and significantly stable over several years. This indicates that our observational markers captured a robust quality of the relationships that unfolded along a fairly stable dyadic trajectory.

Using a broad variety of laboratory paradigms, we also observed rich manifestations of the young children's conscience: moral emotions, moral conduct, and moral cognition. These assessments took place at many points in the children's development—starting in their 2nd year and continuing until early school age. The children's moral emotions, including guilt, discomfort, concern, and empathy, were observed when they were led to believe that they had violated a standard of conduct, or when they witnessed others' distress. While they were unsupervised, either alone or with peers, their moral conduct was assessed in many types of situations in which they faced strong temptations to break various rules and were coaxed to violate standards of behavior. Their moral cognition was measured by presenting them with age-appropriate, hypothetical moral dilemmas and asking them to express their thoughts and feelings about rules and transgressions, and consider moral decisions. We also asked their mothers and teachers to evaluate the children's moral emotions and conduct displayed in environments outside the laboratory—at home and at school.

Both studies supported the view that children who grow up in a context of a highly mutually responsive relationship with their mothers develop strong consciences (Kochanska, 1997; Kochanska, Forman, & Coy, 1999; Kochanska & Murray, 2000). The strength of the replicated findings was striking, given the broad range of the children's ages and the wide variety of conscience measures used.

In both studies, the links between MRO and the development of conscience were both concurrent and longitudinal. The concurrent links were found for both toddlers and preschoolers. The longitudinal findings were robust: MRO in infancy predicted conscience development in the 2nd year, and MRO in toddlerhood predicted children's conscience at preschool age and again at early school age. The history of MRO in the first 2 years predicted conscience at age 5. In short, the beneficial effect of MRO on the development of conscience was evident across diverse measures of conscience involving emotions, conduct, and cognition. It was also evident whether conscience was assessed by observations in the laboratory or reports from mothers and teachers. These results have been replicated by other researchers (Laible & Thompson, 2000).

HOW DOES MRO EXERT ITS IMPACT?

What causal mechanisms may be responsible for these well-established empirical findings? Using statistical approaches (sequences of multiple regressions, as well as structural equations modeling, or SEM) to analyze the causal factors that accounted for the associations in our data, we determined that MRO exerts its influence through at least two mechanisms.

The first mechanism involves promoting the child's positive mood. Early MRO between the parent and the child contributes to the child's positive, happy disposition, and that, in turn, increases his or her broad eagerness to behave prosocially. This finding is consistent with a large body of research in social and developmental psychology (Eisenberg & Fabes, 1998). Adults and children who are in a positive mood have often been found to be more prosocial, altruistic, cooperative, rule abiding, and socially responsive than those who are in neutral or negative moods.

The second mechanism involves promoting the child's responsive stance toward parental influence. We have found that in playlike teaching situations, children in mutually responsive relationships are attuned to their mothers and eagerly follow their lead (Forman & Kochanska, 2001; Kochanska et al., 1999). In discipline situations, they show what we called *committed compliance*—willing, eager, wholehearted cooperation with the parent (Kochanska, Coy, & Murray, 2001). Such a generalized responsive stance may be an intermediate step between simple cooperation with the parent and genuine internalization of parental rules, evident even in the parent's absence. We believe it reflects the child's emerging working model of a cooperative, reciprocal, mutually accommodating relationship in which partners naturally do things for one another without abrogating their autonomy.

FUTURE RESEARCH DIRECTIONS

MRO and Qualities of Individuals

It takes two to develop dyadic MRO. Although the relationship between a parent and child—like any relationship—is more than a simple sum of their characteristics, those characteristics may nevertheless foster or impede the formation of MRO. Recent advances in research on the role of genetics in behavior and on the biological foundations of children's temperament are beginning to be reflected in scientific work in what has been traditionally conceived as the domain of relationships. For example, Deater-Deckard and O'Connor (2000), studying identical and fraternal twins, and biological and adoptive siblings, found that parent-child MRO was driven, in part, by the child's genetically based qualities. In addition, a child's biologically based traits, such as being prone to anger or joy, or being hard or easy to soothe, may facilitate or undermine the evolution of the child's relationships within particular dyads. Being responsive to and having enjoyable interactions with a child may be more challenging if the child is temperamentally difficult than if he or she is easygoing and mellow.

Mothers' traits, some also biologically based, may be important as well. We have found that the more empathic mothers are, the better able they are to form MRO with their children (Kochanska, 1997). A large body of research indicates that depression and high levels of negative emotion in mothers reduce their responsiveness and positive behavior when interacting with their young children.

More complex interplay between biological and relationship factors also deserves future research attention. Our findings indicate that MRO may be particularly beneficial for children with certain temperaments, particularly fearless, thrill-seeking children whose behavior is not easily modified by actual or anticipated punishments and threats. Other interactions between temperament and relationships are also possible.

MRO as a Developmentally Changing System

A mutually responsive relationship between a parent and an infant differs from a mutually responsive relationship between a parent and a preschooler, or between a parent and an adolescent. The contexts and currency of parent-child interactions change. In infancy, those contexts include mostly the contexts of caregiving, play, and daily routines, and the currency of exchange is often nonverbal. Gradually, the contexts expand to include parent-child discussions of events and ideas, and the exchanges are increasingly verbal (Laible & Thompson, 2000). The child's and the parent's relative contributions to the relationship change over time, and so do their cognitive representations, perceptions, and expectations of the relationship and of each other. Psychologists' understanding of the child's side of MRO lags considerably behind their understanding of the parent's side of MRO. How MRO can be assessed in a manner that is developmentally sensitive and yet captures stable qualities of the parent-child dyad over time is one of the future challenges.

MRO and Internal Representations

In research to date, MRO has been inferred from parents' and children's observed behavior and affect during interactions. This outer layer, however, only partially captures the essence of a relationship. Scholars studying relationships have adopted Bowlby's premise that, over time, the parent and the child gradually form inner representations, or internal working models, of their relationship (Collins & Laursen, 1999). Those evolving models include generalized memories of each other's behavior, implicit beliefs and feelings about each other and the relationship, and a sense of what the relationship is like and what to expect from one another. Those generalized products of an individual's experience serve to organize and bias his or her future information processing, behavior, and emotions. In the case of MRO, the parent's and child's internal models entail mutual cooperation and implicit reciprocity, and the child's internal model is thought to underlie his or her willingness to embrace parental rules. Those inner representations, however, are difficult to access and to study. To develop sensitive yet rigorous methodologies that will provide insights into the representational aspect of MRO is an important future challenge.

MRO and the Family System

The relationship between a parent and child is itself nested in a network of family relationships. The importance of studying development in the context of the entire family system has been increasingly acknowledged. In particular, future research should study mother-child and father-child MRO, both separately and as a triadic interconnected system. More generally, family-level variables such as stress, conflict, support, and affective ambience may be significant dimensions of the context in which mutually responsive relationships with the child may flourish or fail.

Recommended Reading

Collins, W.A., & Laursen, B. (Eds.). (1999). (See References)
Kochanska, G. (1997). (See References)
Kochanska, G., & Murray, K.T. (2000). (See References)

Acknowledgments—This research has been sponsored by grants from the National Institute of Mental Health (RO1 MH63096, KO2 MHO1446) and National Science Foundation (DBS-9209559, SBR-9510863) to the author. I gratefully acknowledge the comments of Nazan Aksan, David Forman, and Robert Siegler, and contributions of numerous students, staff, and the families who participated in the studies.

Note

1. Address correspondence to Grazyna Kochanska, Department of Psychology, University of Iowa, Iowa City, IA 52242-1447.

References

Clark, M.S. (1984). Record keeping in two types of relationships. *Journal of Personality and Social Psychology, 47,* 549–557.

Collins, W.A., & Laursen, B. (Eds.). (1999). *Minnesota Symposia on Child Psychology: Vol. 30. Relationships as developmental contexts.* Hillsdale, NJ: Erlbaum.

Collins, W.A., Maccoby, E.E., Steinberg, L., Hetherington, E.M., & Bornstein, M.H. (2000). Contemporary research on parenting: The case for nature and nurture. *American Psychologist, 55,* 218–232.

Deater-Deckard, K., & O'Connor, T.G. (2000). Parent-child mutuality in early childhood: Two behavioral genetic studies. *Developmental Psychology, 36,* 561–570.

Eisenberg, N., & Fabes, R.A. (1998). Prosocial development. In W. Damon (Series Ed.) & N. Eisenberg (Vol. Ed.), *Handbook of child psychology: Vol. 3. Social, emotional, and personality development* (pp. 701–778). New York: Wiley.

Emde, R.N., Biringen, Z., Clyman, R.B., & Oppenheim, D. (1991). The moral self of infancy: Affective core and procedural knowledge. *Developmental Review, 11,* 251–270.

Forman, D.R., & Kochanska, G. (2001). Viewing imitation as child responsiveness: A link between teaching and discipline domains of socialization. *Developmental Psychology, 37,* 198–206.

Grusec, J.E. (1997). A history of research on parenting strategies and children's internalization of values. In J.E. Grusec & L. Kuczynski (Eds.), *Parenting and children's internalization of values: A handbook of contemporary theory* (pp. 3–22). New York: Wiley.

Kochanska, G. (1997). Mutually responsive orientation between mothers and their young children: Implications for early socialization. *Child Development, 68,* 98–112.

Kochanska, G., Coy, K.C., & Murray, K.T. (2001). The development of self-regulation in the first four years of life. *Child Development, 72,* 1091–1111.

Kochanska, G., Forman, G., & Coy, K.C. (1999). Implications of the mother-child relationship in infancy for socialization in the second year of life. *Infant Behavior and Development, 22,* 249–265.

Kochanska, G., & Murray, K.T. (2000). Mother-child mutually responsive orientation and conscience development: From toddler to early school age. *Child Development, 71,* 417–431.

Laible, D.J., & Thompson, R.A. (2000). Mother-child discourse, attachment security, shared positive affect, and early conscience development. *Child Development, 71,* 1424–1440.

Maccoby, E.E. (1999). The uniqueness of the parent-child relationship. In W.A. Collins & B. Laursen (Eds.), *Minnesota Symposia on Child Psychology: Vol. 30. Relationships as developmental contexts* (pp. 157–175). Hillsdale, NJ: Erlbaum.

Reis, H.T., Collins, W.A., & Berscheid, E. (2000). Relationships in human behavior and development. *Psychological Bulletin, 126,* 844–872.

Critical Thinking Questions

1. How might studying mutually responsive orientation in triads, versus dyads, enhance our understanding of early development of conscience? Why might mutually responsive triads be a stronger indication of children's subsequent embracing of their parents' values than mutually responsive dyads?

2. What causal mechanisms are responsible for the influence of mutually responsive orientation on the development of conscience?

3. What sorts of experiences might undermine dyadic mutually responsive orientation?

Understanding Families as Systems

Martha J. Cox[1] and Blair Paley

Department of Psychology and Center for Developmental Science, University of North Carolina at Chapel Hill, Chapel Hill, North Carolina (M.J.C.), and Department of Psychiatry, Neuropsychiatric Institute and Hospital, University of California at Los Angeles, Los Angeles, California (B.P.)

Abstract

In this article, we discuss recent research that has arisen from theoretical and conceptual models that use a systems metaphor for understanding families. We suggest that research stimulated by such models leads social scientists in new and important directions in understanding the social and emotional development of children in their families. These models view development as resulting from the dynamic transactions across multiple levels of family systems, which regulate a child's behavior. Thus, these models are important in considering multiple influences on development and adaptation.

Keywords

family systems; family processes; developmental theory

In response to family systems theory, there has been a change of emphasis in research on children and families. Previous research focused almost exclusively on the parent-child relationship. In contrast, more recently researchers have moved toward viewing individuals within the context of their larger family systems and considering the mutual influences among family subsystems, such as the marital relationship and the parent-child relationship. This change of emphasis has given rise to new lines of research, particularly over the past two decades. These new lines of research follow from applying principles of a general systems theory to study of the family as an organized system. According to such theory, family systems are characterized by (a) wholeness and order (i.e., the whole is greater than the sum of its parts and has properties that cannot be understood simply from the combined characteristics of each part), (b) hierarchical structure (i.e., a family is composed of subsystems that are systems in and of themselves), and (c) adaptive self-organization (i.e., a family, as an open, living system, can adapt to change or challenges).

THE FAMILY SYSTEM AND THE INTERDEPENDENCE OF SUBSYSTEMS

Some of the first impetus for a broader consideration of development within the whole-family system came from the writings of family therapists adopting a family-system view. This work spurred interest in the interdependence between the marital relationship and the parent-child relationships within a family. Therapists had long noted that problems in the parent-child relationship were often associated with marital distress. As a result, parent-child issues were difficult to resolve unless problems in the marriage had first been addressed. Numerous studies have confirmed that marital and parent-child relationships are interrelated. That is, poor parent-child relationships often develop in the context of distressed marriages. These studies have been important in directing researchers to look beyond the mother-child relationship and to consider fathers and their relationships in the family in order to better understand children's development (see review by Cox, Paley, & Harter, 2001). More important, these studies have provided support for the idea that in order to understand children's development, one must gain a broad perspective on the whole family.

Over the past few years, researchers have made important progress in answering one particularly difficult question: How can one conceptualize and measure processes at the whole-family level? This type of research highlights the unique contribution of phenomena that arise at the family level. For example, Deal, Hagan, Bass, Hetherington, and Clingempeel (1999) found that parents behaved differently when the whole family was together than when they were interacting one-on-one with their child. When their child was present, couples were less hostile and less coercive in their behavior toward one another. However, they were also less warm, communicative, and self-disclosing. McHale and his colleagues (e.g., McHale & Rasmussen, 1998) have made valuable contributions in their investigations of how parents interact together with their child (often referred to as co-parenting), demonstrating that such interactions are predictive of children's adjustment. This relationship holds even in analyses that control for factors such as the mother's well-being, the overall quality of the marriage, the mother's and father's warmth when interacting with the child individually, and the quality of parent-child attachment. Clearly, considering interactions among both parents and the child adds information that is important for understanding a child's adjustment.

Other recent studies have advanced knowledge concerning aspects of the marital relationship that are associated with aspects of interactional processes at other levels of the family system, such as parent-child relationships, co-parenting relationships, and whole-family relationships. For example, we (Paley, Cox, Kanoy, Harter, & Margand, 1999) found that the tendency for a husband to withdraw during one-on-one interaction with his wife is related to several features of family-level interactions. Such withdrawal, for example, is associated with an increased likelihood of parent-child alliances within the family. Also, whole-family interactions have lower levels of positive emotions and higher levels of negative emotions and detachment in families characterized by this kind of marital relationship than in other families.

One of the most significant conceptual contributions in the study of family relationships has come from Cummings and his colleagues (e.g., Cummings & Davies, 1995; Cummings & Wilson, 1999). Their work on the emotional-security hypothesis moves beyond the dyadic focus of attachment theory in emphasizing the importance of the broader family context, rather than one-on-one interactions within the family, in shaping the child's sense of emotional security. In particular, they have found that destructive marital conflict (especially conflict that involves violence or aggression between partners or that remains unresolved) threatens the child's sense that he or she can feel safe and emotionally secure in the family. Their work indicates that emotional security is an important factor in the child's regulation and organization of emotion, key processes in the development of early competence in children (i.e., their ability to form positive relationships with others and their ability to explore their environment in a meaningful way).

ADAPTIVE SELF-ORGANIZATION OF FAMILY SYSTEMS

Another important concept of family systems theory is that families have the capacity to reorganize in response to external forces. That is, families can adapt so that they can continue to function in the face of the new circumstances (Sameroff, 1983). This aspect of systems theory is important because it points to the need to consider how the family as a system responds to challenges, in addition to considering how each individual or subsystem responds. The property of adaptive self-organization suggests that there will be challenges to existing patterns of interaction at all levels of the family system during both normative transitions (e.g., birth of a child, a child entering school) and nonnormative transitions (e.g., departure of a spouse, entrance of a new spouse, untimely death of a family member). These challenges affect the family at multiple levels, and changes in activity at each level influence other levels, resulting in a feedback loop that leads to further change. Eventually new patterns emerge as an adaptation to the family's changed circumstances. Sameroff (1983) noted that adoptively reorganized systems are not necessarily more stable than the original systems. They may deal well with the forces that elicited the process of reorganization, but they may not be more resistant to all destabilizing factors in the general environment. Thus, there may be new vulnerabilities in a reorganized family system.

These ideas highlight the importance of looking at transition points in the family life cycle, and have implications for understanding continuity and discontinuity in adult adaptation, child development, and family functioning. The research on the transition to parenthood is a good example of a body of work that has been profitably influenced by family systems theory. Research shows that the birth of a child and the need for the couple to adapt to their new caregiving role affects both spouses individually, as well as interactions between them. Changes at these levels then feed back into the family system. New parents are at increased risk for psychosis, depression, and the "blues" (Cowan & Cowan, 2000; Cowan, Cowan, Herring, & Miller, 1991). Gender roles become more traditional, with women taking over more household tasks and care of the child. Men and women develop diverging attitudes regarding their sense of self as "parent" and "worker" (Cowan & Cowan, 2000; Cowan et al., 1991). These new patterns may be appropriate to providing the child's care, but as Sameroff suggested, they may not be more resilient than previous patterns in response to all stressors or challenges in the general environment. In fact, researchers (e.g., Cowan & Cowan, 2000; Cowan et al., 1991) have found that these increased differences between the roles and attitudes of spouses in response to the task of child rearing set the stage for greater marital dissatisfaction and conflict during the early years after a first child's birth.

94

Moreover, there is good evidence that there are mutual influences among the quality of the adaptation in the marital subsystem, the development of the parent-child relationship, and the quality of the infant's development. The ability of parents to meet their infant's physical and emotional needs seems to be reciprocally related to the support the parents derive from the marital relationship (Cox et al., in press). Qualities of the infant's early regulation (i.e., the infant's innate ability to modulate his or her physical and emotional states) also seem to interact with the caregiving system, with consequent implications for the child's development, particularly the child's social and emotional development. Belsky, Hsieh, and Crnic (1998) found that toddlers whose mothers responded to their irritability with negative affect and intrusive behavior (i.e., inserting their "own goals and agendas upon the child without apparent regard or concern for what the child was doing or feeling," p. 309) were more likely to go on to develop behavior problems than were children whose mothers responded to their irritability with less negative affect and less intrusive behavior or children who had not been irritable as toddlers.

This interplay between levels of the family system can also be seen in the work of Kochanska (e.g., 1995). Her work supports the idea that an infant's temperament affects caregiving practices in the family and also moderates the effects of caregiving on the child. Fearful toddlers may tend not only to stimulate gentle reassurance from mothers, but also to show internalizing behavior (e.g., sadness or anxiety) problems over time if they do not receive this kind of care. Less fearful children, conversely, appear to be less affected if their mothers' caregiving emphasizes power and enforcement rather than gentle guidance. The work of van den Boom (1991) shows similar findings in that mothers of children who were irritable in the first few days of life were more likely to show declining involvement with the infant during the first 6 months than were mothers of less irritable infants. Additionally, this declining involvement was associated with infants' showing less improvement in emotional regulation (i.e., the ability to modulate emotions, especially negative ones such as anger or frustration) over time. Early et al. (2002) found that children who were judged to be extremely shy and withdrawn (top 15%) in response to novel situations at the end of their 1st year and whose mothers were highly sensitive and responsive to them during their preschool years were seen by teachers as no more shy and withdrawn in their initial adjustment to kindergarten than were children who were not classified as shy and withdrawn as 1-year-olds. In contrast, children who had been extremely shy and withdrawn as 1-year-olds and whose mothers were insensitive to their emotional signals during the preschool years were seen by teachers to be shy and withdrawn in the novel kindergarten setting.

Thus, there is evidence that transactions across the multiple levels of a family system are important in regulating a child's behavior and in understanding mothers' and babies' behavior at any one point in time. This evidence points to the limitations of static notions of "difficult temperaments" or "insensitive mothers," labels intended to highlight permanent qualities of an individual. As the research we have summarized shows, the metaphor of the system provides an important perspective on the notion of continuity and discontinuity in individual development. It suggests that continuity cannot be explained as a characteristic of the child. If the child is viewed as a part of an ongoing, dynamic system, then continuity can be located only in the relationship between the child and the family system or caregiving environment. Application of a systems perspective in this research also makes it clear why some individuals do not develop along typical paths, and with good theory, these alternative paths can be seen as lawful. Changes can arise at any level of the family system, and a change at one level can stimulate further change in individuals, relationships, and the whole family system.

CONCLUSIONS AND NEW DIRECTIONS

Process-Oriented Research

These family systems models stimulate researchers to think about the processes of child development in families. There is a dearth of process-oriented research, especially research that considers multiple levels (from the individual up through the whole family) and the interplay between them. These models suggest that researchers should not look for effects at any one level without considering the context of other levels. For example, the work on emotional security in the family (Cummings & Davies, 1995; Cummings & Wilson, 1999) suggests that the extent to which parent-child attachment can support the development of good emotional regulation in a child may be affected by other variables in the family system. Families may differ widely in their interactions at other levels (e.g., marital, co-parenting, or whole-family interactions), and such differences may or may not threaten the child's sense of emotional security. Frightening marital aggression may make it difficult for a parent to foster a secure parent-child attachment, and even a secure parent-child attachment may not lead to a child's ability to regulate his or her emotions in response to the broader family environment if a threat to security is present. That is, the child may react to conflict in the family with distress or anger, or by pushing the parents away (Cummings & Davies, 1995).

An ambitious agenda awaits researchers attempting to realize the potential of these theoretical models. But current research highlights the exciting directions that this work should take in looking at the dynamic interplay of influences at multiple levels over time. For example, Cicchetti and Sroufe (2000) noted that provocative research demonstrates the mutual influence between individual neurobiological development and the relationship experiences of the child. There is considerable work ahead with regard to discovering the processes of development; the central goal of this work will be to clarify the emergence, progressive unfolding, maintenance, and transformation of adaptation and maladaptation over time (Cicchetti & Sroufe, 2000) and at multiple levels of systems such as the family.

The Need for Progress in Measurement and Analysis

The type of research we have described requires good measurement that reflects all the levels of the family system. Researchers have come a long way in improving measurement, but there is more work to be done, particularly in developing methods to measure family subsystems beyond one-on-one relationships, such as parent-child or marital relationships. For example, researchers need to utilize behavioral observation coding schemes that capture the qualities of interactions among multiple members of a family. Studying whole-family interactions can provide important information not only about processes like co-parenting, but also about processes like children's attempts to mediate conflicts and the formation of coalitions or alliances within the family. These processes are likely to have significant implications for children's development, but require a broader measurement of the family system than is seen in the traditional work emphasizing parent-child relationships.

Additionally, systemic models suggest that progress in understanding the development of individuals or relationships in families will come from longitudinal investigations. Such long-term studies are useful for observing and describing the causal processes that reflect the reciprocal influences of various levels of the family system. However, common statistical procedures are not well suited to this task. Advances in statistical techniques are needed. The task of realizing the potential of these models will require efforts in many directions, but, we suggest, will be worth the investment of effort.

Recommended Reading

Bergman, L.R., Cairns, R.B., Nilsson, L., & Nystedt, L. (2000). *Developmental science and the holistic approach*. Mahwah, NJ: Erlbaum.

Sameroff, A.J. (1995), General systems theory and developmental psychopathology. In D. Cicchetti & D.J. Cohen (Eds.), *Developmental psychopathology* (Vol. 1., pp. 659–695). New York: Wiley.

Sroufe, L.A., Duggal, S., Weinfield, N., & Carlson, E. (2000). Relationships, development, and psychopathology. In A.J. Sameroff, M. Lewis, & S.M. Miller (Eds.), *Handbook of developmental psychopathology* (pp. 75–91). New York: Kluwer Academic/ Plenum Publishers.

Note

1. Address correspondence to Martha J. Cox, Center for Developmental Science, CB#8115, University of North Carolina, Chapel Hill, NC 27599-8115.

References

Belsky, J., Hsieh, K., & Crnic, K. (1998). Mothering, fathering, and infant negativity as antecedents of boys externalizing problems and inhibition at age 3 years: Differential susceptibility to rearing experience? *Development and Psychopathology, 10*, 301–320.

Cicchetti, D., & Sroufe, L.A. (2000). The past as prologue to the future: The times, they've been a-changin'. *Development and Psychopathology, 12*, 255–264.

Cowan, C.P., & Cowan, P.A. (2000). *When partners become parents: The big life change for couples*. Mahwah, NJ: Erlbaum.

Cowan, C.P., Cowan, P.A., Herring, G., & Miller, N.B. (1991). Becoming a family: Marriage, parenting, and child development. In P.A Cowan & E.M. Hetherington (Eds,), *Family transitions* (pp. 79–109). Hillsdale, NJ: Erlbaum.

Cox, M.J., Burchinal, M., Taylor, L.C., Frosch, C., Goldman, B., & Kanoy, K. (in press). The transition to parenting: Continuity and change in early parenting behavior and attitudes. In R.D. Conger (Ed.), *Continuity and change: Family structure and process*. Mahwah, NJ: Erlbaum.

Cox, M.J., Paley, B., & Harter, K. (2001). Interparental conflict and parent-child relationships. In J.H. Grych & F.D. Fincham (Eds,), *Interparental conflict and child development* (pp. 249–272). Cambridge, England: Cambridge University Press.

Cummings, E.M., & Davies, P.T. (1995). The impact of parents on their children: An emotional security perspective. *Annals of Child Development, 10,* 167–208.

Cummings, E.M., & Wilson, A. (1999). Contexts of marital conflict and children's emotional security: Exploring the distinction between constructive and destructive conflict from the children's perspective. In M. Cox & J. Brooks-Gunn (Eds.), *Conflict and closeness in families: Causes and consequences* (pp. 105–129). Mahwah, NJ: Erlbaum.

Deal, J.E., Hagan, M.S., Bass, B., Hetherington, E.M., & Clingempeel, G. (1999). Marital interaction in dyadic and triadic contexts: Continuities and discontinuities. *Family Process, 38*(1), 105–115.

Early, D.M., Rimm-Kaufman, S.E., Cox, M.J., Saluja, G., Pianta, R.C., Bradley, R., & Payne, C.C. (2002). Maternal sensitivity and child wariness in the transition to kindergarten. *Parenting: Science and Practice, 2,* 355–377.

Kochanska, G. (1995). Children's temperament, mothers' discipline, and security of attachment: Multiple pathways to emerging internalization. *Child Development, 66,* 597–615.

McHale, J.P., & Rasmussen, J.L. (1998). Coparental and family group-level dynamics during infancy: Early family precursors of child and family functioning during preschool. *Development and Psychopathology, 10,* 39–59.

Paley, B., Cox, M.J., Kanoy, K., Harter, K.S.M., & Margand, N. (1999, April). *Adult attachment stance and marital quality as predictors of whole family interactions.* Paper presented at the biennial meeting of the Society for Research in Child Development, Albuquerque, NM.

Sameroff, A. (1983). Developmental systems: Context and evolution, In P.H. Mussen & W. Kessen (Eds.), *Handbook of child psychology: Vol. 1. History, theory, and methods* (4th ed., pp. 237–294). New York: Wiley.

van den Boom, D.C. (1991). The influence of infant irritability on the development of the mother-infant relationship in the first six months of life. In J.K. Nugent, B.M. Lester, & T.B. Brazelton (Eds.), *The cultural context of infancy (pp. 63–89). Norwood, NJ: Ablex.*

Critical Thinking Questions

1. If the whole is greater than the sum of its parts, can individual-level findings contribute to family-level conclusions?

2. How might changes in the marital subsystem affect changes in the sibling subsystem, and vice versa?

3. Why is the concept "goodness of fit" very relevant to the conceptualization of the family as a system?

Peers and Social Context

Peers provide an important set of experiences to the developing child. It is through peer interaction that children learn the social norms of behavior. They learn to share, to test out roles, and they learn a great deal about themselves and their values. Peer relations have been found to play a significant role in children's' social and emotional functioning. The study of peer relations has been a major area in developmental psychology, and the articles in this section highlight some of the most current findings.

Steven Asher and Julie Paquette consider the concept of loneliness, that is, when there is an awareness of a deficiency in one's social and personal relationships leading to reactions of sadness, emptiness, or longing. They present a differentiated view of loneliness and assert that it is a subjective and internal emotional state that is not directly influenced by peer relationships. For example, they note that it is possible to have many friends, be accepted by peers, and still feel lonely. Asher and Paquette present the nuances of how loneliness is conceptualized and measured and what it means for overall child functioning. One of their conclusions is that the only way to fully understand the dynamics and import of loneliness for development is to focus on children's subjective representations of their experiences.

Both positive and negative aspects of peer relationships have been studied in order to discern their role in development. On the negative side, much attention has been paid to the study of peer maltreatment, or physical victimization. Nicki Crick and her colleagues present a more comprehensive understanding of peer maltreatment by presenting an overview of relational victimization. In relational victimization harm is done through the manipulation of relationships rather than through physical aggression. They note that research in this area has just begun, but the implications of relational aggression for development are beginning to be understood. The typical form of relational aggression is when a child or adolescent attempts to harm the victim by threatening to withdraw affection unless the victim complies with what the aggressor wants him or her to do. Alternatively, the victim may be excluded from important social gatherings or activities, or may be the target of rumors and gossip that are designed so that peers will reject him or her. This type of aggression is more likely to be found in samples of girls, and thus, future research efforts should lead researchers to a deeper understanding of peer victimization and to a more enhanced view of the social development of girls.

Thomas Berndt presents the nuances of quality friendships and how they affect the social development of children. He defines a high-quality friendship as one with high levels of prosocial behavior and intimacy, and low levels of conflicts and rivalry. For some time, it has been assumed that friendship quality has a direct effect on many aspects of children's social development. Berndt reviews recent research that reveals that friendship quality primarily affects children's success in the world of peers, and notes that high quality friendships may enhance children's development regardless of the characteristics of those friends. He also presents evidence that friendship quality may have differential effects from childhood to adulthood, with high quality friendships influencing mental health and self-esteem for adults but not for children.

As we noted above, child development takes place in a system, with the family being a central setting for children. More recent attention has been paid to another setting, the neighborhood context. Tama Leventhal and Jeanne Brooks-Gunn give an overview of the research that has examined the impact of the neighborhood setting on child development. Overall, their review reveals that neighborhoods do influence child development, and stronger effects are found in experimental studies. Specifically, youth in higher SES neighborhoods show higher verbal and scholastic ability, controlling for family influences. Leventhal and Brooks-Gunn present theoretical models to explain the potential pathways of neighborhood influences.

While romantic relationships are a central part of the lives of adolescents, it has only been in the last decade that research efforts have been aimed at examining them. Wyndol Furman presents the developmental course of such relationships, and notes that while romantic relationships have the potential to affect development positively, they also place adolescents at risk for problems. While early work in this area was primarily descriptive, more recent efforts have been aimed at delineating the content and processes involved in such relationships, and how they change and impact development. Furman notes that research efforts need to integrate the fields of romantic relationships and sexual behavior in adolescence. In addition, the ways that adolescent relationships are linked to relationships with parents and peers, as well as the diversity of these relationships are discussed.

The articles in this section all relate to the social context of child development, more specifically, the impact of peers and neighborhood. To end this section, Reed Larson discusses another social context factor that has an influence on the developing child—how children and adolescents spend their time. The recent national concern about how children spend their time has prompted child developmentalists to evaluate children's activities and time spent in them, and what it does and does not tell us about their development. While a simple look at how children spend their time does not necessarily uncover the socialization experiences that children have within each activity, it does give us a starting point for the examination of such experiences. We know that there has been a remarkable increase in discretionary time for children and adolescents, and studies need to assess whether this is a developmental asset or liability. Taken together, these articles illuminate the import of the social context of development and of the experiences that children have while interacting with peers, in their neighborhoods, and while engaging in a diverse array of activities, from school to leisure.

Loneliness and Peer Relations in Childhood

Steven R. Asher[1] and Julie A. Paquette

Department of Psychology, Duke University, Durham, North Carolina

Abstract

Although loneliness is a normative experience, there is reason to be concerned about children who are chronically lonely in school. Research indicates that children have a fundamental understanding of what it means to be lonely, and that loneliness can be reliably measured in children. Most of the research on loneliness in children has focused on the contributions of children's peer relations to their feelings of well-being at school. Loneliness in children is influenced by how well accepted they are by peers, whether they are overtly victimized, whether they have friends, and the durability and quality of their best friendships. Findings from this emerging area of research provide a differentiated picture of how children's peer experiences come to influence their emotional well-being.

Keywords

loneliness; peer acceptance; friendship

The study of children's peer-relationship difficulties has become a major focus of contemporary developmental and child-clinical psychology (see Rubin, Bukowski, & Parker, 1998). As part of this focus, increasing attention is being given to the internal, subjective, and emotional sides of children's social lives. Human beings have fundamental needs for inclusion in group life and for close relationships (e.g., Baumeister & Leary, 1995), so it is fitting to examine what happens when social needs go unmet. It is clear that a variety of strong affective consequences can result. In this article, we focus on one such emotional reaction, loneliness, and we describe what has been learned about the association between loneliness and various indicators of the quality of children's social lives with peers.

PERSPECTIVES ON LONELINESS

Loneliness is typically defined by researchers as involving the cognitive awareness of a deficiency in one's social and personal relationships, and the ensuing affective reactions of sadness, emptiness, or longing. For example, Parkhurst and Hopmeyer (1999) described loneliness as "a sad or aching sense of isolation, that is, of being alone, cut-off, or distanced from others . . . associated with a felt deprivation of, or longing for, association, contact, or closeness" (p. 58). Likewise, many other authors emphasize the perceived deficiencies in the qualitative or quantitative aspects of social relationships and the accompanying emotional discomfort or distress that results.

The subjective experience of loneliness should not be viewed as interchangeable with more objective features of children's peer experiences, such as how well accepted they are by peers, whether they have friends, and what their friendships are like. So, for example, it is possible to have many friends and still feel lonely. Likewise, it is possible to be poorly accepted by the peer group or to lack friends and yet to not feel lonely. Loneliness is an internal emotional state that can be strongly influenced by features of one's social life, but it is not to be confused with any particular external condition.

It is also important to note that loneliness in itself is not pathological. Loneliness is actually quite normative in that most people feel lonely at some point during their lives. As social animals who participate extensively in social relationships, humans open themselves up to the possibility of loneliness. This can occur not only when people lack ongoing relationships with others, but even when they have meaningful relationships that take negative turns. For example, loneliness can be a response to separations, such as when a friend is unavailable to play or moves away. These situational or short-term experiences of loneliness are typically not causes for concern. Chronic loneliness, however, is associated with various indices of maladjustment in adolescents and adults, such as dropping out of school, depression, alcoholism, and medical problems. At least 10% of elementary school-aged children report feeling lonely either always or most of the time (Asher, Hymel, & Renshaw, 1984), which suggests a level of loneliness that places children at risk for poor outcomes.

Systematic research on children's loneliness partially grew out of an earlier line of research on the effects of teaching social-relationship skills to children who were highly rejected by their peers. The question that emerged was whether the children who were the focus of these intensive intervention efforts were themselves unhappy with their situation in school. The research was also inspired by very interesting work on adults' loneliness. The study of loneliness in childhood offers unique opportunities that are typically not available to researchers who explore loneliness in adulthood. Much of children's social lives takes place in a "closed" full-time environment, the school, so it is much easier to capture children's peer world. The presence of a child's "colleagues" makes it possible to learn about a child not just by studying that child, but also by querying his or her interactive partners or directly observing the social interactions the child has with peers. By contrast, adults' relationships take place over more contexts, making it harder to get access to most of their social network. Furthermore, it is usually easier to gain research access to schools than the adult workplace.

CAN LONELINESS BE MEANINGFULLY STUDIED WITH CHILDREN?

Some people might think that the concept of loneliness does not have much meaning to children or that they cannot give reliable information about their subjective well-being in this regard. Indeed, Harry Stack Sullivan (the famous American psychiatrist who wrote eloquently about the role of "chumship" in middle childhood) argued that children cannot experience true loneliness until early adolescence, when they develop a need for intimacy within the context of close friendships. However, research indicates that children as young as 5 or 6 years of age have at least a rudimentary understanding of the concept of loneliness

(Cassidy & Asher, 1992). Their understanding that loneliness involves having no one to play with and feeling sad corresponds fairly well to typical definitions of loneliness in the literature in that children grasp that loneliness involves a combination of solitude and depressed affect. We call this a rudimentary understanding because young children do not yet appreciate that one can be "lonely in a crowd" or even when with a significant other.

Children's basic understanding of loneliness is accompanied by the ability to respond in meaningful ways to formal assessments of loneliness. The most widely used measures have children respond to some items that assess their feelings of loneliness and other items that involve appraisals of whether they have friends, whether they are good at making friends and getting along with others, and whether their basic relationship needs are being met. Because most of these self-report measures for children contain diverse item content that goes beyond loneliness per se (as does the widely used UCLA Loneliness Scale for adults), caution must be used when interpreting results. Some investigators (e.g., Asher, Gorman, Gabriel, & Guerra, 2003; Ladd, Kochenderfer, & Coleman, 1997; Parker & Asher, 1993) have therefore calculated "pure loneliness" scores by using only items that directly assess feelings of loneliness (e.g., "I am lonely at school"; "I feel left out of things at school"; "I feel alone at school").

Researchers in the field have examined whether, within a particular measure, children respond in an internally consistent manner from one loneliness item to another (e.g., Asher et al., 1984). They have also examined whether there is stability in children's reports of loneliness from one time of assessment to another (e.g., Renshaw & Brown, 1993). Several studies indicate that children's reports of loneliness are highly reliable by both of these criteria. Accordingly, researchers have used these methodologically sound measures to examine whether acceptance by peers and friendships influence children's feelings of loneliness.

PEER ACCEPTANCE AND LONELINESS

The preponderance of research on children's loneliness has focused on the influence of acceptance versus rejection by peers. Peer acceptance in school is typically assessed using sociometric measures in which children either nominate schoolmates they like most and like least or use a rating scale to indicate how much they like each of their peers. Regardless of method, there is a consistent association between acceptance by peers and loneliness. Children who are poorly accepted report experiencing greater loneliness. This finding holds whether loneliness is measured in classroom, lunchroom, playground, or physical education contexts (Asher et al., 2003), suggesting that there is no safe haven at school for poorly accepted children. The finding that rejected children experience more loneliness than other children holds for age groups ranging from kindergartners to elementary-school children to middle schoolers. Furthermore, these associations have been found in research in many different countries and for both genders (with mean differences in loneliness between boys and girls rarely significant).

Although rejected children report the most loneliness, there is considerable within-group variability. Researchers have found that there are distinct subgroups of rejected children. Withdrawn-rejected children consistently report greater loneliness than aggressive-rejected children, although in the elementary-school years both groups report more loneliness than children with an average degree of acceptance by their peers. One factor that may account for variability in rejected children's feelings of loneliness is overt victimization. Not all highly disliked children are overtly victimized, but those who are victimized are more likely than others to report elevated loneliness (for relevant research, see Boivin & Hymel, 1997; Ladd et al., 1997).

FRIENDSHIP AND LONELINESS

Variability in loneliness among children rejected by their peers also arises from the partial independence of acceptance and friendship. One way researchers assess whether children have friends is by giving them a roster of the names of their classmates and asking them to circle the names of their friends. Researchers typically consider that a friendship exists when two children identify one another as friends. With this mutual-nomination criterion, half of the children who are poorly accepted by their peers prove to have friends, making it possible to learn whether friendship has a buffering effect on the influence of low peer acceptance.

In studies of the connection between friendship and loneliness, children without friends report experiencing more loneliness than children with friends (Parker & Asher, 1993; Renshaw & Brown, 1993). This beneficial effect of friendship occurs for children at all levels of peer acceptance and for both boys and girls. Even children with deviant friends (i.e., friends who participate in delinquent behavior) report less loneliness than friendless children (Brendgen, Vitaro, & Bukowski, 2000).

There is no evidence to date that the number of friends children have (beyond one friend!) relates to loneliness; however, it is important for children to have friendships that endure. In a camp-based study, Parker and Seal (1996) found that children's ability to maintain, as well as form, friendships was related to loneliness. Children who frequently made new friends but who did not maintain their friendships experienced higher levels of loneliness than other children.

The quality of children's friendships also plays an important role in children's feelings of loneliness. Features such as the degree of companionship, help and guidance, intimacy, conflict, and ease of conflict resolution can all be reliably measured among elementary-school children. Children who participate in high-quality friendships experience less loneliness than other children (Parker & Asher, 1993); this result is found even in analyses that statistically control for level of peer acceptance. Furthermore, the effects of friendship quality on loneliness are comparable for boys and girls. One indicator of friendship quality is whether friends engage in relational aggression toward one another. Crick and Nelson (2002) recently found that among both boys and girls, having friends who ignored them when angry or tried to influence them by threatening termination of the friendship was associated with increased loneliness.

There is a need for research on how the influence of specific qualities of friendship might differ for children of different ages. As discussed by Parkhurst and Hopmeyer (1999), the experience of loneliness at different ages might be influenced by cognitive-developmental changes, changes in the kinds of closeness or associations that are meaningful, and changes in the value that children place on certain kinds of relationships. Thus, what causes a 5- or 6-year-old child to feel lonely will likely be different from what causes an adolescent to feel lonely. For example, kindergartners might feel lonely if there is no one to play with, whereas older youth might feel lonely if they do not have someone with whom to discuss personal thoughts and feelings. These types of developmental predictions need direct tests.

FUTURE DIRECTIONS

Research to date consistently indicates that both acceptance by peers and friendship processes influence children's feelings of loneliness at school. However, acceptance and friendship variables, as typically measured, still leave much of the variance in loneliness unexplained. Partly this is because of the frequent reliance on single-shot assessments of key constructs. When repeated assessments of rejection or victimization are conducted, the associations with loneliness become stronger. Children who chronically experience negative peer relations are unquestionably at greater risk than children whose adverse circumstances are more short term (e.g., Kochenderfer-Ladd & Wardrop, 2001). Repeated assessments help to account for more of the variance in children's loneliness.

At the same time, psychologists will never fully understand the dynamics of loneliness if they look only at objective indicators of children's adjustment and ignore children's subjective representations of their experiences. Little is known about the role of beliefs and expectations in children's loneliness. For example, children who have idealized views that friends will always "be there for them," will never fail to keep a commitment, or will never hurt their feelings are likely to experience disappointments in their friendships even when other people with different beliefs and expectations might think those friendships are going well. Likewise, children who believe that conflict is a sign of impending dissolution of a friendship are likely to experience higher levels of loneliness than other children because some level of conflict is virtually inevitable in all close relationships. Examining children's beliefs and expectations may shed light on why some children who are highly accepted and have what seem to be high-quality friendships nevertheless are lonely.

Finally, there is a need for intervention research aimed at helping children who experience chronic loneliness. An earlier generation of intervention studies found that teaching children social-relationship skills had beneficial effects on children's peer acceptance (see Asher, Parker, & Walker, 1996, for a review). However, these studies generally predated the more recent research on loneliness in children and therefore did not assess whether the interventions had positive effects on loneliness. Intervention research not only would offer a potential aid to children, but also could be useful for testing specific hypotheses about the processes that lead particular kinds of children to become lonely. For example, intervention research is a way to learn whether increasing the social skills of poorly accepted children who lack friends leads to parallel increases in acceptance and friendship that in turn result in reductions in loneliness. Likewise, for children who are well accepted and have friends yet are lonely, interventions aimed at modifying their thoughts and beliefs about relationships can experimentally test hypothesized linkages between particular representations and loneliness.

Recommended Reading

Asher, S.R., Rose, A.J., & Gabriel, S.W. (2001). Peer rejection in everyday life. In M.R. Leary (Ed.), *Interpersonal rejection* (pp. 105–142). New York: Oxford University Press.

Ernst, J.M., & Cacioppo, J.T. (1999). Lonely hearts: Psychological perspectives on loneliness. *Applied & Preventive Psychology, 8,* 1–22.

Peplau, L.A., & Perlman, D. (Eds.). (1982). *Loneliness: A sourcebook of current theory, research, and therapy.* New York: Wiley.

Rotenberg, K.J., & Hymel, S. (Eds.). (1999). *Loneliness in childhood and adolescence.* New York: Cambridge University Press.

Note

1. Address correspondence to Steven R. Asher, Department of Psychology: Social and Health Sciences, Duke University, Box 90085, Durham, NC 27708-0085; e-mail: asher@duke.edu.

References

Asher, S.R., Gorman, A.H., Gabriel, S.W., & Guerra, V.S. (2003). *Children's loneliness in different school contexts.* Manuscript submitted for publication.

Asher, S.R., Hymel, S., & Renshaw, R.D. (1984). Loneliness in childhood. *Child Development, 55,* 1456–1464.

Asher, S.R., Parker, J.G., & Walker, D.L. (1996). Distinguishing friendship from acceptance: Implications for intervention and assessment. In W.M. Bukowski, A.F. Newcomb, & W.W. Hartup (Eds.), *The company they keep: Friendship during childhood and adolescence* (pp. 366–405). New York: Cambridge University Press.

Baumeister, R.F., & Leary, M.R. (1995). The need to belong: Desire for interpersonal attachments as a fundamental human motivation. *Psychological Bulletin, 117,* 497–529.

Boivin, M., & Hymel, S. (1997). Peer experiences and social self-perceptions: A sequential model. *Developmental Psychology, 33,* 135–145.

Brendgen, M., Vitaro, F., & Bukowski, W.M. (2000). Deviant friends and early adolescents' emotional and behavioral adjustment. *Journal of Research on Adolescence, 10,* 172–189.

Cassidy, J., & Asher, S.R. (1992). Loneliness and peer relations in young children. *Child Development, 63,* 350–365.

Crick N.R., & Nelson, D.A. (2002). Relational and physical victimization within friendships: Nobody told me there'd be friends like these. *Journal of Abnormal Child Psychology, 30,* 599–607.

Kochenderfer-Ladd, B.J., & Wardrop, J.L. (2001). Chronicity and instability of children's peer victimization experiences as predictors of loneliness and social satisfaction trajectories. *Child Development, 72,* 134–151.

Ladd, G.W., Kochenderfer, B.J., & Coleman, C.C. (1997). Classroom peer acceptance, friendship, and victimization: Distinct relational systems that contribute uniquely to children's school adjustment? *Child Development, 68,* 1181–1197.

Parker, J.G., & Asher, S.R. (1993). Friendship and friendship quality in middle childhood: Links with peer group acceptance and feelings of loneliness and social dissatisfaction. *Developmental Psychology, 29,* 611–621.

Parker, J.G., & Seal, J. (1996). Forming, losing, renewing, and replacing friendships: Applying temporal parameters to the assessment of children's friendship experiences. *Child Development, 67,* 2248–2268.

Parkhurst, J.T., & Hopmeyer, A. (1999). Developmental change in the source of loneliness in child-hood and adolescence: Constructing a theoretical model. In K.J. Rotenberg & S. Hymel (Eds.), *Loneliness in childhood and adolescence* (pp. 56–79). New York: Cambridge University Press.

Renshaw, P.D., & Brown, P.J. (1993). Loneliness in middle childhood: Concurrent and longitudi-nal predictors. *Child Development, 64,* 1271–1284.

Rubin, K.H., Bukowski, W., & Parker, J.G. (1998). Peer interactions, relationships, and groups. In W. Damon (Editor-in-Chief) & N. Eisenberg (Vol. Ed.), *Handbook of child psychology: Vol. 3. Social, emotional, and personality development* (pp. 619–700). New York: Wiley.

Critical Thinking Questions

1. If loneliness is not necessarily the result of an external condition, will social interventions be effective?

2. Why might it be easier to study loneliness in children than in adults?

3. Why might some children describe themselves as lonely, yet are well accepted and have friends?

Toward a More Comprehensive Understanding of Peer Maltreatment: Studies of Relational Victimization

Nicki R. Crick,[1] Juan F. Casas, and David A. Nelson

Institute of Child Development, University of Minnesota, Twin Cities Campus, Minneapolis, Minnesota (N.R.C.); Department of Psychology, University of Nebraska, Omaha, Nebraska (J.F.C.); and Department of Marriage, Family, and Human Development, Brigham Young University, Provo, Utah (D.A.N.)

Abstract

Although many past studies of peer maltreatment have focused on physical victimization, the importance of an empirical focus on relational victimization has only recently been recognized. In relational victimization, the perpetrator attempts to harm the target through the manipulation of relationships, threat of damage to them, or both. We review what is currently known about relational victimization with three issues in mind: (a) developmental changes in the manifestation of relational victimization, (b) gender differences in the likelihood of being victimized, and (c) evidence that relational victimization is harmful.

Keywords

victimization; gender; relational aggression

Although victimization by peers has long been considered a significant area of empirical inquiry in other countries (e.g., Olweus, 1978), in the United States it has only recently emerged as a "hot" research topic. In this country, increased interest has likely been fueled by several horrific episodes of peer violence that have attracted significant national media attention (e.g., the school shootings in Littleton, Colorado). These events have highlighted the importance of increasing understanding of peer victimization so that people can intervene before troubled interactions escalate to fatal proportions. Interestingly, even in the cases that ended in serious physical injuries and death to the victims, perpetrators (or persons close to them) often cited relational slights (e.g., being excluded from salient social groups, which is one kind of relational victimization) as significant motivating factors in their physically aggressive acts (e.g., Johnson & Brooke, 1999).

Although many past studies of peer maltreatment have focused on physical victimization (e.g., Olweus, 1978; Perry, Kusel, & Perry, 1988), the importance of an empirical focus on relational victimization has only recently been recognized (for a review, see Crick et al., 2001). Anecdotal evidence for the salience of this construct abounds, but this research area is still in its infancy.

WHAT IS RELATIONAL VICTIMIZATION?

In contrast to physical victimization, which involves being the frequent target of peers' physically aggressive acts, relational victimization involves being the frequent target of peers' relationally aggressive strategies. Relationally aggressive behaviors are those in which the perpetrator attempts to harm the victim through the manipulation of relationships, threat of damage to them, or both (Crick et al., 2001). Thus, for example, a relational victim may have friends who threaten to withdraw their affection unless he or she does what they want, may be excluded from important social gatherings or activities when a peer is angry with him or her, or may be the target of nasty rumors within the peer group that are designed to motivate peers to reject him or her.

Relationally aggressive acts deprive children of opportunities to satisfy their social needs for closeness, acceptance, and friendship in peer relationships, social psychological experiences that have been shown to be critical for children's development and well-being (for a review, see Baumeister & Leary, 1995). A certain degree of exposure to these behaviors is likely to be normative for most children (and adults), and is unlikely to be detrimental for most individuals. It is the children who are targeted at extreme levels that we are concerned about and whom we consider to be relationally victimized. In our studies, we have defined "extreme" as referring to greater exposure than what is average in a relevant, same-age peer group (e.g., in elementary-school classroom).

Studies of relational victimization are important not only because of the hypothesized salience of relational victimization for all children, but also because of their potential for increasing knowledge of the social development of girls (Crick & Grotpeter, 1996). This is because studies of physical victimization have shown the targets to be primarily boys, but relational victimization is more likely than physical victimization to involve girls as victims. We review what is currently known about relational victimization with three issues in mind: (a) developmental changes in the manifestation of relational victimization, (b) gender differences in the likelihood of being victimized, and (c) evidence that relational victimization is harmful. This discussion is organized with respect to three developmental periods: preschool, middle childhood, and adolescence.

DEVELOPMENTAL CHANGES IN THE MANIFESTATION OF RELATIONAL VICTIMIZATION

The manifestation of relational victimization changes with development, reflecting the social, cognitive, and emotional changes that occur with increasing maturity (Crick et al., 2001). Thus, for example, relational victimization among preschool children tends to involve direct, face-to-face behaviors, such as threatening to exclude someone from a birthday party (e.g., "You can't come to my birthday party unless you let me play in your group") or signaling ignoring by holding one's hands over one's ears (i.e., the preschool equivalent of the "silent treatment"). During middle childhood, relationally victimized children encounter more sophisticated manifestations of peer maltreatment, including both indirect and direct relationally aggressive acts. For example, a peer may spread rumors about them (an indirect act) or may refuse to choose them as team members during gym class as retaliation for a past grievance (a direct act).

These types of victimizing behaviors continue into adolescence (with increasing complexity and subtlety). In addition, the increased salience of opposite-sex friendships and romantic relationships during this developmental period provides new contexts for the expression of relational victimization. For example, a relationally victimized adolescent may find that a peer "gets even" with her for a past grievance by stealing her boyfriend. Or she may discover that her best friend has "shared" negative information about her with her boyfriend in an attempt to damage her romantic relationship. Further, her boyfriend himself may give her the silent treatment when he wants to control or manipulate her (e.g., "I won't talk to you until you do what I want"). Although cross-sectional studies show these developmental trends (Crick et al., 2001), it should be noted that no longitudinal studies of developmental changes in the manifestations of relational victimization have yet been conducted.

GENDER DIFFERENCES IN RELATIONAL VICTIMIZATION

The study of relational victimization was initiated to generate a more gender-balanced view of peer maltreatment, so it is not surprising that several studies have been conducted to evaluate whether there are indeed gender differences in relational victimization. Among preschool-age children, existing findings are mixed with regard to this issue, at least in the case of studies that have assessed victimization by using reports of teachers or peers. Specifically, results of one study showed that girls were more relationally victimized than boys (Crick, Casas, & Ku, 1999), whereas two other studies yielded no gender differences (Bonica, Yershova, & Arnold, 1999; Hart et al., 1999). In contrast, studies that have employed observational methods have shown that girls are significantly more relationally victimized than boys (e.g., Ostrov, Woods, Jansen, Casas, & Crick, 2002).

Research findings for middle childhood and adolescence are also conflicting. Studies in which children and adolescents have been asked to describe the aggressive interchanges that take place in their peer interactions indicate that relational aggression most commonly takes place in female-female interactions (e.g., Crick, Bigbee, & Howes, 1996; French, Jansen, & Pidada, in press). However, studies that have assessed victimization by asking children and adolescents or their teachers to answer more standardized questionnaires have yielded mixed findings, with some studies indicating that girls are more relationally victimized than boys and others showing no gender differences (Crick et al., 2001).

Given the paucity of research in this area, it is difficult to draw firm conclusions regarding gender differences in the frequency of relational victimization. However, the salience of relational victimization for increasing understanding of maltreated girls cannot be judged solely on the basis of gender differences in exposure. At least two additional issues must be considered. First, it is important to note that assessing relational victimization results in the identification of significantly more peer-victimized girls than does focusing on physical victimization only, as was done in the past (Crick & Bigbee, 1998). Second, given evidence that females are more likely than males to become distressed by negative interpersonal events (Leadbeater, Blatt, & Quinlan, 1995), the consequences of relational victimization may be more serious for girls than for boys. Thus, regardless of whether or not future research indicates the existence of gender differences in the frequency of relational victimization, the study of relational victimization is likely to have significant utility for enhancing knowledge of the social development of females.

RELATIONAL VICTIMIZATION AND SOCIAL PSYCHOLOGICAL HARM

Two approaches have been taken to establish a link between relational victimization and social psychological harm. In the first, children and adolescents have been asked to describe the types of aggressive harmful behaviors that they have observed in their peer groups (e.g., Crick et al., 1996; French et al., in press). These studies have shown that relationally aggressive acts are among the most commonly cited mean behaviors, a finding that provides evidence of the hurtful nature of relational victimization.

The second approach to assessing the potentially damaging consequences of relational victimization has focused on evaluation of the association between this type of peer maltreatment and indices of social psychological adjustment. These studies have demonstrated that, during the preschool, middle-childhood, and adolescent years, relational victimization within the general peer group is associated with significant concurrent adjustment problems, such as poor peer relationships, internalizing problems (e.g., depressive symptoms), and externalizing difficulties (e.g., delinquent behavior; for a review, see Crick et al., 2001). Recent research has also demonstrated that relational victimization predicts future difficulties such as peer rejection (Crick et al., 2001).

CONCLUSIONS AND FUTURE DIRECTIONS

Given the potentially harmful nature of relational victimization, it will be important to identify factors that predict individual differences in children's risk for exposure to this type of maltreatment and in their propensity for developing other problems related to these experiences (e.g., depressive symptoms). For example, it may be that children who have been exposed to particular kinds of aversive family environments (e.g., parental rejection or neglect, relational victimization by siblings) are more sensitive than other children to relational victimization by peers or are more likely to be viewed within the peer group as easy targets (e.g., peers may sense that these children are more vulnerable than others to social exclusion). For these children, even relatively low levels of relational victimization may be distressing and likely to result in other adjustment difficulties, as well as additional victimization in the future. In contrast, some children may be relatively resilient when confronted with relational victimization, perhaps because of supportive family environments, and may not react negatively to these experiences. This, in turn, may make them less likely to encounter relational victimization in the future (e.g., because they do not react in ways that are rewarding to the perpetrators). These and other factors warrant attention so that researchers can build theoretical models of the processes involved in relational victimization.

A number of future research directions are suggested by existing research and theory. One of the most urgent needs is for longitudinal studies. It is clear from existing studies that relational victimization is associated with concurrent difficulties in adjustment, as well as with difficulties in the short-term future; however, long-term prospective investigations are necessary to establish that relational victimization results in lasting harm. This type of research is also needed to discover whether, as we suggested in the introduction, relational victimization sometimes plays a rote in physical violence directed toward peers. Studies of the factors that contribute to relational victimization (e.g., family factors, contextual factors, individual characteristics) are also sorely needed so that empirically based intervention programs can be developed for children who experience this type of peer abuse.

Studies utilizing observational approaches for assessing relational victimization are also needed, along with studies that directly compare the utility and validity of various measures of relational victimization. In addition, it would be useful for future research to evaluate chronicity and severity of relational victimization and their relative contributions to social psychological difficulties. Another important avenue for future work involves generating and applying theory to guide exploration of the impact of relational victimization on children's development. For example, this aversive peer treatment may influence children's interpretations of future peer interactions in negative ways (e.g., they may begin to interpret peers' behavior as intentionally hostile, even when it is not). Social information processing models may be useful for understanding this phenomenon.

Finally, another issue that warrants attention in future research concerns the role of the relationship context in which victimization occurs. Most previous investigations of relational victimization have evaluated maltreatment in a large, peer-group context (e.g., a classroom). However, given recent evidence that relational peer abuse can also occur in smaller groups or dyads, such as between best friends or in a romantic relationship (for a review, see Crick et al., 2001), future research that considers and systematically compares these various contexts is needed. This may be particularly important for females because relational victimization within the dyadic context has been shown to be particularly problematic for girls (Crick & Nelson, in press).

Recommended Reading

Crick, N.R., & Bigbee, M.A. (1998). (See References)
Crick, N.R., Casas, J.F., & Ku, H. (1999). (See References)
Crick, N.R., & Grotpeter, J.K. (1996). (See References)
Crick, N.R., Nelson, D.A., Morales, J.R., Cullerton-Sen, C., Casas, J.F., & Hickman, S. (2001). (See References)
Juvonen, J., & Graham, S. (Eds.). (2001). *School-based peer harassment: The plight of the vulnerable and victimized.* New York: Guilford Press.

Acknowledgments—Preparation of this essay was supported by a FIRST Award from the National institute of Mental Health (MH53524) and a Faculty Scholars Award from the William T. Grant Foundation to the first author and by a Child Psychology Training Grant Fellowship from the National institute of Mental Health (T32MH15755) to the third author.

Note

1. Address correspondence to Nicki R. Crick, Institute of Child Development, University of Minnesota, 51 East River Rd., Minneapolis, MN 55455; e-mail: crick001@umn.edu.

References

Baumeister, R.F., & Leary, M.R. (1995). The need to belong: Desire for interpersonal attachments as a fundamental human motivation. *Psychological Bulletin, 117,* 497–529.

Bonica, C., Yershova, K., & Arnold, D. (1999, April). *Relational aggression, relational victimization, and language development in preschool.* Poster presented at the biennial meeting of the Society for Research in Child Development, Albuquerque, NM.

Crick, N.R., & Bigbee, M.A. (1998). Relational and overt forms of peer victimization: A multiinformant approach. *Journal of Consulting and Clinical Psychology, 66,* 337–347.

Crick, N.R., Bigbee, M.A., & Howes, C. (1996). Gender differences in children's normative beliefs about aggression: How do I hurt thee? Let me count the ways. *Child Development, 67,* 1003–1014.

Crick, N.R., Casas, J.F., & Ku, H. (1999). Physical and relational peer victimization in preschool. *Developmental Psychology, 35,* 376–385.

Crick, N.R., & Grotpeter, J.K. (1996). Children's treatment by peers: Victims of relational and overt aggression. *Development and Psychopathology, 8,* 367–380.

Crick, N.R., & Nelson, D.A. (in press). Relational and physical victimization within friendships: Nobody told me there'd be friends like this. *Journal of Abnormal Child Psychology.*

Crick, N.R., Nelson, D.A., Morales, J.R., Cullerton-Sen, C., Casas, J.F., & Hickman, S. (2001). Relational victimization in childhood and adolescence: I hurt you through the grapevine. In J. Juvonen & S. Graham (Eds.), *School-based peer harassment: The plight of the vulnerable and victimized* (pp. 196–214). New York: Guilford Press.

French, D.C., Jansen, E.A., & Pidada, S. (in press). U.S. and Indonesian children's and adolescents' reports of relational aggression by disliked peers. *Child Development.*

Hart, C.H., Nelson, D.A., Robinson, C.C., Olsen, S.F., McNeilly-Choque, M.K., Porter, C.L., & McKee, T. (1999). Russian parenting styles and family processes: Linkages with subtypes of victimization and aggression. In K.A. Kerns (Ed.), *Explaining associations between family and peer relationships* (pp. 47–84). New York: Greenwood/Praeger.

Johnson, D., & Brooke, J. (1999, April 22). Terror in Littleton: The suspects; portrait of outcases seeking to stand out. *The New York Times,* p. A1.

Leadbeater, B.J., Blatt, S.J., & Quinlan, D.M. (1995). Gender-linked vulnerabilities to depressive symptoms, stress, and problem behaviors in adolescents. *Journal of Research in Adolescence, 5,* 1–29.

Olweus, D. (1978). *Aggression in the schools: Bullies and whipping boys.* Washington, DC: Hemisphere.

Ostrov, J., Woods, K., Jansen, E., Casas, J.F., & Crick, N.R. (2002). *An observational study of aggression, victimization, and social-psychological adjustment: "This white crayon doesn't work."* Manuscript submitted for publication.

Perry, D.G., Kusel, S.J., & Perry, L.C. (1988). Victims of peer aggression. Developmental Psychology, 24, 807–814.

Critical Thinking Questions

1. Why might an empirical focus on relational victimization be important to a comprehensive understanding of peer maltreatment?

2. Given that the manifestation of relational victimization changes with development, what will be the challenges in designing a longitudinal study?

3. What factors are likely to mitigate the effect of relational victimization on children?

Friendship Quality and Social Development

Thomas J. Berndt[1]

Department of Psychological Sciences, Purdue University,
West Lafayette, Indiana

Abstract

A high-quality friendship is characterized by high levels of prosocial behavior, intimacy, and other positive features, and low levels of conflicts, rivalry, and other negative features. Friendship quality has been assumed to have direct effects on many aspects of children's social development, including their self-esteem and social adjustment. Recent research suggests, however, that friendship quality affects primarily children's success in the social world of peers. Friendship quality could also have indirect effects, by magnifying or diminishing the influence of friends on each other's attitudes and behaviors. Having high-quality friendships may lessen children's tendencies to imitate the behavior of shy and withdrawn friends, but little evidence supports the hypothesis that high-quality friendships magnify friends' influence.

Keywords

friendship; social development; peer influence; self-esteem

Do good friendships enhance children's social development? What if those good friendships are with bad friends, friends who often misbehave in school or show other signs of poor social or psychological adjustment? Do good friendships with friends like those have a positive or a negative influence on children?

Similar questions about the effects of friends and friendships have been discussed in theoretical writings for decades. Only in recent years, however, have answers to the questions begun to emerge from empirical research. The recent advances have resulted in part from researchers' success in defining, conceptually and operationally, what a good friendship is. In much of the literature, good friendships are now defined as friendships high in quality (e.g., Berndt, 1996).

High-quality friendships may enhance children's development regardless of the characteristics of those friends. Research on this hypothesis can be described as examining the direct effects of friendship quality. But another possibility is that friendship quality most often has indirect effects on children, effects that depend on the friends' characteristics. For example, when friendships are high in quality, the influence of the friends' characteristics may be magnified. I review evidence for both types of effects in this article, but it is necessary to begin by defining the construct of friendship quality more precisely.

A DEFINITION OF FRIENDSHIP QUALITY

The old proverb says, "A friend in need is a friend indeed." That is, friends help and share with each other. Children agree with adults that these types of prosocial behavior are expected among friends. Children also agree with adults that good friends praise each other's successes and encourage each other after failures, thereby bolstering each other's self-esteem.

Some features of high-quality friendships are recognized by adolescents but not by young children. Adolescents often say that best friends tell each other everything, or disclose their most personal thoughts and feelings. These personal self-disclosures are the hallmark of an intimate friendship. Adolescents also say that friends will stick up for one another in a fight, demonstrating their loyalty.

A few researchers have described various positive features of good friendships, including prosocial behavior, self-esteem support, intimacy, loyalty, plus others, and investigated the associations between these features by asking questions assessing them. For example, to assess intimacy, researchers have asked children how often they tell a particular friend things about themselves that they would not tell most other people (Berndt & Keefe, 1995). Such research has found that children who say that their friendship has a high level of one positive feature, such as intimacy, typically say that their friendship is high in all other positive features. These results suggest that all positive features are linked to a single dimension of friendship quality.

Even best friendships can have negative features. Most children admit that best friends sometimes have conflicts with each other. In addition, children typically think of themselves as equal to their friends, but equality can be more an ideal than a reality. Children sometimes say that their friends try to boss them around, or dominate them. Children say that their friends "try to prove they're better than me," or engage in rivalry. When asked about actual friendships, children usually report the co-occurrence of conflicts, dominance attempts, and rivalry. Thus, all negative features seem to be linked to a single dimension of friendship quality. Scores on this negative dimension are only weakly correlated with those on the positive dimension (Berndt, 1996), so both dimensions must be considered when defining the quality of a friendship.

DIRECT EFFECTS OF FRIENDSHIP QUALITY

Most writers on friendship have assumed that high-quality friendships have positive effects on children: fostering their self-esteem, improving their social adjustment, and increasing their ability to cope with stressors (see Hartup & Stevens, 1999). Moreover, the correlations of friendship quality with indicators of social adjustment are consistent with that assumption. For example, among early adolescents, having friendships with more positive features correlates with greater involvement in school, higher self-perceived social acceptance, and higher general self-esteem (Berndt & Keefe, 1995; Keefe & Berndt, 1996).

Still, a significant correlation between two variables is only weak evidence that one affects the other. To test hypotheses about the effects of friendship quality more conclusively, researchers have assessed children's friendships and their adjustment on two or more occasions months or years apart (e.g., Ladd, Kochenderfer, & Coleman, 1996). Then the researchers have examined whether the quality of children's friendships on the first occasion predicted the changes over time in their adjustment. If so, the researchers tentatively have concluded that friendship quality affected the changes in children's adjustment.

In one study of this type (Ladd et al., 1996), kindergarten children who had high-quality friendships in January of the school year improved by the following May in their liking for school and in their perceptions of their classmates' support. In another study (Berndt, Hawkins, & Jiao, 1999), classmates rated students' sociability and leadership in sixth grade and again in seventh grade. Students whose sixth-grade friendships were high in positive features improved between sixth and seventh grade in peer-rated sociability and leadership, but only if their sixth-grade friendships were stable over time. These findings are consistent with hypotheses about the direct effects of high-quality friendships, but other data are not. In one study (Berndt et al., 1999), my colleagues and I found that friendship quality did not significantly affect the changes over time in students' general self-esteem. In three earlier longitudinal studies (see Keefe & Berndt, 1996), friendship quality also was not significantly related to changes in general self-esteem. These data cast doubt on the hypothesis that good friendships enhance children's self-esteem. Stated more strongly, the repeated failures to confirm the hypothesis that high-quality friendships increase children's self-esteem suggest a need for less sweeping and more specific hypotheses about the benefits of good friendships.

One possibility is that friendships high in positive features affect primarily children's success in the social world of peers. Thus, good friendships can improve children's views of their classmates and improve their classmates' views of them. A speculative explanation for these effects can also be offered. Having a few good friendships may help children make positive contacts with several other classmates. Those positive contacts may then lead to positive relationships that are not as close best friendships but that affect the children's attitudes toward their classmates and vice versa.

The effects of negative friendship features have also been examined. In one study (Ladd et al., 1996), kindergarten boys who had many conflicts with friends in the middle of a school year exhibited a decrease by the end of the year in liking for school and engagement in classroom activities, but an increase in loneliness. In another study (Berndt & Keefe, 1995), seventh graders whose friendships were high in negative features in the fall of a year reported increased disruptive behavior at school the following spring. Moreover, those students whose friendships were also high in positive features reported the greatest increase in disruptive behavior.

One possible explanation of these findings focuses on the likely effects of negative interactions between friends. Friends who frequently get into conflicts with each other, or who often try to dominate or assert their superiority over one another, are practicing a repertoire of negative social behaviors that may generalize to interactions with other peers and adults. Moreover, the closer a friendship is, the more the friends interact and the more frequently they practice their negative social repertoire. Naturally, the students' negative behaviors provoke negative reactions from classmates and teachers. Those negative reactions encourage the students to disengage from classmates and classroom activities, to feel more lonely, and to like school less.

These explanations are only possibilities because the recent longitudinal studies do not provide evidence on the processes responsible for the effects of friendship quality. Examining these processes must be a major goal of future research (Hartup, 1999). Information about processes would be especially valuable as researchers seek to replace theories about the general effects of friendship quality with theories that explain the effects of each dimension of friendship quality on specific aspects of social development.

INDIRECT EFFECTS OF FRIENDSHIP QUALITY

For decades, researchers from a variety of disciplines have tested the hypothesis that children and adolescents are influenced by the attitudes and behaviors of their peers. Not all studies have provided support for the hypothesis, but the available data convincingly show that close friends influence many facets of children's and adolescents' social behavior and adjustment (Collins & Laursen, 1999). In most studies, researchers have not assessed the quality of the friendships among the peers who were influencing one another. But when the issue has been raised, researchers have often suggested that the magnitude of friends' influence should be affected by the quality of their friendships. In this way, friendship quality can have an indirect effect on children's social development—affecting how much children are influenced by their friends' characteristics.

For example, according to the differential-association theory of delinquent behavior, adolescents who spend time with delinquent friends are expected to commit delinquent acts themselves (see Agnew, 1991). Moreover, delinquent friends are assumed to have more influence the more positive the relationships with those friends are. That is, having high-quality friendships with delinquent friends is assumed to increase the influence of those friends, thereby increasing the degree to which adolescents become like their friends over time.

Many other theories include the hypothesis that friends' influence is magnified when friendships are higher in quality (see Berndt, 1999). For example, social learning theory suggests that observational learning from friends is enhanced when friends have more positive relationships. Other theories suggest that friends' influence should be greater the more friends trust each other, and trust is another facet of the positive dimension of friendship quality.

Given the plausibility of the hypothesis about the magnifying effect of friendship quality, the scarcity of evidence for it is surprising. Some evidence consistent with the hypothesis was obtained in one longitudinal study of adolescents' delinquent behavior (Agnew, 1991). Among all the adolescents whose friends engaged in serious delinquent acts, only those who were closely attached to those friends became more seriously delinquent themselves. However, the comparable effect of attachment to friends who engaged in minor delinquency was nonsignificant. Other studies have yielded equally equivocal support for the hypothesis (Berndt et al., 1999), or no support at all (Berndt & Keefe, 1995; Poulin, Dishion, & Haas, 1999). In short, the general hypothesis that high friendship quality magnifies friends' influence must currently be viewed as doubtful.

Under certain conditions, having high-quality friendships may lessen rather than magnify friends' influence on each other. Consider, in particular, children who have good friendships with peers who are shy and withdrawn. Would those friendships increase the children's tendencies to imitate their friends' shy and withdrawn behavior? Alternatively, would those friendships enhance children's confidence in social situations and make them less prone to social withdrawal?

These questions were addressed in a longitudinal study of early adolescents whose shyness and social withdrawal were judged by their classmates (Berndt et al., 1999). Adolescents whose friends showed above-average shyness and withdrawal became more shy and withdrawn themselves over time only if those friendships were average or low in quality. Having shy and withdrawn friends did not influence changes in students' shyness and withdrawal when those friendships were high in quality. Apparently, the support that the students received from their friends offset any tendencies to imitate the friends' patterns of social behavior.

The hypothesis that variations in friendship quality affect the magnitude of friends' influence on each other can be evaluated only in studies that include measures of friends' characteristics and of friendship quality. Unfortunately, researchers interested in exploring the benefits of friendships have seldom examined what those friends are like, and researchers interested in exploring friends' influence have seldom examined the types of relationships those friends have. Consequently, the evidence necessary for answering questions about indirect effects is very limited. This gap in the literature creates serious problems, because researchers may misjudge either the effects of friendship quality or the influence of friends by not exploring how friends' influence is moderated by friendship quality.

Understanding of indirect effects would increase if researchers more often probed the processes responsible for those effects (Hartup, 1999). Typically, researchers use interviews or questionnaires to assess friendship quality and the characteristics of children and their friends, without ever seeing how the friends behave toward each other. But a few researchers have shown that rich and compelling data can be obtained by observing the social interactions between friends (e.g., Dishion, Andrews, & Crosby, 1995). These observations can reveal both the features of children's friendships and the relations of those features to the friends' influence on each other. Such observational studies can be a valuable complement to interview-questionnaire studies. When used in combination, the two research strategies should greatly expand knowledge about the indirect effects of friendship quality and the processes responsible for those effects.

CONCLUSIONS

Children prize friendships that are high in prosocial behavior, intimacy, and other positive features. Children are troubled by friendships that are high in conflicts, dominance, rivalry, and other negative features. Friendships are high in quality when they have high levels of positive features and low levels of negative features.

High-quality friendships have often been assumed to have positive effects on many aspects of children's social development. However, the direct effects of friendship quality appear to be quite specific. Having friendships high in negative features increases disagreeable and disruptive behaviors, probably because the interactional style that children practice with friends generalizes to interactions with other peers and adults. Having friendships high in positive features enhances children's success in the social world of peers, but it apparently does not affect children's general self-esteem. These findings are surprising because numerous studies with adults suggest that friendships and other supportive relationships enhance many aspects of adults' physical and mental health, including their self-esteem (e.g., Uchino, Uno, & Holt-Lunstad, 1999). If future research confirms that friendship quality has only narrow and specific effects in childhood but has broad and general effects in adulthood, the reasons for this difference should be thoroughly explored.

High-quality friendships may also have indirect effects on children's social development. Most theories of social influence include some form of the hypothesis that children are more strongly influenced by their friends' characteristics the higher the quality of those friendships. An alarming corollary of this hypothesis is that good friendships with bad friends (e.g., friends with poor social or psychological adjustment) should have especially negative effects on children's behavior and development. However, recent research provides equivocal support for this hypothesis. Often, the influence of friends' characteristics has varied little with the quality of these friendships.

More extensive tests of this hypothesis are necessary, for both theoretical and practical reasons. If the hypothesis is not supported in future research, most theories of social influence in childhood will need to be reevaluated. By contrast, if future studies do support the hypothesis, interventions to improve children's friendships will need to be carefully designed to ensure that they do not inadvertently magnify the negative influence of poorly adjusted friends. More generally, a fuller understanding of the joint effects of friendship quality and friends' characteristics will be crucial for enhancing the positive contributions of friendships to children's social development.

Recommended Reading

Bukowski, W.M., Newcomb, A.F., & Hartup, W.W. (Eds.). (1996). *The company they keep: Friendship in childhood and adolescence.* Cambridge, England: Cambridge University Press.
Collins, W.A., & Laursen, B. (Eds.). (1999). (See References)
Hartup, W.W. (1996). The company they keep: Friendships and their developmental significance. *Child Development, 67,* 1–13.

Note

1. Address correspondence to Thomas J. Berndt, Department of Psychological Sciences, Purdue University, W. Lafayette, IN 47907.

References

Agnew, R. (1991). The interactive effects of peer variables on delinquency. *Criminology, 29,* 47–72.
Berndt, T.J. (1996). Exploring the effects of friendship quality on social development. In W.M. Bukowski, A.F. Newcomb, & W.W. Hartup (Eds.), *The company they keep: Friendship in childhood and adolescence* (pp. 346–365). Cambridge, England: Cambridge University Press.
Berndt, T.J. (1999). Friends' influence on students' adjustment to school. *Educational Psychologist, 34,* 15–28.
Berndt, T.J., Hawkins, J.A., & Jiao, Z. (1999). Influences of friends and friendships on adjustment to junior high school. *Merrill-Palmer Quarterly, 45,* 13–41.
Berndt, T.J., & Keefe, K. (1995). Friends' influence on adolescents' adjustment to school. *Child Development, 66,* 1312–1329.

Collins, W.A., & Laursen, B. (Eds.). (1999). *Relationships as developmental contexts.* Mahwah, NJ: Erlbaum.

Dishion, T.J., Andrews, D.W., & Crosby, L. (1995). Antisocial boys and their friends in early adolescence: Relationship characteristics, quality, and interactional process. *Child Development, 66,* 139–151.

Hartup, W.W. (1999). Constraints on peer socialization: Let me count the ways. *Merrill-Palmer Quarterly, 45,* 172–183.

Hartup, W.W., & Stevens, N. (1999). Friendships and adaption across the life span. *Current Directions in Psychological Science, 8,* 76–79.

Keefe, K., & Berndt, T.J. (1996). Relations of friendship quality to self-esteem in early adolescence. *Journal of Early Adolescence, 16,* 110–129.

Ladd, G.W., Kochenderfer, B.J., & Coleman, C.C. (1996). Friendship quality as a predictor of young children's early school adjustment. *Child Development, 67,* 1103–1118.

Poulin, F., Dishion, T.J., & Haas, E. (1999). The peer influence paradox: Friendship quality and deviancy training within male adolescent friendships. *Merrill-Palmer Quarterly, 45,* 42–61.

Uchino, B.N., Uno, D., & Holt-Lunstad, J. (1999). Social support, physiological processes, and health. *Current Directions in Psychological Science, 8,* 145–148.

Critical Thinking Questions

1. How does the quality of a friendship differentially affect behavior when the characteristics of the individuals are either positively or negatively perceived?

2. What distinctions between the direct and indirects of friendship does the author make?

3. How might the instruments used (i.e., self-report questionnaire, teacher report, and observation) affect the results and, in turn, our understanding of childhood friendships?

Children and Youth in Neighborhood Contexts

Tama Leventhal[1] and Jeanne Brooks-Gunn

National Center for Children and Families, Teachers College, Columbia University, New York, New York

Abstract

Neighborhoods are increasingly studied as a context where children and youth develop; however, the extent of neighborhoods' impact remains debatable because it is difficult to disentangle this impact from that of the family context, in part because families have some choice as to where they live. Evidence from randomized experiments, studies using advanced statistical models, and longitudinal studies that control for family characteristics indicates that neighborhoods do matter. In nonexperimental studies, small to moderate associations were found, suggesting that children and adolescents living in high-income neighborhoods had higher cognitive ability and school achievement than those living in middle-income neighborhoods, and children and adolescents living in low-income neighborhoods had more mental and physical health problems than those living in middle-income neighborhoods. The home environment has been shown to be partly responsible for the link between neighborhood and children's development. For adolescents, neighborhood effects are partially accounted for by community social control. Experimental studies in which families were randomly assigned to move to low-poverty neighborhoods from housing projects found larger neighborhood effects than nonexperimental research, particularly for boys' outcomes. Additional issues reviewed are relevant neighborhood characteristics, theoretical models explaining the pathways underlying neighborhood effects, methods for research assessing neighborhood processes, and policy implications.

Keywords

neighborhood; community; achievement; health; income/socioeconomic status; policy

Historical trends document the declining economic conditions in which children grow up. Compared with their predecessors, children today are more likely to be raised in poor families (i.e., those whose incomes fall below a federally established threshold), as well as to live in poor neighborhoods (i.e., 20% or more of residents poor). Almost half of poor families reside in urban neighborhoods that are increasingly marked by concentrated poverty. Both family and neighborhood poverty are rooted in demographic shifts in family composition and labor-force participation, changes in migration and residential patterns, declines in industrialization, and housing segregation (Massey & Denton, 1993; Wilson, 1987). Responding to these trends, both academic scholars and policymakers developed a rising interest in the contexts in which children are reared, including larger social environments beyond the family, notably neighborhoods. By the mid-1980s, questions such as the following were raised: Does neighborhood residence influence children's well-being? How do neighborhoods affect children and youth? What can be done to alleviate neighborhood disadvantage and its potentially harmful effects on children's development? In response to these questions, scholars from various disciplines—economics, epidemiology, demography, sociology, and psychology—launched a field of study that has become known as neighborhood research (Brooks-Gunn, Duncan, & Aber, 1997).

NONEXPERIMENTAL STUDIES OF NEIGHBORHOOD EFFECTS ON DEVELOPMENT

Most neighborhood research has used census-based measures of neighborhood structural or sociodemographic characteristics in conjunction with data collected on children and families, often from large national data sets (e.g., Panel Study of Income Dynamics, National Longitudinal Survey of Youth-Child Supplement), to examine associations among neighborhood residence and child and adolescent outcomes. Data from the U.S. Census come from the forms the population fills out on April 1 of the 1st year of every decade. Thus, census information is limited to structural characteristics, such as median household income, percentage of residents with a high school diploma, racial composition, and percentage of homeowners. The census tract is the most frequently used definition of "neighborhood" in these studies. Tract boundaries are identified by local communities working under Census Bureau guidelines and reflect salient physical and social features that demarcate neighborhoods, such as major streets, railroads, and ethnic divisions; census tracts contain approximately 3,000 to 8,000 individuals.

Neighborhood income or socioeconomic status (SES)—a combination of social and economic indicators—is the most commonly investigated neighborhood characteristic. In these studies, researchers often use two separate measures of SES, because the presence of poor and affluent neighbors may have differential associations with child and adolescent outcomes (Jencks & Mayer, 1990). High-SES/affluence measures may take into consideration indicators such as income, percentage professionals, and percentage of residents who are college educated; low-SES/poverty measures may take into consideration indicators such as percentage poor, percentage of households headed by females, percentage on public assistance, and percentage unemployed. Other structural characteristics frequently examined include racial-ethnic mix (e.g., percentage Black, percentage Latino, and percentage foreign-born) and residential instability (e.g., percentage moved in last 5 years, percentage of households in their current home less than 10 years, and percentage renters).

Studies investigating neighborhood effects on children's development also account for family characteristics, such as income, composition, and parents' education, age, and race or ethnicity, to demonstrate whether neighborhood effects go "above and beyond" family influences. Because families have some choice as to where they live, adjusting for these background factors also minimizes the possibility that unmeasured individual and family characteristics associated with neighborhood residence (i.e., selection bias) might account for observed neighborhood effects. Some researchers also have addressed selection problems by using various advanced analytic strategies, such as comparisons of siblings or first cousins, which hold family characteristics constant; instrumental variable analyses, which minimize unmeasured correlations between neighborhood characteristics and child outcomes; and behavior genetics models, which differentiate between genetic and environmental influences.

We recently conducted a large-scale review of the neighborhood research (Leventhal & Brooks-Gunn, 2000). Findings reported in that review as well as subsequent work revealed consistent patterns of neighborhood effects on children's and adolescents' development, comparable findings have been documented in U.S. and Canadian samples and in cross-sectional and longitudinal studies that control for family characteristics. Across these studies, neighborhood effects were small to moderate in size. For preschool and school-age children, the presence of affluent or high-income neighbors was positively associated with children's verbal ability, IQ scores, and school achievement. In contrast, the presence of low-income or low-SES neighbors was associated with children's mental health problems. For adolescents, living in a high-income neighborhood was also associated with high school achievement and educational attainment, particularly for males. Residence in low-income neighborhoods was associated with adverse mental health, criminal and delinquent behavior, and unfavorable sexual and fertility outcomes for adolescents. For both children and adolescents, these patterns of results also have been found in studies employing advanced statistical techniques, although effect sizes are typically reduced.

EXPERIMENTAL STUDIES OF NEIGHBORHOOD EFFECTS ON DEVELOPMENT

Although nonexperimental neighborhood research has yielded fairly consistent patterns of findings, it has been criticized on the grounds that families have some choice as to the neighborhoods in which they live, resulting in selection bias (even after accounting for family characteristics). Experimental and quasi-experimental studies that randomly assign families to live in certain types of neighborhoods overcome the selection problem in nonexperimental research. Although such designs may seem implausible, they have been possible in the context of housing programs that randomly select families for assistance in relocating from public housing to less poor neighborhoods (e.g., they may receive vouchers to rent housing in the private market or be offered public housing built in nonpoor neighborhoods).

The oldest and most well known quasi-experimental study is the Gautreaux Program, enacted following a court order to desegregate Chicago's public housing. Families were given vouchers to move, and assignment of families to neighborhoods was random, based on housing availability (see Rubinowitz & Rosenbaum, 2000, for a review). A 10-year follow-up found that youth who moved to more affluent suburban neighborhoods fared better academically than youth who moved to poor urban neighborhoods.

In 1994, partially in response to positive findings reported in the Gautreaux Program, the U.S. Department of Housing and Urban Development initiated the Moving to Opportunity Program in five cities across the country. Approximately 4,600 families were randomly assigned vouchers to move out of public housing in high-poverty neighborhoods into private housing of their choice or into private housing in low-poverty neighborhoods (with special assistance); a subset of families remained in public housing. Although initial evaluations were conducted independently in each city, there is some overlap in the outcomes examined in

123

different cities, so that it is possible to draw some preliminary conclusions from this research (Goering, in press). Findings from these experimental studies revealed that several years into the program, children and youth who moved to less poor neighborhoods had higher educational achievement and superior physical and mental health compared with their peers who remained in high-poverty neighborhoods (Katz, Kling, & Liebman, 2001; Leventhal & Brooks-Gunn, 2002, in press). In addition, arrests for violent crime were lower among male youth who moved to less poor neighborhoods than among peers who stayed in high-poverty neighborhoods (Ludwig, Duncan, & Hirschfield, 2001). Neighborhood effects in these experimental studies were large. In addition, larger effects were generally seen for children and youth who moved to low-poverty neighborhoods than for those who moved to moderately poor neighborhoods, and effects were more pronounced for boys than girls.

THEORETICAL MODELS OF NEIGHBORHOOD EFFECTS

The experimental and nonexperimental studies we have reviewed illuminated specific neighborhood characteristics that were associated with particular outcomes. These studies, however, do not address the mechanisms through which neighborhood effects occur. We have proposed several theoretical models to explain potential pathways of neighborhood influences (Leventhal & Brooks-Gunn, 2000). These models highlight different underlying processes operating at various levels (individual, family, school, peer, and community). This work draws heavily from a review and analysis by Jencks and Mayer (1990); from research on family stress, economic hardship, and unemployment; and from literature on community social organization and urban sociology.

The first model, *institutional resources*, posits that neighborhood influences operate by means of the quality, quantity, and diversity of learning, recreational, social, educational, health, and employment resources in the community. The second model, *relationships and ties*, highlights families as a potential mechanism of neighborhood effects. Important variables in this model include parental attributes (e.g., mental and physical health, coping skills, and efficacy), social networks, and behavior (e.g., supervision-monitoring, warmth, and harshness), as well as characteristics of the home environment (e.g., learning and physical environments, family routines, and violence). The last model, *norms and collective efficacy*, hypothesizes that neighborhood influences are accounted for by the extent of formal and informal social institutions in the community and the degree to which they monitor or control residents' behavior in accordance with socially accepted practices and the goal of maintaining public order (Sampson, Raudenbush, & Earls, 1997). This model includes influences such as peer groups and physical threats in the neighborhood (e.g., violence, availability of illegal and harmful substances). The models are intended to be complementary rather than conflicting, with the utility of each model for explaining neighborhood effects on children's well-being depending on both the particular outcome studied and the age group examined.

An emerging body of research, focused largely on adolescent problem behavior, substantiates the norms-and-collective-efficacy model. At both the community and the individual levels, mechanisms of social control have been found to

124

account, in part, for associations among neighborhood structure and rates of problem behavior among adolescents (e.g., Elliott et al., 1996; Sampson et al., 1997). There has been scant research relevant to the other models, although several studies of young children support the relationships-and-ties model; quality of the home environment was found to partially account for associations between neighborhood structure and children's achievement and behavioral outcomes (Klebanov, Brooks-Gunn, McCarton, & McCormick, 1998).

CONCLUSIONS AND IMPLICATIONS

Evidence from randomized experiments, studies employing advanced statistical models, and longitudinal studies controlling for family characteristics indicates that neighborhoods, and particularly their socioeconomic composition, do matter. The size of neighborhood effects reported in the nonexperimental literature has typically been small to modest (after background characteristics are accounted for). However, neighborhood effects reported in the limited set of experimental studies were large, likely because the changes in neighborhood conditions were substantial (when families initiate their own moves, the changes are usually not so large, particularly among low-income families). To determine whether nonexperimental research is underestimating neighborhood effects, it will be necessary to try to replicate the experimental findings by undertaking natural studies where radical changes in neighborhood economic conditions have occurred. In addition, suggestive evidence from nonexperimental studies reveals that neighborhood residence may be differentially associated with outcomes for Latinos compared with European and African Americans, pointing to acculturation as a potentially important and unexplored variable moderating the effects of neighborhood structure.

The impact of neighborhood residence is also likely to vary across development; however, because much of the neighborhood research is cross-sectional or based on neighborhood residence at a single point in time, this issue has not been adequately addressed. This relatively static view of neighborhood influences extends to neighborhood conditions. Researchers often ignore the fact that families move across neighborhoods and that even when families do not move, neighborhood structure changes, for example, through gentrification and immigration (Leventhal & Brooks-Gunn, 2001).

What else remains unclear is how neighborhoods matter. Our proposed models—institutional resources, relationships and ties, and norms and collective efficacy—provide a framework intended to aid empirical investigations of theoretically driven neighborhood research. To test theoretical models, it is necessary to move beyond census measures of SES and directly assess underlying processes. Alternative data sources are required to measure neighborhood-level processes, in particular. Useful data will come from (a) city, state, and federal records (e.g., vital statistics from health departments, crime reports from police departments, school records from education departments, and child abuse and neglect records from social service departments); (b) systematic social observations by trained observers using a structured format to characterize neighborhoods along a range of social and physical attributes; (c) community surveys in which non-study participants (i.e., an independent sample) are interviewed about their neighborhoods (usually about their neighborhoods' social organization); and (d) neighborhood-expert surveys in which key community leaders are interviewed about neighborhood political and social organization (see Leventhal & Brooks-Gunn, 2001, for additional details). Recent studies designed specifically with neighborhood influences in mind are collecting longitudinal and process-oriented data on children, families, and neighborhoods and are well suited for exploring mechanisms through which neighborhoods influence child well-being, as well as addressing dynamic models of neighborhood influences.

Several policy implications may be drawn from the existing neighborhood research. The research suggests that it would be beneficial to develop programs that foster moving poor families out of poor neighborhoods. In line with this goal are efforts to reduce housing discrimination in nonpoor neighborhoods. What Moving to Opportunity and other such programs have demonstrated is that without special assistance, poor families who are given vouchers do not necessarily move out of poor neighborhoods. A complementary approach is to build scattered-site public housing in nonpoor neighborhoods, as was done in Yonkers, New York. However, if the most advantaged poor families move out of poor neighborhoods, what remains are concentrations of poor families, and possibly of those with the most mental and physical health problems, poor coping skills, and low literacy—all barriers to economic self-sufficiency.

An alternative strategy is to move nonpoor families into poor neighborhoods to change the mix and reduce poverty concentration and segregation. Gentrification also typically entails providing services (e.g., good-quality schools) and jobs in these neighborhoods. It is still unclear if poor families (or which poor families) benefit from this transformation or if they are forced out.

In summary, future research will likely lead to better answers to the original questions posed by academic scholars and policymakers, as well as to the design of more effective policies.

Recommended Reading

Brooks-Gunn, J., Duncan, G.J., & Aber, J.L. (Eds.). (1997). (See References)
Burton, L.M., & Jarrett, R.L. (2000). In the mix, yet on the margins: The place of families in urban neighborhood and child development research. *Journal of Marriage and the Family, 62,* 1114–1135.
Goering, J. (Ed.). (in press). (See References)
Leventhal, T., & Brooks-Gunn, J. (2000). (See References)
Sampson, R.J., Raudenbush, S.W., & Earls, F. (1997). (See References)

Note

1. Address correspondence to Tama Leventhal, National Center for Children and Families, Teachers College, Columbia University, New York, NY 10027; e-mail: tl91@columbia.edu.

References

Brooks-Gunn, J., Duncan, G.J., & Aber, J.L. (Eds.). (1997). *Neighborhood poverty* (2 vols.). New York: Russell Sage Foundation Press.
Elliott, D., Wilson, W.J., Huizinga, D., Sampson, R., Elliott, A., & Rankin, B. (1996). The effects of neighborhood disadvantage on adolescent development. *Journal of Research in Crime and Delinquency, 33,* 389–426.

Goering, J. (Ed.). (in press). *Choosing a better life? How public housing tenants selected a HUD experiment to improve their lives and those of their children: The Moving to Opportunity Demonstration Program.* Washington, DC: Urban Institute Press.

Jencks, C., & Mayer, S. (1990). The social consequences of growing up in a poor neighborhood. In L.E. Lynn & M.F.H. McGeary (Eds.), *Inner-city poverty in the United States* (pp. 111–186). Washington, DC: National Academy Press.

Katz, L.F., Kling, J.R., & Liebman, J.B. (2001). Moving to Opportunity in Boston: Early results of a randomized mobility experiment. *Quarterly Journal of Economics, 116,* 607–654.

Klebanov, P.K., Brooks-Gunn, J., McCarton, C., & McCormick, M.C. (1998). The contribution of neighborhood and family income to developmental test scores over the first three years of life. *Child Development, 69,* 1420–1436.

Leventhal, T., & Brooks-Gunn, J. (2000). The neighborhoods they live in: The effects of neighborhood residence upon child and adolescent outcomes. *Psychological Bulletin, 126,* 309–337.

Leventhal, T., & Brooks-Gunn, J. (2001). Changing neighborhoods: Understanding how children may be affected in the coming century. *Advances in Life Course Research, 6,* 263–301.

Leventhal, T., & Brooks-Gunn, J. (2002). *A randomized study of neighborhood effects on low-income children's educational outcomes.* Manuscript submitted for publication.

Leventhal, T., & Brooks-Gunn, J. (in press). Moving to Opportunity: An experimental study of neighborhood effects on mental health. *American Journal of Public Health.*

Ludwig, J., Duncan, G.J., & Hirschfield, P. (2001). Urban poverty and juvenile crime: Evidence from a randomized housing-mobility experiment. *Quarterly Journal of Economics, 116,* 655–679.

Massey, D.S., & Denton, N.A. (1993). *American apartheid: Segregation and the making of the underclass.* Cambridge, MA: Harvard University Press.

Rubinowitz, L.S., & Rosenbaum, J.E. (2000). *Crossing the class and color lines: From public housing to white suburbia.* Chicago: University of Chicago Press.

Sampson, R.J., Raudenbush, S.W., & Earls, F. (1997). Neighborhoods and violent crime: A multilevel study of collective efficacy. *Science, 277,* 918–924.

Wilson, W.J. (1987). *The truly disadvantaged: The innercity, the underclass, and public policy.* Chicago: University of Chicago Press.

Critical Thinking Questions

1. What types of research questions regarding the influence of neighborhood context on child development would be most easily and effectively translated into policies?

2. Given that it is unethical to randomly assign families to live in certain types of neighborhoods, how are experimental and quasi-experimental studies conducted without compromising ethical standards?

3. What are the theoretical models proposed by the authors that attempt to address the mechanisms through which neighborhood effects occur? How do they complement one another?

The Emerging Field of Adolescent Romantic Relationships

Wyndol Furman[1]

Department of Psychology, University of Denver, Denver, Colorado

Abstract

Romantic relationships are central in adolescents' lives. They have the potential to affect development positively, but also place adolescents at risk for problems. Romantic experiences change substantially over the course of adolescence; the peer context plays a critical role as heterosexual adolescents initially interact with the other sex in a group context, then begin group dating, and finally have dyadic romantic relationships. Adolescents' expectations and experiences in romantic relationships are related to their relationships with their peers as well as their parents. Although research on adolescents' romantic relationships has blossomed in the past decade, further work is needed to identify the causes and consequences of romantic experiences, examine the diversity of romantic experiences, and integrate the field with work on sexuality and adult romantic relationships.

Keywords

romantic relationships; attachment; love; friendships; adolescent adjustment

A review of the literature on adolescent romantic relationships a decade ago would have uncovered little empirical research. The work that had been conducted consisted primarily of descriptive studies on the frequency of dating other romantic behaviors. A substantial amount of work on sexual behavior had been conducted, but much of that was descriptive as well, and did not say much about the relational context in which the sexual behavior occurred. In other words, the literature contained a lot of information about the proportions of adolescents of different ages or backgrounds who were sexually active, but much less about who their partners were and what their relationships with them were like.

Happily, the field has changed substantially in the past decade. A cadre of social scientists have been studying adolescents' romantic relationships, and the number of articles and conference presentations seems to increase each year. The fields of adolescent romantic relationships and sexual behavior are still not well integrated, but the connections between them are increasing. Most of the work has been done on heterosexual relationships, but research on lesbian, gay, and bisexual relationships is beginning as well.

The increasing interest in adolescents' romantic relationships may partially stem from a recognition that these relationships are not simply trivial flings. As young people move from preadolescence through late adolescence, their romantic relationships become increasingly central in their social world. Preadolescents spend an hour or less a week interacting with the other sex. By the 12th grade, boys spend an average of 5 hr a week with the other sex, and girls spend an average of 10 hr a week. Furthermore, 12th-grade boys and girls spend an additional 5 to 8 hr a week thinking about members of the other sex when not with them (Richards, Crowe, Larson, & Swarr, 1998). Romantic partners are also a major source of support for many adolescents. Among 10th graders, only close friends provide more support. During the college years, romantic relationships are the most supportive relationships for males, and among the most supportive relationships for females (Furman & Buhrmester, 1992).

Romantic relationships may also affect other aspects of adolescents' development. For example, they have been hypothesized to contribute to the development of an identity, the transformation of family relationships, the development of close relationships with peers, the development of sexuality, and scholastic achievement and career planning (Furman & Shaffer, in press). One particularly interesting question is whether adolescent romantic experiences influence subsequent romantic relationships, including marriages. Unfortunately, there is limited empirical data on these possible impacts.

Adolescent romantic relationships are not, however, simple "beds of roses." One fifth of adolescent women are victims of physical or sexual abuse by a dating partner (Silverman, Raj, Mucci, & Hathaway, 2001). Breakups are one of the strongest predictors of depression (Monroe, Rhode, Seeley, & Lewinsohn, 1999). Sexually transmitted diseases and teenage pregnancy are also major risks.

Of course, the benefits and risks of particular romantic experiences vary. Having romantic experience at an early age and having a high number of partners are associated with problems in adjustment (see Zimmer-Gembeck, Siebenbruner, & Collins, 2001), although researchers do not know yet the direction of the influence. That is, the romantic experiences may lead to the difficulties, but it is also possible that adolescents who are not well adjusted are more likely than their better adjusted peers to become prematurely or overly involved in romantic relationships. Moreover, little is known about how the length or qualities of romantic relationships may be linked to adjustment.

DEVELOPMENTAL COURSE

Adolescents vary widely in when they become interested in romantic relationships, and the experiences they have once they begin dating. Accordingly, there is not one normative pattern of development. Some commonalities in the nature and sequence of heterosexual experiences can be seen, however. Prior to adolescence, boys and girls primarily interact with same-sex peers. In early adolescence, they begin to think more about members of the other sex, and then eventually to interact more with them (Richards et al., 1998). Initial interactions typically occur in mixed boy-girl groups; then group dating begins, with several pairs engaging in some activity together; finally, dyadic romantic relationships begin to form (Connolly, Goldberg, & Pepler, 2002). Having a large network of other-sex friends increases the likelihood of developing a romantic relationship with someone (Connolly, Furman, & Konarski, 2000).

The developmental course of romantic experiences for gay, lesbian, and bisexual youths is less charted, but is likely to be somewhat different. Most have some same-sex sexual experience, but relatively few have same-sex romantic relationships because of both the limited opportunities to do so and the social disapproval such relationships may generate from families or heterosexual peers

(Diamond, Savin-Williams, & Dubé, 1999). Many sexual-minority youths date other-sex peers; such experiences can help them clarify their sexual orientation or disguise it from others.

The nature of heterosexual or homosexual romantic relationships changes developmentally. Early relationships do not fulfill many of the functions that adult romantic relationships often do. Early adolescents do not commonly turn to a partner for support or provide such caregiving for a partner. In fact, what may be important is simply having such a relationship, especially if the partner is a popular or desired one.

Eventually, adolescents develop some comfort in these interactions and begin to turn to their partners for specific social and emotional needs. Wehner and I proposed that romantic relationships become important in the functioning of four behavioral systems—affiliation, sex-reproduction, attachment, and caregiving (Furman & Wehner, 1994). The affiliative and sexual-reproductive systems are the first to become salient, as young adolescents spend time with their partners and explore their sexual feelings. The attachment and caretaking systems become more important during late adolescence and early adulthood, as relationships become more long term. Several findings are consistent with our proposal. When asked to describe their romantic relationships, adolescents mention affiliative features more often than attachment or caregiving features (Feiring, 1996). Similarly, in another study, young adults retrospectively described their romances in adolescence in terms of companionship and affiliation, and described their relationships in young adulthood in terms of trust and support (Shulman & Kipnis, 2001).

The work on the developmental course of romantic experiences illustrates several important points. First, these relationships do not occur in isolation. Relationships with peers typically serve as a social context for the emergence of heterosexual relationships, and often are a deterrent for gay and lesbian relationships. Second, adolescents' romantic relationships are more than simple sexual encounters; at the same time, one could not characterize most of them as the full-blown attachment relationships that committed adult relationships become (Shaver & Hazan, 1988). Affiliation, companionship, and friendship seem to be particularly important aspects of most of these relationships. Finally, the developmental changes in these relationships are striking. Although at first they are based on simple interest, in the course of a decade, adolescents go from simply being interested in boys or girls to having significant relationships that are beginning to be characterized by attachment and caregiving. Because the changes are qualitative as well as quantitative, they present challenges for investigators trying to describe them or to compare the experiences of different adolescents. Wehner and I (Furman & Wehner, 1994) have tried to provide a common framework for research by examining adolescents' expectations for and beliefs about these relationships, a point I discuss more extensively in the next section.

LINKS WITH OTHER RELATIONSHIPS

Much of the current research on adult romantic relationships has been guided by attachment theory. More than a decade ago, Shaver and Hazan (1988) proposed that committed romantic relationships could be characterized as attachments, just as relationships between parent and child were. Moreover, they suggested that experiences with parents affect individuals' expectations of romantic relationships. Individuals who had secure relationships with parents would be likely to have secure expectations of romantic relationships and, in fact, would be likely to develop secure romantic attachments, whereas those who had adverse experiences with parents would be expected to develop insecure expectations of romantic relationships.

Although researchers generally emphasized the links between relationships with parents and romantic relationships, Wehner and I suggested that friendships would be related to romantic relationships as well (Furman & Wehner, 1994). Friendships and romantic relationships are both egalitarian relationships characterized by features of affiliation, such as companionship and mutual intimacy. Accordingly, we proposed that adolescents' experiences with friends and expectations concerning these relationships influence their expectations of romantic relationships. Subsequently, several studies using multiple methods of assessment demonstrated links between adolescents' expectations of friendships and romantic relationships (see Furman, Simon, Shaffer, & Bouchey, 2002). In fact, these links were more consistent than those between parent-child relationships and romantic relationships. Interestingly, the latter links were found to strengthen over the course of adolescence. Such a developmental shift may occur as the attachment and caregiving features of romantic relationships become increasingly salient.

These studies were cross-sectional, and thus cannot support inferences about causality. However, the findings again underscore the importance of recognizing that romantic relationships are peer relationships and thus, links with friendships are likely as well.

At the same time, various types of relationships have only moderate effects on one another. Experiences in other relationships may influence romantic relationships, but romantic relationships also present new challenges, and thus past experiences are not likely to be simply replicated. What influence do past romantic relationships have on future romantic relationships? Individuals' perceptions of support and negative interaction in their romantic relationships have been found to be stable over the span of a year, even across different relationships (Connolly et al., 2000), but otherwise researchers know little about what does and does not carry over from one romantic relationship to the next.

CURRENT AND FUTURE DIRECTIONS

The existing literature on romantic relationships has many of the characteristics of initial research on a topic. One such characteristic is the methodologies used to date: Investigators have principally relied on questionnaires, administered at one point in time. Interview and observational studies are now beginning to appear, though, and investigators conducting longitudinal studies have begun to report their results concerning adolescent romantic relationships. For example, Capaldi and Clark (1998) found that having a parent whose behavior is antisocial and who is unskilled in parenting is predictive of antisocial behavior in midadolescence, which in turn is predictive of aggression toward dating partners in late adolescence. Reports from other ongoing longitudinal studies of the childhood precursors of adolescent romantic relationships and the consequences of these relationships for subsequent development should appear shortly.

In this article, I have described some of the common developmental changes characteristic of adolescent romantic relationships and how these relationships may be influenced by relationships with friends and parents. At the same time, the diversity of romantic experiences should be underscored. The links between romantic experiences and adjustment vary as a function of the timing and degree of romantic involvement (Zimmer-Gembeck et al., 2001). Investigators are beginning to examine how romantic experiences may be associated with characteristics of the adolescent, such as antisocial or bullying behavior, health status, or sensitivity to being rejected. To date, most of the work has focused on heterosexual youths from middle-class Euro-American backgrounds, and further work with other groups is certainly needed. Additionally, almost all of the research has been conducted in Western societies, yet romantic development is likely to be quite different in other societies where contacts with the other sex are more constrained, and marriages are arranged.

Efforts to integrate the field with related ones are needed. Just as research on sexual behavior could profit from examining the nature of the relationships between sexual partners, investigators studying romantic relationships need to examine the role of sexual behavior in romantic relationships. Ironically, few investigators have done so, and instead these relationships have been treated as if they were platonic. Similarly, research on adolescent relationships could benefit from the insights of the work on adult romantic relationships, which has a rich empirical and theoretical history. At the same time, investigators studying adult relationships may want to give greater consideration to the developmental changes that occur in these relationships and to their peer context—themes that have been highlighted by adolescence researchers. In sum, research on adolescent romantic relationships has blossomed in the past decade, but a broad, integrative perspective will be needed to fully illuminate their nature.

Recommended Reading

Bouchey, H.A., & Furman, W. (in press). Dating and romantic experiences in adolescence. In G.R. Adams & M. Berzonsky (Eds.), *The Blackwell handbook of adolescence*. Oxford, England: Blackwell.

Florsheim, P. (Ed.). (in press). *Adolescent romantic relations and sexual behavior: Theory, research, and practical implications*. Mahwah, NJ: Erlbaum.

Furman, W., Brown, B.B., & Feiring, C. (Eds.). (1999). *The development of romantic relationships in adolescence*. New York: Cambridge University Press.

Shulman, S., & Collins, W. (Eds.). (1997). *Romantic relationships in adolescence: Developmental perspectives*. San Francisco: Jossey-Bass.

Shulman, S., & Seiffge-Krenke, I. (Eds.). (2001). Adolescent romance: From experiences to relationships [Special issue]. *Journal of Adolescence, 24*(3).

Acknowledgments—Preparation of this manuscript was supported by Grant 50106 from the National Institute of Mental Health.

Note

1. Address correspondence to Wyndol Furman, Department of Psychology, University of Denver, Denver, CO 80208; e-mail: wfurman@nova.psy.du.edu.

References

Capaldi, D.M., & Clark, S. (1998). Prospective family predictors of aggression toward female partners for at-risk young men. *Developmental Psychology, 34,* 1175–1188.

Connolly, J., Furman, W., & Konarski, R. (2000). The role of peers in the emergence of romantic relationships in adolescence. *Child Development, 71,* 1395–1408.

Connolly, J., Goldberg, A., & Pepler, D. (2002). *Romantic development in the peer group in early adolescence.* Manuscript submitted for publication.

Diamond, L.M., Savin-Williams, R.C., & Dubé, E.M. (1999). Sex, dating, passionate friendships, and romance: intimate peer relations among lesbian, gay, and bisexual adolescents. In W. Furman, B.B. Brown, & C. Feiring (Eds.), *The development of romantic relationships in adolescence* (pp. 175–210). New York: Cambridge University Press.

Feiring, C. (1996). Concepts of romance in 15-year-old adolescents. *Journal of Research on Adolescence, 6,* 181–200.

Furman, W., & Buhrmester, D. (1992). Age and sex differences in perceptions of networks of personal relationships. *Child Development, 63,* 103–115.

Furman, W., & Shaffer, L. (in press). The role of romantic relationships in adolescent development. In P. Florsheim (Ed.), *Adolescent romantic relations and sexual behavior: Theory, research, and practical implications.* Mahwah, NJ: Erlbaum.

Furman, W., Simon, V.A., Shaffer, L., & Bouchey, H.A. (2002). Adolescents' working models and styles for relationships with parents, friends, and romantic partners. *Child Development, 73,* 241–255.

Furman, W., & Wehner, E.A. (1994). Romantic views: Toward a theory of adolescent romantic relationships. In R. Montemayor, G.R. Adams, & G.P. Gullota (Eds.), *Advances in adolescent development: Vol. 6. Relationships during adolescence* (pp. 168–175). Thousand Oaks, CA: Sage.

Monroe, S.M., Rhode, P., Seeley, J.R., & Lewinsohn, P.M. (1999). Life events and depression in adolescence: Relationship loss a a prospective risk factor for first onset of major depressive disorder. *Journal of Abnormal Psychology, 108,* 606–614.

Richards, M.H., Crowe, P.A., Larson, R., & Swarr, A. (1998). Developmental patterns and gender differences in the experience of peer companionship during adolescence. *Child Development, 69,* 154–163.

Shaver, P., & Hazan, C. (1988). A biased overview of the study of love. *Journal of Social and Personal Relationships, 5,* 473–501.

Shulman, S., & Kipnis, O. (2001). Adolescent romantic relationships: A look from the future. *Journal of Adolescence, 24,* 337–351.

Silverman, J.G., Raj, A., Mucci, L.A., & Hathaway, J.E. (2001). Dating violence against adolescent girls and associated substance use, unhealthy weight control, sexual risk behavior, pregnancy, and suicidality. *Journal of the American Medical Association, 285,* 572–579.

Zimmer-Gembeck, M.J., Siebenbruner, J., & Collins, W.A. (2001). Diverse aspects of dating: Associations with psychosocial functioning from early to middle adolescence. *Journal of Adolescence, 24,* 313–336.

Critical Thinking Questions

1. What are the domains of romantic relationships suggested by the author? How does he propose they develop over both age and time?

2. In what ways do romantic relationships in adolescence resemble the social interactions of young children?

3. How might the social modeling of single parents who are dating effect the romantic relationships of their adolescents?

How U.S. Children and Adolescents Spend Time: What It Does (and Doesn't) Tell Us About Their Development

Reed W. Larson[1]

Department of Human and Community Development, University of Illinois, Urbana, Illinois

Abstract

Young people develop as "the sum of past experiences," and data on their time use are one means of quantifying those experiences. U.S. children and adolescents spend dramatically less time than in the agrarian past in household and income-generating labor. Because such labor is usually repetitive and unchallenging, this reduction has probably not deprived youths of crucial developmental experience. The school-work replacing this time has a clearer relationship to developmental outcomes. American teens, however, spend less time on schoolwork than teens in other industrialized countries. American teenagers have more discretionary time, much spent watching television or interacting with friends; spending large amounts of time in these activities is related to negative developmental outcomes. Increasing amounts of young people's discretionary time, however, appear to be spent in structured voluntary activities, like arts, sports, and organizations, which may foster initiative, identity, and other positive developmental outcomes.

Keywords

time use; developmental experiences

Children's and adolescents' use of time, a topic of public debate since the 1920s, has reemerged as an issue of national concern. Alarm is voiced that American youths do too little homework, spend too little time with their parents, and spend too much time watching television and, now, playing computer games or surfing the Internet. The after-school hours have been identified as a time of risk, when unsupervised children are endangered and teenagers use drugs, commit crimes, and have sex. The underlying question is whether young people are spending their time in ways that are healthy and prepare them for adulthood in the competitive, global world of the 21st century. Another, related question is whether young people are being overscheduled and denied the creative, exploratory freedom of youth.

Time, as economists tell us, is a resource—one that can be used productively or squandered. For developmental psychologists, study of children's and adolescents' use of this resource offers a means to examine their portfolio of daily socialization experiences. Data on their time spent in different activities provide estimates of how much they are engaged with the information, social systems, developmental opportunities, and developmental liabilities associated with each context. Of course, information on time spent in specific activities is only a rough proxy for actual socialization experiences. The impact of watching TV for 2 hr depends on whom a child is with, what the child watches, and how the child interprets it. Even two siblings eating supper with their parents each night may have much different experiences of this time. Nonetheless, assessment of time spent in different activities provides a useful starting point for evaluating a population's set of developmental experiences.

A LIFTED BURDEN OF REPETITIVE DRUDGERY

If we look back over the past 200 years, the most striking historic change in young people's use of time is that youths spend much less time on labor activities today than they did in America's agrarian past. In current nonindustrialized agrarian settings, household and income-generating labor fills 6 hr a day by middle childhood and reaches full adult levels of 8 or more hours per day by the early teens. By comparison, in the contemporary United States, time spent on household chores averages 15 to 30 min per day in childhood and 20 to 40 min in adolescence; income-generating activities account for little or no time, except among employed older teenagers (Larson & Verma, 1999).

Has this dramatic reduction in labor taken away valuable developmental experiences? In a comprehensive review, Goodnow (1988) found remarkably little evidence that household chores foster development. Children gain activity-specific skills (e.g., cooking skills), and care of younger children, if well-supervised, may bring positive outcomes. But evidence for broader developmental gains is thin. In reality, much time spent on chores in traditional agrarian settings involved highly repetitive activities, like carrying water and weeding fields; likewise, in contemporary America, most chores are mundane, with little challenge or developmental content. Evidence on the developmental benefits of U.S. adolescents' employment is more positive but also mixed. Definitive longitudinal studies indicate that employment during adolescence increases likelihood of employment and wages in early adulthood; however, teen employment over 20 hr per week is associated with greater delinquency, school misconduct, and substance use (Mortimer, Harley, & Aronson, 1999). Except in atypical circumstances in which youths have intellectually challenging jobs, it is hard to argue that more than 15 to 20 hr of employment per week brings additional developmental gains. Certainly, spending some time in chores and, especially, employment may provide useful learning experiences, but the dramatic reduction in youths' time in these repetitive labor activities appears to be a developmental plus.

Historically, this large burden of labor has been replaced by schooling, and schooling has clearer benefits. Young people often feel bored and unmotivated while doing schoolwork, as they do during chores and employment, and many experience schoolwork, too, as drudgery. But unlike labor activities, schoolwork brings experiences of high challenge and concentration. Amount of time spent in education correlates with youths' knowledge, intelligence, and subsequent adult earnings (Ceci & Williams, 1997), and is related to growth of a society's economy. Thus, economically and in other ways, the displacement of labor by schoolwork is a positive change in young people's time use.

American youths, however, spend less time on schoolwork than youths in most industrialized nations. As with other activities, the largest cross-national differences occur in adolescence (Table 1). U.S. teens spend approximately three fifths the amount of time on schoolwork that East Asian teens do and four fifths

Table 1. *Average daily time use of adolescents in 45 studies*

Activity	Nonindustrial, unschooled populations	Postindustrial, schooled populations		
		United States	Europe	East Asia
Household labor	5–9 hr	20–40 min	20–40 min	10–20 min
Paid labor	0.5–8 hr	40–60 min	10–20 min	0–10 min
Schoolwork	—	3.0–4.5 hr	4.0–5.5 hr	5.5–7.5 hr
Total work time	6–9 hr	4–6 hr	4.5–6.5 hr	6–8 hr
TV viewing	*insufficient data*	1.5–2.5 hr	1.5–2.5 hr	1.5–2.5 hr
Talking	*insufficient data*	2–3 hr	*insufficient data*	45–60 min
Sports	*insufficient data*	30–60 min	20–80 min	0–20 min
Structured voluntary activities	*insufficient data*	10–20 min	1.0–20 min	0–10 min
Total free time	4–7 hr	6.5–8.0 hr	5.5–7.5 hr	4.0–5.5 hr

Note. The estimates in the table are averaged across a 7-day week, including weekdays and weekends. Time spent in maintenance activities like eating, personal care, and sleeping is not included. The data for non-industrial, unschooled populations come primarily from rural peasant populations in developing countries. Adapted from Larson and Verma (1999).

the time that European teens do. These differences are mostly attributable to American teens doing less homework, estimated at 20 to 40 min per day, as compared with 2.0 to 4.0 hr in East Asia and 1.0 to 2.5 hr in Europe. These figures do not take into account national differences in length of the school year (it is shortest in the United States) and overlook differences between individual students and school districts—some U.S. schools and state legislatures have recently taken action to increase homework. These figures also overlook possible differences in quality of instruction: An hour of schoolwork may yield more learning in one country than in another. Nonetheless, they provide one explanation for American students' lower test scores and raise questions about whether American youths are being disadvantaged in the new competitive global marketplace.

THE EXPANSE OF FREE TIME

What American youths, especially adolescents, have in greater quantities than young people in other industrialized nations is discretionary time. Studies carried out since the 1920s have found that 40 to 50% of U.S. teenagers' waking time (not counting summer vacations) is spent in discretionary activities. Current estimates are 25 to 35% in East Asia and 35 to 45% in Europe. Whether this time is a liability or gives American youths an advantage depends largely on what they do with it.

Media Use

American teens spend much of their free time using media, particularly watching television. Studies indicate that TV viewing is American youths' primary activity for 1.5 to 2.5 hr per day on average. Curiously, the averages in other nations are quite similar. Within the United States, rates of viewing are found to be highest in late childhood and among boys, youths of low socioeconomic status (SES), and African Americans across income levels.

Current theories emphasize that viewers are active, not passive—they "use" media. Research indicates, however, that TV is rarely used for positive developmental experiences and that viewing is associated with developmental liabilities. A high amount of time watching entertainment TV—which constitutes most of youths' viewing—is associated with obesity and changed perceptions of sexual norms. Watching more than 3 to 4 hr per day is associated with lower school grades. Controlled longitudinal studies show that rates of viewing violence predict subsequent aggression (Strasburger, 1995). TV watching may sometimes be used for relaxation: Much viewing occurs in the late evening, when young people wind down before bed. But, on balance, TV time is developmentally unconstructive.

The new kid on the block, of course, is computer and Internet use, and we know little about developmental impacts of these new media. Rates of use in the United States are still small, but are increasing steadily. A recent national survey found recreational computer use to account for an average of 30 min per day for youths over age 8, with greater use among higher-SES youngsters (Roberts, Foehr, Rideout, & Brodie, 1999). Children spend more time playing computer games, whereas adolescents devote more time to e-mail and other Internet activities. As with television, there are important concerns: about effects of violent and pornographic content, commercial exploitation, participation in deviant Internet groups, and social isolation among frequent users. At the same time, computers and the Internet permit more active individualized use than television and thus have more developmental promise. Young people can use these media to obtain information, develop relationships with people different from themselves, learn job skills, and even start companies, irrespective of their age, gender, ethnicity, and physical appearance. The question of developmental benefits versus liabilities for this use of time is not likely to have a singular conclusion; answers are likely to differ across uses and users.

Unstructured Leisure

The largest amount of U.S. youths' free time is spent playing, talking, hanging out, and participating in other unstructured leisure activities, often with friends. Play is more frequent in childhood than in adolescence, accounting for 1.5 to 3.0 hr per day in the elementary years. It is gradually displaced by talking, primarily with peers. U.S. first graders appear to spend about as much time playing as first graders in Japan and Taiwan, but play falls off more quickly with age in East Asia (Stevenson & Lee, 1990).

Abundant theory and research suggest that play promotes positive development. Piaget viewed play as an arena for experimentation and adaptation of mental schemas (including concepts and strategies) to experience. Research substantiates that play has relationships to children's cognitive, linguistic, social, and emotional development (Fisher, 1992). McHale, Crouter, and Tucker (2000), however, found that among 10-year-olds, more time spent in outdoor play was associated with lower school grades and more conduct problems. Thus, more time playing does not necessarily facilitate more development.

Adolescents' talking, it can be argued, is play at a symbolic level. Social interaction is an arena for exploration and development of emotional, interpersonal, and moral schemas. Therefore, we might expect time spent interacting with peers to be associated with developmental gains similar to those for time spent playing. Little research has directly addressed this question, but longitudinal research shows that spending more time interacting with friends in unstructured contexts predicts higher rates of problem behavior (Osgood, Wilson, O'Malley, Bachman, & Johnston, 1996). This relationship is undoubtedly complex, depending on the content of interaction, individual dispositions, and numerous other factors. But these findings certainly contradict the argument that youths need large amounts of unstructured, free time.

Structured Leisure Activities

U.S. adolescents stand out from East Asian youths in time spent in voluntary structured activities, like sports, arts, music, hobbies, and organizations. (Insufficient comparative data exist for younger children.) Even so, the current media image of "overscheduled kids" is misleading. Among American teens, the average amount of time spent in these activities per day is measured in minutes, not hours (Table 1), although there is mixed evidence suggesting this time is increasing (Fishman, 1999; Zill, Nord, & Loomis, 1995).

What are the developmental benefits and costs of spending time in these activities? When participating, young people report experiencing high challenge, concentration, and motivation. This combination, which rarely occurs elsewhere in youths' lives, suggests they are engaged and invested in ways that provide unique opportunities for growth. Theory and a partial body of research suggest that these activities are associated with development of identity and initiative, reduced delinquency, and positive adult outcomes (Larson, 2000; Mahoney, 2000), although some studies have found sports participation increases alcohol use. More research is needed, but there is good reason to hypothesize that, under the right conditions, structured activities provide unique developmental experiences.

CONCLUSIONS

Are U.S. children and adolescents spending their time in ways consistent with optimal development? This question, I confess, makes me cringe. Taken to its logical conclusion, it suggests submitting every moment of youth to utilitarian "time and motion study." We know too well from current trends in education that when things can be measured—for example, by test scores—policy discussions focus on measures as ends in themselves, irrespective of more important harder-to-measure variables. Given our limited state of knowledge and the loose relationship between how time is spent and what youths actually experience, overemphasis on time allocation is certain to mislead. It also overlooks individual and cultural differences in learning processes and developmental goals. Human development is not a board game that can be won by having one's pieces spend the most time on selected squares. Developmental science needs models that conceptualize time as one among many variables affecting growth.

With these cautions firmly in mind, it seems important to consider quantities of time as part of the package when appraising young people's portfolio of developmental experiences. Should U.S. teenagers' schoolwork time be lengthened to match that of East Asian teens? In fact, East Asian societies are engaged in intense public debates about the stress and developmental costs associated with their adolescents' exclusionary focus on school achievement. Recent U.S. efforts to require more homework for all young people are probably justified, and there are empirical rationales for experiments with lengthening the school year and redistributing summer vacation throughout the calendar. But I think the most pressing issue for U.S. youths is not further increasing schoolwork time, but ensuring consistent quality in what happens during this time. My research shows that adolescents, including honor students, are frequently bored during schoolwork (this is also true in East Asia). It may be less important to pack more studying into the day than for researchers and practitioners to find ways to increase the quality of engagement for all students.

Are Americans' large quantities of discretionary time—40 to 50% of waking hours—a developmental asset or liability? A romantic view sees large blocks of unstructured time giving youths opportunities to explore, create structure on their own, learn to think outside the box, and perhaps "find themselves" in the existential ground zero of free choice. The underlying reality is that, left to themselves, children and adolescents often choose to spend time in unchallenging activities, like hanging out with friends and watching TV. Although some social interaction and time for relaxation are undoubtedly useful, it seems unlikely that spending many hours in unchallenging contexts fosters development. The hypothesis that youths need and benefit from unstructured free time, nonetheless, remains worthy of creative research, especially if the time they spend on schoolwork increases.

The small but possibly growing amount of time children and adolescents spend in structured voluntary activities provides more developmentally promising use for some of these discretionary hours. In these activities, youths often experience challenge and exercise initiative. When adult leaders give responsibility to youths, they may provide better contexts for learning to create structure and think outside the box than can be found in free play or social interaction (Heath, 1999). In the absence of better knowledge, however, the current rush to create activities for afterschool hours is unwise. Research is needed to determine the features of these activities associated with positive outcomes and how to fit participation to individuals' developmental readiness. A fundamental question is how to create activities with enough structure to contain and channel behavior without compromising youths' sense of agency.

Ultimately, development is probably best served by combinations of complementary activities, including those that shape good habits, teach literacy, build interpersonal relationships, foster initiative, and provide relaxation. The task of future research is to illuminate how quantities and qualities of experiences in different activities act in combination to affect development. Certainty, development is much more than an additive "sum of past experiences." We need to consider how individuals interpret, synthesize, and grow from experiences. Evaluation of time allocation is a useful entry point for examining links between experience and development, but only one small piece of a much more complex inquiry.

Recommended Reading

Larson, R., & Verma, S. (1999). (See References)

Robinson, J., & Bianchi, S. (1997). The children's hours. *American Demographics, 19*(12), 20–24.

Stevenson, H.W., & Stigler, J.W. (1992). *The learning gap.* New York: Simon & Schuster.

Wartella, E., & Mazzarella, S. (1990). A historical comparison of children's use of leisure time. In R. Butsch (Ed.), *For fun and profit: The transformation of leisure into consumption* (pp. 173–194). Philadelphia: Temple University Press.

Note

1. Address correspondence to Reed W. Larson, Department of Human and Community Development, University of Illinois, 1105 W. Nevada St., Urbana, IL 61801; e-mail: larsonr@uiuc.edu.

References

Ceci, S.J., & Williams, W.M. (1997). Schooling, intelligence, and income. *American Psychologist, 52*, 1051–1058.

Fisher, E.P. (1992). The impact of play on development: A meta-analysis. *Play & Culture, 5*, 159–181.

Fishman, C. (1999). The smorgasbord generation. *American Demographics, 21*(5), 55–60.

Goodnow, J.J. (1988). Children's household work: Its nature and functions. *Psychological Bulletin, 103*, 5–26.

Heath, S.B. (1999). Dimensions of language development: Lessons from older children. In A.S. Masten (Ed.), *The Minnesota Symposium on Child Psychology: Vol. 29. Cultural processes in child development* (pp. 59–75). Mahwah, NJ: Erlbaum.

Larson, R. (2000). Towards a psychology of positive youth development. *American Psychologist, 55*, 170–183.

Larson, R., & Verma, S. (1999). How children and adolescents spend time across cultural settings of the world: Work, play and developmental opportunities. *Psychological Bulletin, 125*, 701–736.

Mahoney, J.L. (2000). School extracurricular activity participation as a moderator in the development of antisocial patterns. *Child Development, 71*, 502–516.

McHale, S.M., Crouter, A.C., & Tucker, C.J. (2000, March). *Free time activities in middle childhood: Links with adjustment in early adolescence.* Paper presented at the biannual meeting of the Society for Research on Adolescence, Chicago.

Mortimer, J.T., Harley, C., & Aronson, P. (1999). How do prior experiences in the workplace set the stage for transitions to adulthood? In A. Booth, A.C. Crouter, & M.J. Shanahan (Eds.), *Transitions to adulthood in a changing economy: No work, no family, no future?* (pp. 131–159). Westport, CT: Praeger.

Osgood, D.W., Wilson, J.K., O'Malley, P.M., Bachman, J.G., & Johnston, L.D. (1996). Routine activities and individual deviant behavior. *American Sociological Review, 61*, 635–655.

Roberts, D.F., Foehr, U.G., Rideout, V.J., & Brodie, M. (1999). *Kids & media @ the new millennium.* Menlo Park, CA: Kaiser Family Foundation.

Stevenson, H.W., & Lee, S. (1990). Context of achievement. *Monographs of the Society for Research in Child Development, 55*(1–2).

Strasburger, V.C. (1995). *Adolescents and the media.* Thousand Oaks, CA: Sage.

Zill, N., Nord, C.W., & Loomis, L.S. (1995). *Adolescent time use, risky behavior, and outcomes: An analysis of national data.* Rockville, MD: Westat.

Critical Thinking Questions

1. What seem to be the benefits and drawbacks of structured and unstructured activities?

2. Why does the author believe that using only time use data is insufficient?

3. Although Larsons' work suggests that the direct effect of jobs may not be beneficial to development, how could the indirect effects be considered (e.g., the satisfaction of contributing to a household income)?

Adulthood and Aging

The change in the age composition of the population has attracted significant scientific attention to the development of older adults. In the year 2000 there were 36 million Americans 64 years old and older, and there is a rapid increase expected between 2010 and 2030, when the "baby boom" generation reaches the age of 65. While normative adult development has been of interest to scholars of human development for some time, recent attention has also focused on the problems of aging and older Americans. In this section, we look at some recent efforts in research aimed at understanding the social and cognitive development of the adult and aging population.

Emotions and how we experience and interpret them affect our personal, social, and physical functioning. James Gross presents some new research that shows that adults have a considerable amount of control over their emotions. He points out that the timing and strategies that we use in emotion regulation are significant. Specifically, if we have an experience that triggers an emotional response, it is more effective to employ a reappraisal strategy early in the emotion-generative process, than it is to use suppression to inhibit the outward signs of emotion and how they are experienced. Cognitive reappraisal decreases the experience and behavioral expression of emotion and has no impact on memory. On the other hand, suppression decreases the behavioral expression but fails to decrease the experience of emotion, and impairs memory. Laboratory studies using dyads reveal that when one person suppresses emotions, they evoke large physiological responses in the other person, such as high blood pressure. This research has implications for how individuals learn to cope with situations that provoke negative emotions and in addition, lends insight to the emotion regulation process in adulthood.

Turning to a topic of considerable importance to the aging population, Robert Wilson and David Bennett discuss the recent research that suggests that frequent participation in cognitively stimulating activities may reduce the risk of Alzheimer's disease. They report that the link may stem from the fact that cognitively active persons begin old age at a higher level of cognitive functioning than less cognitively active people. More active individuals, therefore, have to experience more cognitive decline before they reach a level of impairment as is seen in dementia. What is interesting about this research is that studies reveal that the skills that cognitively active people possess may also be less subject to decline. New questions from this research center on whether the protective effects of cognitive activity depend on when it occurs during the life span.

The evidence that has emerged showing a decline in cognitive abilities is augmented by evidence that suggests that age-related decline in cognition could sometimes be reduced through experience, cognitive training, and other interventions. Arthur Kramer and Sherry Willis review research that reveals that the cognitive vitality of older adults can be enhanced through cognitive training, in the form of domain-relevant expertise or laboratory training, and improved fitness. However, these results are not seen in all studies, and they urge researchers to further investigate when the benefits are and are not produced. In addition, they note that there may in fact be age-related enhancements in cognitive efficiency, through a process of selective optimization with compensation. These authors note the need for theory-guided research and the development of new methods to ascertain the mechanisms underlying both cognitive decline and cognitive enhancement.

The article by Shu-Chen Li continues with the topic of cognitive aging, but reviews the research at the biological, information processing and behavioral levels. Li notes that a new integrative theory has been advanced that postulates that age-related deficiencies in neurotransmission cause increased noise in information processing and less distinctive cortical representation, which in turn lead to cognitive deficits. This biological underpinning of many cognitive aging deficits is just beginning to be understood, and the link between biology and cognitive aging deficits await direct and vigorous study. Overall, these studies reveal remarkable advances in our understanding of both development and cognitive decline during adulthood.

Emotion Regulation in Adulthood: Timing Is Everything

James J. Gross[1]

Department of Psychology, Stanford University, Stanford, California

Abstract

Emotions seem to come and go as they please. However, we actually hold considerable sway over our emotions: We influence which emotions we have and how we experience and express these emotions. The process model of emotion regulation described here suggests that how we regulate our emotions matters. Regulatory strategies that act early in the emotion-generative process should have quite different outcomes than strategies that act later. This review focuses on two widely used strategies for down-regulating emotion. The first, reappraisal, comes early in the emotion-generative process. It consists of changing how we think about a situation in order to decrease its emotional impact. The second, suppression, comes later in the emotion-generative process. It involves inhibiting the outward signs of emotion. Theory and research suggest that reappraisal is more effective than suppression. Reappraisal decreases the experience and behavioral expression of emotion, and has no impact on memory. By contrast, suppression decreases behavioral expression, but fails to decrease the experience of emotion, and actually impairs memory. Suppression also increases physiological responding in both the suppressors and their social partners.

Keywords

emotion; mood; regulation

Some goon in a sports car careens across your lane. You brake hard. You feel like yelling, throwing something, or even ramming that idiot. Do you? Probably not. Instead, you *regulate* your emotions, and do something else that you think is more appropriate. Psychological research on emotion regulation examines the strategies we use to influence which emotions we have and how we experience and express these emotions. This research grows out of two earlier traditions, the psychoanalytic tradition and the stress and coping tradition (Gross, 1999b).[2] In this review, I describe a process model of emotion regulation that distinguishes two major kinds of emotion regulation. I illustrate each focusing on two common forms emotion down-regulation—reappraisal and suppression—and demonstrate how these two regulation strategies differ in their affective, cognitive, and social consequences.

A PROCESS MODEL OF EMOTION REGULATION

Emotion regulation includes all of the conscious and nonconscious strategies we use to increase, maintain, or decrease one or more components of an emotional response (Gross, 1999a). These components are the feelings, behaviors, and physiological responses that make up the emotion.

A moment's reflection suggests there are many ways to go about regulating emotions. How can we make sense of the potentially limitless number of emotion-regulation strategies? According to my process model of emotion regulation (Gross, 1998b), specific strategies can be differentiated along the timeline of the unfolding emotional response. That is, strategies differ in *when* they have their primary impact on the emotion-generative process, as shown in Figure 1.

At the broadest level, we can distinguish between *antecedent-focused* and *response-focused* emotion-regulation strategies. Antecedent-focused strategies refer to things we do before response tendencies have become fully activated and have changed our behavior and physiological responses. An example of antecedent-focused regulation is viewing an admissions interview at a school you have applied to as an opportunity to see how much you like the school, rather than a test of your worth. Response-focused strategies refer to things we do once an emotion is already under way, after response tendencies have been generated. An example of response-focused regulation is keeping a poker face while holding a great hand during an exciting card game.

As shown in Figure 1, five more specific emotion-regulation strategies can be located within this broad scheme. The first is *situation selection*, illustrated in Figure 1 by the solid arrow pointing toward Situation 1 (S1) rather than Situation 2 (S2). For example, you may decide to have dinner with a friend who always makes you laugh the night before a big exam (S1), rather than going to the last-minute study session with other nervous students (S2).

Once selected, a situation may be tailored so as to modify its emotional impact (e.g., S1x, S1y, and S1z in Fig. 1). This constitutes *situation modification*.

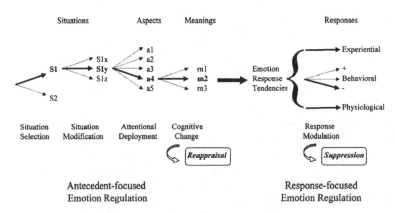

Fig. 1. A process model of emotion regulation. According to this model, emotion may be regulated at five points in the emotion-generative process: (a) selection of the situation, (b) modification of the situation, (c) deployment of attention, (d) change of cognitions, and (e) modulation of experiential, behavioral, or physiological responses. The first four of these processes are antecedent-focused, and the fifth is response-focused. The number of response options shown at each of these five points in the illustration is arbitrary, and the heavy lines indicate the particular options selected in the example given in the text. Two specific emotion-regulation strategies—reappraisal and suppression—are the primary focus of this review (Gross, 1998b).

For example, at dinner, if your friend asks whether you are ready for the exam, you can make it clear that you would rather talk about something else.

Third, situations have different aspects (e.g., a1–a5 in Fig. 1), and *attentional deployment* is used to select which aspect of the situation you focus on. An example is distracting yourself from a conversation that has taken an upsetting turn by counting ceiling tiles.

Once you have focused on a particular aspect of the situation, *cognitive change* refers to selecting which of the many possible meanings (e.g., m1–m3 in Fig. 1) you will attach to that aspect. For example, if your upcoming test is mentioned during the dinner conversation, you might remind yourself that "it's only a test," rather than seeing the exam as a measure of your value as a human being. The personal meaning you assign to the situation is crucial because it determines which experiential, behavioral, and physiological response tendencies will be generated.

Finally, *response modulation* refers to attempts to influence these response tendencies once they have been elicited, illustrated in Figure 1 by the solid arrow pointing toward decreasing expressive behavior. In our example, response modulation might take the form of hiding your embarrassment after bombing the exam. It might also take the form of altering experiential or physiological components of emotion.

CONTRASTING TWO FORMS OF EMOTION REGULATION: REAPPRAISAL AND SUPPRESSION

Antecedent-focused strategies change the emotion trajectory very early on. By contrast, response-focused strategies occur after response tendencies have already been generated. This difference in timing predicts rather different consequences for these two kinds of emotion regulation. To test this idea, my colleagues and I have focused on two specific strategies used to down-regulate emotion. One is *reappraisal*. As shown in Figure 1, this is a type of cognitive change, and thus antecedent-focused. Reappraisal means that the individual reappraises or cognitively reevaluates a potentially emotion-eliciting situation in terms that decrease its emotional impact. The second strategy we have focused on is *suppression*, a type of response modulation, and thus response-focused. Suppression means that an individual inhibits ongoing emotion-expressive behavior.[3] In the following sections, I describe our findings concerning the affective, cognitive, and social consequences of reappraisal and suppression.

Affective Consequences of Emotion Regulation

Reappraisal occurs early in the emotion-generative process and involves cognitively neutralizing a potentially emotion-eliciting situation. Thus, reappraisal should decrease experiential, behavioral, and physiological responding. By contrast, suppression occurs later and requires active inhibition of the emotion-expressive behavior that is generated as the emotion unfolds. Thus, suppression should not change emotion experience at all, but should increase physiological activation as a result of the effort expended in inhibiting ongoing emotion-expressive behavior.

To test these predictions, we needed to elicit emotion in the laboratory. Researchers have used a variety of methods, including music, obnoxious confederates, and films, to elicit emotion. Films have the advantage of being readily standardized, and of provoking high levels of emotion in an ethically acceptable way (Gross & Levenson, 1995). To examine the affective consequences of emotion regulation, we used a short film that showed a disgusting arm amputation (Gross, 1998a). In the reappraisal condition, participants were asked to think about the film they were seeing in such a way (e.g., as if it were a medical teaching film) that they would not respond emotionally. In the suppression condition, participants were asked to hide their emotional reactions to the film. In the natural condition, participants simply watched the film.

As expected, suppression decreased disgust-expressive behavior, but also increased physiological activation. For example, participants in the suppression condition had greater constriction of their blood vessels than participants in the natural condition. Like suppression, reappraisal decreased expressive behavior. Unlike suppression, however, reappraisal had no observable physiological consequences.[4] Another predicted difference was that reappraisal decreased the experience of disgust, whereas suppression did not.

Related studies have confirmed and extended these findings. Increases in physiological activation also have been found when participants suppress amusement and sadness (Gross & Levenson, 1993, 1997). Note that there are no such increases in physiological activation when people "suppress" during a neutral film. This shows that the physiological impact of suppression grows out of pitting attempts to inhibit expression against strong impulses to express. Absent a stimulus that produces emotional impulses, suppression has no impact on physiological responding. The finding that reappraisal decreases emotional responding has recently been replicated using a behavioral measure (the magnitude of a startle response to a loud noise burst) as an index of emotional state (Jackson, Maimstadt, Larson, & Davidson, 2000).

Cognitive Consequences of Emotion Regulation

Suppression is a form of emotion regulation that requires self-monitoring and self-corrective action throughout an emotional event. Such monitoring requires a continual outlay of cognitive resources, reducing the resources available for processing events so that they can be remembered later. Reappraisal, by contrast, is evoked early on in the emotion-generative process. Therefore, this strategy typically does not require continual self-regulatory effort during an emotional event. This would make costly self-regulation unnecessary, leaving memory intact.

We tested these predictions in several interlocking studies (Richards & Gross, 2000). In one study, participants viewed slides under one of three conditions: reappraisal, suppression, or a "just watch" control. Slides depicted injured men, and information concerning each man was provided orally as each slide was presented. Suppression led to worse performance on a memory test for information presented during slide viewing. Reappraisal did not.

To see whether our laboratory findings would generalize to everyday life, we examined memory and individual differences in emotion regulation, measured with the Emotion Regulation Questionnaire (Gross & John, 2001). Individuals with high scores on the Suppression scale of the questionnaire reported having worse memory than individuals with low Suppression scores. They also performed worse on an objective memory test in which participants were asked to recall events they had listed in a daily diary 1 week earlier. By contrast, Reappraisal scores had no relationship to either self-reported or objective memory. Together, these findings suggest that whereas suppression is cognitively costly, reappraisal is not.

Social Consequences of Emotion Regulation

Emotions serve important social functions. Thus, emotion regulation should have social consequences, and different regulation strategies should have different consequences. As postulated in my model, reappraisal selectively alters the meaning of an emotion-eliciting situation. In emotionally negative situations, reappraisal decreases negative emotion-expressive behavior, but does not decrease positive behavior. Suppression, by contrast, decreases both negative and positive emotion-expressive behavior. This decrease in positive emotion-expressive behavior should interfere with social interaction, leading to negative reactions in other individuals.

To test this prediction, we asked unacquainted pairs of women to view an upsetting film, and then discuss their reactions (Butler, Egloff, Wilhelm, Smith, & Gross, 2001). Unbeknownst to the other, one member of each dyad had been asked to either suppress her emotions, reappraise the meaning of the film, or interact naturally with her conversation partner. We expected suppression to decrease both negative and positive emotion-expressive behavior in the regulator. Positive emotion expressions are a key element of social support, and social support decreases physiological responses to stressors (Uchino, Cacioppo, & Kiecolt-Glaser, 1996). We therefore reasoned that the diminished positive emotion-expressive behavior shown by participants who suppressed their emotions would produce large physiological responses in their interaction partners. By contrast, we did not expect participants given the reappraisal instructions to show decreased positive emotion-expressive behavior. We therefore expected that their interaction partners would have physiological responses comparable to those of the partners of participants who acted naturally.

Figure 2 shows that partners of participants asked to suppress their emotions had greater increases in blood pressure than partners of participants given reappraisal instructions or asked to act naturally. Interacting with a partner who shows little positive emotion is more physiologically activating than interacting with a partner who shows greater positive emotion. This finding extends prior work by Fredrickson and Levenson (1998), who showed that positive emotions speed cardiovascular recovery from negative emotions. Emotion-regulation strategies that increase (or at least maintain) positive emotion should be calming for both the regulator and the interaction partner, whereas strategies that diminish positive emotion should increase physiological responses of both the regulator and the interaction partner.

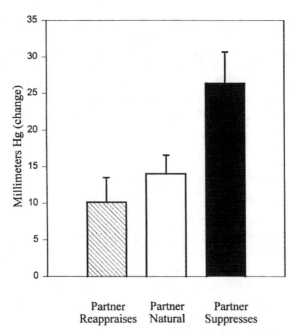

Fig. 2. Social consequences of emotion regulation. Mean change in blood pressure is shown separately for individuals whose conversation partners were asked to reappraise the situation, act naturally, or suppress their emotions (Butler, Egloff, Wilhelm, Smith, & Gross, 2001).

DIRECTIONS FOR FUTURE RESEARCH

My model suggests that adjustments made early in the emotion trajectory are more effective than adjustments made later on. The findings I have reviewed support this prediction. Reappraisal decreases expressive behavior and emotion experience, and does not adversely affect physiological responding, memory, or the regulator's interaction partner. Suppression, by contrast, has no impact on emotion experience, impairs memory, and increases physiological responding in both the regulator and the partner.

One direction for future research is to learn more about emotion regulation at each step in the emotion-generative process. This review has focused on one type of cognitive change and one type of response modulation. Do other forms of cognitive change and response modulation have similar consequences? Moreover, what are the differences among the antecedent-focused strategies of situation selection, situation modification, cognitive change, and attentional deployment? Similarly, what are the differences among the response-focused strategies?

A second important direction for future research is to explore the long-term consequences of differing emotion-regulation strategies. I have largely focused here on the immediate effects of reappraisal and suppression. However, if there are consistent individual differences in emotion and emotion regulation, such differences might have cumulative effects. For example, each time emotion is suppressed, physiological responses are magnified. Any one physiological response of increased intensity is unlikely to have deleterious consequences. But if such responses recur day after day after day, there might be adverse health consequences. A recent study illustrates how such a hypothesis might be tested. Heart attack survivors were divided into four groups, depending on their distress and their tendency to suppress emotion (Denollet et al., 1996). The subgroup scoring high on both distress and suppression had a significantly higher death rate (27%) than other patients (7%). This finding suggests that suppression indeed has important cumulative health consequences.

A third direction for future research is to explore whether people regulate emotional impulses in the same way as physical impulses such as hunger, aggression, and sexual arousal. Do strategies that help people stay emotionally cool also help them avoid eating that extra piece of cake, or steer clear of that tempting adulterous relationship? Or must each type of impulse be handled differently? Answers to such questions are of rich theoretical interest, and will also have great practical value for education and therapy.

Recommended Reading

Gross, J.J. (1998a). (See References)
Gross, J.J. (1999a). (See References)
Richards, J.M., & Gross, J.J. (2000). (See References)

Acknowledgments—Preparation of this article was supported by Grant MH53859 from the National Institute of Mental Health, I would like to thank Jo-Anne Bachorowski, Lisa Feldman Barrett, Barb Fredrickson, Oliver John, Ann Kring, Sonja Lyubomirsky, Jane Richards, Steve Sutton, and Jeanne Tsai for their helpful comments.

Notes

1. Address correspondence to James J. Gross, Department of Psychology, Stanford University, Stanford, CA 94305-2130; e-mail: james@psych.stanford.edu; http://www.psych.stanford.edu/~psyphy/.

2. This review focuses on emotion regulation in adults. For a recent review of emotion regulation in childhood, see Eisenberg, Fabes, Guthrie, and Reiser (2000).

3. The term "reappraisal" has a long history. Although some researchers find it confusing because it suggests that there is an initial appraisal that is then reworked, I use it for historical continuity. My focus here is on reappraisal that is used to cognitively transform a potentially negative-emotion-inducing situation so as to reduce its emotional impact. The term "suppression" also has a long history. It has been used to refer to inhibiting feelings, behavior, or thoughts. Here I use it to refer to inhibiting emotion-expressive behavior.

4. One puzzle is why reappraisal did not decrease physiological responding in this study. The potency and brevity of the surgical film may have made it difficult for participants to curtail their physiological responses in the time specified.

References

Butler, E.A. Egloff, B., Wilhelm, F.H., Smith, N.C., & Gross, J.J. (2001). *The social consequences of emotion regulation.* Manuscript submitted for publication.

Denollet, J., Sys, S.U., Stroobant, N., Rombouts, H., Gillebert, T.C., & Brutsaert, D.L. (1996). Personality as independent predictor of long-term mortality in patients with coronary heat disease. *The Lancet, 347*, 417–421.

Eisenberg, N., Fabes, R.A., Guthrie, I.K., & Reiser, M. (2000). Dispositional emotionality and regulation: Their role in predicting quality of social functioning. *Journal of Personality and Social Psychology, 78*, 136–157.

Fredrickson, B.L., & Levenson, R.W. (1998). Positive emotions speed recovery from the cardiovascular sequelae of negative emotions. *Cognitive & Emotion, 12*, 191–220.

Gross, J.J. (1998a). Antecedent- and response-focused emotion regulation: Divergent consequences for experience, expression, and physiology. *Journal of Personality and Social Psychology, 74*, 224–237.

Gross, J.J. (1998b). The emerging field of emotion regulation: An integrative review. *Review of General Psychology, 2*, 271–299.

Gross, J.J. (1999a). Emotion and emotion regulation. In L.A. Pervin & O.P. John (Eds.), *Handbook of personality: Theory and research* (2nd ed., pp. 525–552). New York: Guilford.

Gross, J.J. (1999b). Emotion regulation: Past, present, future. *Cognition & Emotion, 13*, 551–573.

Gross, J.J., & John, O.P. (2001). *Individual differences in emotion regulation processes: Consequences affect, well-being, and relationships.* Manuscript submitted for publication.

Gross, J.J., & Levenson, R.W. (1993). Emotional suppression: Physiology, self-report, and expressive behavior. *Journal of Personality and Social Psychology, 64*, 970–986.

Gross, J.J., & Levenson, R.W. (1995). Emotion elicitation using films. *Cognition & Emotion, 9*, 87–108.

Gross, J.J., & Levenson, R.W. (1997). Hiding feelings: The acute effects of inhibiting positive and negative emotions. *Journal of Abnormal Psychology, 106*, 95–103.

Jackson, D.C., Malmstadt, J.R., Larson, C.L., & Davidson, R.J. (2000). Suppression and enhancement of emotional responses to unpleasant pictures. *Psychophysiology, 37*, 515–522.

Richards, J.M., & Gross, J.J. (2000). Emotion regulation and memory: The cognitive costs of keeping one's cool. *Journal of Personality and Social Psychology, 79*, 419–424.

Uchino, B.N., Cacioppo, J.T., & Kiecolt-Glaser, J.K. (1996). The relationship between social support and physiological processes: A review with emphasis on underlying mechanisms and implications for health. *Psychological Bulletin, 119*, 488–531.

Critical Thinking Questions

1. Is reappraisal or suppression more effective in the healthful regulation of emotion? How do their affective, cognitive, and social consequences differ?

2. Why does the unit of analysis matter when considering the effectiveness of reappraisal versus suppression?

3. How might findings from longitudinal research studies on emotion-regulation strategies extend the conclusions made in this article?

Cognitive Activity and Risk of Alzheimer's Disease

Robert S. Wilson[1] and David A. Bennett

*Rush Alzheimer's Disease Center (R.S.W., D.A.B.)
and Departments of Neurological Sciences (R.S.W., D.A.B.)
and Psychology (R.S.W.), Rush-Presbyterian-St. Luke's Medical
Center, Chicago, Illinois*

Abstract

Recent research suggests that frequent participation in cognitively stimulating activities may reduce risk of Alzheimer's disease in old age. We review epidemiological evidence of such an association. We then consider whether cognitive activity can account for the association between higher educational, and occupational attainment and reduced risk of Alzheimer's disease. Finally, we discuss the behavioral and neurobiological mechanisms that may underlie the association between cognitive activity and risk of Alzheimer's disease.

Keywords

Alzheimer's disease; cognitive activity; longitudinal studies

Recent scientific data suggest that people with higher educational and occupational attainment tend to have a lower risk of developing Alzheimer's disease than do people with lower educational and occupational attainment (Stem et al., 1994). The mechanism underlying this pattern is unknown. One hypothesis is that the effects of education and occupation are due to their association with frequency of participation in cognitively stimulating activities (Evans et al., 1997). Although the idea that frequent intellectual activity might help one's mental faculties in old age predates the Roman empire, it has only recently become the subject of rigorous scientific investigation.

COGNITIVE ACTIVITY AND ALZHEIMER'S DISEASE

The first problem encountered in this line of research is defining the construct of cognitive activity. Most human activities involve some degree of cognitive function, but it is uncertain how best to quantify that degree, particularly when comparing persons from diverse cultural and socioeconomic backgrounds. Nonetheless, researchers have developed a number of scales to measure frequency of cognitive activity. For these measures, respondents rate their current or past frequency of participation in activities judged to primarily involve seeking or processing information. These activities range from pursuits that most people would agree are cognitively stimulating (e.g., reading a book or playing a game like chess or checkers), to pursuits that seem less cognitively demanding (e.g., listening to the radio or watching television), but that also involve information processing that may be important, especially in old age, when physical infirmities and social isolation may limit access to certain kinds of activities. Various summary measures of frequency of participation in cognitively stimulating activities have been shown to be related to educational level and performance on cognitive tests, so they appear to have some validity (Wilson, Barnes, & Bennett, in press; Wilson et al., 1999, 2000).

Several prospective studies have examined the association between summary measures of participation in cognitively stimulating activities and risk of developing Alzheimer's disease. In one of these studies (Wilson, Mendes de Leon, et al., 2002), older[2] Catholic clergy members who did not have dementia rated how frequently they participated in several cognitively stimulating activities at the beginning of the study. During an average of about 5 years of follow-up, persons reporting frequent participation in cognitively stimulating activities had only half the risk of developing Alzheimer's disease compared with those reporting infrequent cognitive activity. This association between cognitive activity and incidence of Alzheimer's disease has been confirmed in several studies of older persons from geographically defined communities (Scarmeas, Levy, Tang, Manly, & Stern, 2001; Wang, Karp, Winblad, & Fratiglioni, 2002; Wilson, Bennett, et al., 2002).

Because Alzheimer's disease is the leading cause of dementia in older persons and few potentially modifiable risk factors have been identified, understanding the basis of the association between cognitive activity and disease incidence is a matter of substantial public health significance. In the remainder of this article, we examine three issues bearing on this association. We first consider whether cognitive activity accounts for the association between educational and occupational attainment and risk of Alzheimer's disease. We then discuss what is known about the behavioral and neurobiological mechanisms underlying the association between cognitive activity and Alzheimer's disease.

COGNITIVE ACTIVITY AND EDUCATION

Because cognitive activity is related to both risk of Alzheimer's disease and education, in a recent study we examined whether cognitive activity could explain the association between educational attainment and disease risk (Wilson, Bennett, et al., 2002). In this 4-year longitudinal study of older residents of a biracial community, those who had completed more years of schooling had a reduced risk of developing Alzheimer's disease compared with those who had less educational attainment. The prestige of a resident's main occupation had a similar association with disease risk. When frequency of participation in cognitive activity was added to the analysis, however, the associations of educational and occupational attainment with disease risk were substantially reduced and no longer statistically significant. By contrast, the association between frequency of cognitive activity and disease risk was not substantially affected by adding educational level, occupational prestige, or both to the statistical model. These findings suggest that the association between educational attainment and risk of Alzheimer's disease may in large part be due to the fact that persons with more education tend to be more cognitively active than persons with less education.

BEHAVIORAL MECHANISMS UNDERLYING THE ASSOCIATION

What might account for the association between cognitive activity and risk of Alzheimer's disease? It seems likely that the positive correlation between cognitive activity and cognitive function is one contributing factor. On average, cognitively active persons are apt to begin old age at a higher level of cognitive function than their less cognitively active counterparts. As a result, a cognitively active person would need to experience more cognitive decline than a less active person before reaching a level of cognitive impairment commensurate with dementia.

A more fundamental way in which cognitive activity might affect risk of Alzheimer's disease is through an association with the primary manifestation of the disease, progressive cognitive decline. That is, not only might cognitively active people begin old age with better cognitive skills than less cognitively active people, but those skills may also be less subject to decline. Two studies have demonstrated such an effect (Hultsch, Hertzog, Small, & Dixon, 1999; Wilson, Mendes de Leon, et al., 2002). In each, frequent cognitive activity was associated with reduced cognitive decline in analyses that controlled for initial level of cognitive function. Thus, the higher level of cognitive function and reduced rate of cognitive decline that are associated with frequent cognitive activity probably both contribute to the association between frequent cognitive activity and reduced risk of Alzheimer's disease.

Cognitive training programs that provide strategic instruction and practice have been shown to have substantial and long-lasting beneficial effects on cognitive function in older persons (Ball et al., 2002), further supporting the idea that level of cognitive activity may be causally linked with risk of Alzheimer's disease. The benefits of cognitive training appear quite specific, with improved performance restricted to the skill that was trained.

Evidence of this specificity can also be discerned in observational studies. Thus, some studies have found that frequency of cognitive activity, but not of physical activity, is related to risk of Alzheimer's disease (Wilson, Bennett, et al., 2002; Wilson, Mendes de Leon, et al., 2002). In addition, cognitive activity appears to be primarily associated with reduced decline in processing skills like perceptual speed and working memory (Hultsch et al., 1999; Wilson, Mendes de Leon, et al., 2002). These skills are notable for being involved in nearly all kinds of intellectual activity, so it makes sense that they would benefit most from the frequency of such activity. Further, among people who already have Alzheimer's disease, level of reading activity prior to the onset of dementia is related to decline in verbal abilities but not nonverbal abilities (Wilson et al., 2000), providing further evidence that a particular cognitive activity benefits mainly the skills involved in that activity.

NEUROBIOLOGICAL MECHANISMS UNDERLYING THE ASSOCIATION

The neurobiological mechanisms through which cognitive activity reduces the risk of Alzheimer's disease are unclear. One possibility is that cognitive activity actually reduces the accumulation of pathology associated with cognitive impairment, such as neuritic plaques and neurofibrillary tangles,[3] which are forms of Alzheimer's disease pathology, or cerebral infarction (i.e., stroke). Alternatively, cognitive activity may influence risk of Alzheimer's disease by affecting the development or maintenance of the interconnected neural systems that underlie different forms of cognitive processing.

Scientific interest has focused on the latter possibility for two main reasons. First, recent studies have found that the correlation of quantitative measures of Alzheimer's disease pathology with cognitive impairment or dementia are modest in size, which suggests that other neurobiological mechanisms are involved. Second, an extensive body of research has shown that environmental complexity is related to a variety of changes in the brains of adult animals, including formation of new neurons and connections between neurons, in brain regions that are critically involved in memory and thinking (Kempermann, Gast, & Gage, 2002; Shors et al., 2001). In humans, therefore, some researchers have hypothesized that cognitive activity contributes to structural and functional organization and reorganization that make selected neural systems more difficult to disrupt, so that more Alzheimer's disease pathology is needed to impair the skills mediated by those systems (Cummings, Vinters, Cole, & Khachaturian, 1998).

Support for this idea comes from a recent study (Bennett et al., in press) that examined the relation of education and a summary measure of Alzheimer's disease pathology to level of cognitive function near the time of death. Both years of education and amount of Alzheimer's disease pathology were related to level of cognitive function. Education was not related to measures of Alzheimer's disease pathology, but influenced the association between Alzheimer's disease pathology and cognitive function: A given amount of Alzheimer's disease pathology was associated with less cognitive impairment in a person with more education than in a person with less education. In other words, the deleterious impact of Alzheimer's disease pathology on cognitive function was reduced in persons with more education compared with those with less education. These data suggest that education—or variables related to education, such as cognitive activity—affects risk of cognitive impairment and dementia by somehow enhancing the brain's capacity to tolerate Alzheimer's disease pathology, rather than by altering the accumulation of the pathology itself.

Because Alzheimer's disease is thought to develop gradually over a period of years, another possibility is that a low level of cognitive activity is an early sign of the disease rather than an independent risk factor. The early-sign hypothesis is inconsistent with several observations, however. For example, excluding people with memory impairment, usually the first sign of Alzheimer's disease, or controlling for a well-established genetic risk factor for the disease (i.e., possession of an ε4 allele from a gene on chromosome 19 that codes apolipoprotein E, a plasma protein involved in cholesterol transport), does not appear to substantially affect the association between cognitive activity and Alzheimer's disease. In addition, the specificity of the association between frequency of participation in cognitive activity and level of function in different domains of cognition is not easily reconciled with the early-sign hypothesis. Thus, although early Alzheimer's disease may contribute to reduced cognitive activity, such an effect does not appear to be sufficient to explain the association between cognitive activity and disease incidence.

CONCLUSIONS

Several large prospective studies have found an association between frequency of cognitive activity and subsequent risk of developing dementia or Alzheimer's disease. Evidence from observational studies and cognitive intervention research suggests that the association of cognitive activity with disease incidence may be causal. Because few potentially modifiable risk factors for Alzheimer's disease have been identified, this area of research has important public-health implications. Much remains to be learned, however.

A central question is whether the protective effect of cognitive activity depends on when it occurs during the life span. In particular, it is uncertain to what extent cognitive stimulation in late life, as opposed to early life or adulthood, is critical. Answers to this question are likely to require advances in how researchers assess cognitive activity and features of the environment that support it (Wilson et al., in press). Such research could help determine the feasibility of large-scale trials of cognitive intervention.

Another challenge is to elucidate the structural, biochemical, and molecular mechanisms that underlie individual differences in the ability to tolerate Alzheimer's disease pathology. These mechanisms may differ for cognitive activity during development compared with cognitive activity in adulthood and old age. For example, in experimental animal studies, environmental experiences during development appear to affect mainly the number of neurons that survive into adulthood, whereas experiences late in life may affect cognition more by maintaining neural connections than by changing their number. Understanding these mechanisms may make it possible to develop new preventive strategies aimed at augmenting the ability of the brain to withstand the deleterious effects of Alzheimer's disease pathology and possibly other neurodegenerative conditions as well. To that end, we have recently begun a large epidemiological study of older persons who have a wide range of educational and occupational backgrounds and have agreed to annual clinical evaluation and brain donation at death.

Finally, short-term clinical trials are needed to identify efficient and practical ways to train and strengthen cognitive skills. In addition, clinical trials of several years' duration are needed to determine whether cognitive training can reduce cognitive decline in old age.

Recommended Reading

Ball, K., Berch, D.B., Helmers, K.F., Jobe, J.B., Leveck, M.D., Marsiske, M., Morris, J.N., Rebok, G.W., Smith, D.M., Tennstedt, S.L., Unverzagt, F.W., & Willis, S.L. (2002). (See References)

Kempermann, G., Gast, D., & Gage, F.H. (2002). (See References)

Wilson, R.S., Bennett, D.A., Bienias, J.L., Aggarwal, N.T., Mendes de Leon, C.F., Morris, M.C., Schneider, J.A., & Evans, D.A. (2002). (See References)

Wilson, R.S., Mendes de Leon, C.F., Barnes, L.L., Schneider, J.A., Bienias, J.L., Evans, D.A., & Bennett, D.A. (2002). (See References)

Acknowledgments—This research was supported by National Institute on Aging Grants P30 AG10161, R01 AG15819, and R01 AG17917.

Notes

1. Address correspondence to Robert S. Wilson, Rush Alzheimer's Disease Center, 1645 West Jackson Blvd., Suite 675, Chicago, IL 60612; e-mail: rwilson@rush.edu.

2. We use "older" to refer to persons who are 65 years of age or older.

3. Neuritic plaques accumulate outside neurons and consist mainly of an abnormal protein called beta-amyloid. Neurofibrillary tangles are found inside neurons and are composed primarily of an abnormal protein called tau that appears like a tangled mass of filaments under a microscope. If sufficient numbers of plaques and tangles are present, a pathological diagnosis of Alzheimer's disease can be made.

References

Ball, K., Berch, D.B., Helmers, K.F., Jobe, J.B., Leveck, M.D., Marsiske, M., Morris, J.N., Rebok, G.W., Smith, D.M., Tennstedt, S.L., Unverzagt, F.W., & Willis, S.L. (2002). Effects of cognitive training interventions with older adults: A randomized controlled trial. *Journal of the American Medical Association, 288,* 2271–2281.

Bennett, D.A., Wilson, R.S., Schneider, J.A., Evans, D.A., Mendes de Leon, C.F., Arnold, S.E., Barnes, L.L., & Bienias, J.L. (in press). Education modifies the relation of AD pathology to level of cognitive function in older persons. *Neurology.*

Cummings, J., Vinters, H., Cole, G., & Khachaturian, Z. (1998). Alzheimer's disease: Etiologies, pathophysiology, cognitive reserve, and treatment opportunities. *Neurology, 51*(Suppl. 1), S2–Sl7.

Evans, D.A., Hebert, L.E., Beckett, L.A., Scherr, P.A., Albert, M.A., Chown, M.J., Pilgrim, D.M., & Taylor, J.0. (1997). Education and other measures of socioeconomic status and risk of incident Alzheimer's disease in a defined population of older persons. *Archives of Neurology, 54,* 1399–1405.

Hultsch, D., Hertzog, C., Small, B., & Dixon, R. (1999). Use it or lose it: Engaged lifestyle as a buffer of cognitive decline in aging? *Psychology and Aging, 14,* 245–263.

Kempermann, G., Gast, D., & Gage, F.H. (2002). Neuroplasticity in old age: Sustained fivefold induction of hippocampal neurogenesis by long-term environmental enrichment. *Annals of Neurology, 52,* 135–143.

Scarmeas, N., Levy, G., Tang, M.-X., Manly, J., & Stem, Y. (2001). Influence of leisure activity on the incidence of Alzheimer's disease. *Neurology, 57,* 2236–2242.

Shors, T.J., Miesegaes, G., Beylin, A., Zhao, M., Rydel, T., & Gould, E. (2001). Neurogenesis in the adult is involved in the formation of trace memories. *Nature, 410,* 372–376.

Stern, Y., Gurland, B., Tatemichi, T.K., Tang, M.-X, Wilder, D., & Mayeux, R. (1994). Influence of education and occupation on the incidence of Alzheimer's disease. *Journal of the American Medical Association, 271,* 1004–1010.

Wang, H.-H., Karp, A., Winblad, B., & Fratiglioni, L. (2002). Late-life engagement in social and leisure activities is associated with a decreased risk of dementia: A longitudinal study from the Kungsholmen Project. *American Journal of Epidemiology, 155,* 1081–1087.

Wilson, R.S., Barnes, L.L., & Bennett, D.A. (in press). Assessment of lifetime participation in cognitively stimulating activities. *Journal of Clinical and Experimental Neuropsychology.*

Wilson, R.S., Bennett, D.A., Beckett, L.A., Morris, M.C., Gilley, D.W., Bienias, J.L., Scherr, P.A., & Evans, D.A. (1999). Cognitive activity in older persons from a geographically defined population. *Journal of Gerontology: Psychological Sciences, 54B,* P155–P160.

Wilson, R.S., Bennett, D.A., Bienias, J.L., Aggarwal, N.T., Mendes de Leon, C.F., Morris, M.C., Schneider, J.A., & Evans, D.A. (2002). Cognitive activity and incident AD in a population-based sample of older persons. *Neurology, 59,* 1910–1915.

Wilson, R.S., Bennett, D.A., Gilley, D.W., Beckett, L.A., Barnes, L.L., & Evans, D.A. (2000). Premorbid reading activity and patterns of cognitive decline in Alzheimer's disease. *Archives of Neurology, 56,* 1718–1723.

Wilson, R.S., Mendes de Leon, C.F., Barnes, L.L., Schneider, J.A., Bienias, J.L., Evans, D.A., & Bennett, D.A. (2002). Participation in cognitively stimulating activities and risk of incident Alzheimer's disease. *Journal of the American Medical Association, 287,* 742–748.

Critical Thinking Questions

1. What variables might moderate the relationship between cognitive activity and risk of Alzheimer's disease?

2. How might the findings in this article apprise preventive and therapeutic interventions for Alzheimer's disease?

Enhancing the Cognitive Vitality of Older Adults

Arthur F. Kramer[1] and Sherry L. Willis

Beckman Institute, University of Illinois, Urbana, Illinois (A.F.K.), and Department of Human Development and Family Studies, Pennsylvania State University, University Park, Pennsylvania (S.L.W.)

Abstract

Aging is associated with decline in a multitude of cognitive processes and brain functions. However, a growing body of literature suggests that age-related decline in cognition can sometimes be reduced through experience, cognitive training, and other interventions such as fitness training. Research on cognitive training and expertise has suggested that age-related cognitive sparing is often quite narrow, being observed only on tasks and skills similar to those on which individuals have been trained. Furthermore, training and expertise, fits are often realized only after extensive practice with specific training strategies. Like cognitive training, fitness training has narrow effects on cognitive processes, but in the case of fitness training, the most substantial effects are observed for executive-control processes.

Keywords

aging; plasticity; cognitive enhancement

One of the most ubiquitous findings in research on cognition and aging is that a wide variety of cognitive abilities show an increasing decline across the life span. Declines in cognitive function over the adult life span have been found in both cross-sectional and longitudinal studies for a variety of tasks, abilities, and processes. Cross-sectional studies, which compare the performance of one age group with that of another, have found linear decreases in a number of measures of cognition over the adult life span (Salthouse, 1996). Longitudinal studies, which range in length from a few years to more than 40 years, have found that the rate and onset of decline is variable, depending on the ability, and that accelerated decline occurs in the late 70s (Schaie, 2000). Although there are a number of factors that may be responsible for the different results obtained in the cross-sectional and longitudinal studies (e.g., differential attrition, non-age-related differences between age groups in cross-sectional studies, effects of practice, and study length in longitudinal studies), the important common observation is a reduction in cognitive efficiency with age.

Although age-related cognitive decline is quite broad, there are some notable exceptions. It has generally been observed that knowledge-based abilities (also called crystallized abilities) such as verbal knowledge and comprehension continue to be maintained or improve over the life span. In contrast, process-based abilities (also called fluid abilities) display age-related declines.

An important current issue concerns the source (or sources) of age-related declines in process-based abilities. A large number of mostly cross-sectional studies have found that age-related influences on different skills are highly related, prompting the suggestion that a common factor may be responsible for age-related declines (Salthouse, 1996). Many proposals concerning the source or mechanism responsible for this general decline have been advanced. For example, reduced processing speed, decreased attentional resources, sensory deficits, reduced working memory[2] capacity, impaired frontal lobe function, and impaired neurotransmitter function have all been cited as possible mechanisms of age-related cognitive decline.

Contrary to the general-decline proposals, a growing body of literature has pointed out a number of situations in which age-related differences remain after a general age-related factor has been statistically or methodologically controlled for (Verhaeghen, Khegl, & Mayr, 1997). Such data suggest that a variety of different mechanisms may be responsible for age-related declines in information processing and that these mechanisms may be differentially sensitive to age.

DOES EXPERIENCE MODULATE AGE-RELATED COGNITIVE DECLINE?

Over the past several decades, researchers have examined whether previous experience in content areas (domains) such as driving, flying, and music serves to (a) reduce age-related decline in basic abilities, (b) aid in the development of domain-specific strategies that can compensate for the effects of aging on basic abilities, or (c) both reduce decline and help develop compensating strategies. In general, these studies have found that well- learned skills can be maintained at relatively high levels of proficiency, well into the 70s. However, these same studies have found that general perceptual, cognitive, and motor processes are not preserved in these highly skilled individuals. Thus, preservation of cognitive abilities for highly skilled individuals appears to be domain-specific and compensatory in nature. For example, Salthouse (1984) examined the performance of young and old adult typists and found a significant age-related decline in the performance of general psychomotor tasks, but no age-related deficit in measures of typing proficiency. Furthermore, the older typists were better able than the young typists to use preview of the text to decease their interkeystroke times, thereby enhancing their typing. Thus, the older typists were able to employ their accrued knowledge of the task domain to implement a strategy that compensated for declines in processing speed.

Krampe and Ericsson (1996) examined how amateur and expert pianists' expertise influenced their general processing speed, as well as performance on music-related tasks (i.e., single-hand and bimanual finger coordination). The general processing-speed measures showed an age-related decrement, regardless of the level of the individuals' music expertise. However, in the case of the music-related tasks, age-related effects were abolished for the expert pianists, although not for the amateur pianists. Furthermore, among the experts, high levels of deliberate practice over the past 10 years were found to be associated with decreases in age-related differences in music-related performance.

Despite the impressive cognitive sparing observed in the studies just discussed, as well as other studies, a variety of studies have failed to demonstrate an effect of expertise on age-related decline. The variability of the findings could be the result of several factors, including (a) the recency and amount of deliberate practice, (b) the degree to which the criterion tasks were specific to the domain of expertise, and (c) the age and health of the study participants.

In summary, the answer to the question of whether experience can reduce age-related cognitive decline is affirmative. However, this answer must be qualified. Sparing seems to be domain-specific, rather than general, and appears to depend on deliberate practice of the relevant skills and possibly also development of compensatory strategies.

CAN LABORATORY-BASED TRAINING REDUCE COGNITIVE DECLINE?

In this section, we discuss the results of laboratory-based practice and training studies on development and improvement of cognitive skills. We also address the specificity of these skills. We begin with a discussion of cross- sectional studies of the effects of training and conclude with an examination of longitudinal studies, in which specific individuals served as their own controls.

Cross-Sectional Training Studies

In general, old and young adults have been found to learn new tasks and skills at approximately the same rate and to show the same magnitude of benefit from training. Such data clearly suggest that older adults can learn new skills. However, given that older adults' baseline performance on most tasks is lower than that of younger adults, these data also suggest that age-related differences in level of performance will be maintained after training.

There have, however, been some interesting exceptions to these general observations. For example, Baron and Mattila (1989) examined the influence of training on the speed and accuracy with which young and older adults performed a memory search task; that is, the subjects memorized a set of items and then compared a newly presented item to the items in memory, to decide whether the new item was a member of the original memory set or not. Subjects were trained for 44 hr with a deadline procedure in which they were required to constantly increase the speed with which they performed the task. Prior to training, young and older adults performed the task with comparable accuracy, but the older adults were substantially slower. During training with the deadline procedure, both young and older adults performed more quickly, but with a substantially elevated error rate. Interestingly, when the deadline procedure was relaxed, the young and older adults performed with equivalent accuracies, and the speed differences between the groups were substantially reduced. Thus, these data suggest that the older adults improved their speed of responding more than the younger adults did.

A similar pattern of results was obtained in a study of training effects on dual-task performance (Kramer, Larish, Weber, & Bardell, 1999). Young and old adults were trained to concurrently perform two tasks, a pattern-learning task and a tracking task (i.e., a task that involved using a joystick to control the position of an object so that it constantly matched the position of a computer-controlled object), with either of two training strategies. In the fixed-priority training condition, subjects were asked to treat the two tasks as equal in importance. In the variable- priority training condition, subjects were required to constantly vary their priorities between the two tasks. In both training conditions, subjects received continuing feedback on their performance.

Several interesting results were obtained. First, as in previous studies, young and old adults improved their dual-task performance at the same rate when using the fixed-priority training strategy. Second, variable-priority training led to faster learning of the tasks, a higher level of mastery, superior transfer of learning to new tasks, and better retention than did fixed-priority training. Finally, age-related differences in the efficiency of dual-task performance were substantially reduced for individuals trained in the variable-priority condition.

Although these studies and several others found that training decreased age-related performance differences, other studies have failed to demonstrate such training effects. What is the reason for these seemingly contradictory results? Although there is quite likely not a single answer to this question, one possibility centers on the nature of the training procedures. The training strategies in the two studies we just summarized explicitly focused on aspects of performance on which young and older adults showed large differences. For example, the deadline strategy employed by Baron and Mattila encourages individuals to emphasize speed rather than accuracy, something older adults are hesitant to do. Similarly, older adults have been observed to have difficulty in flexibly setting and modifying processing priorities among concurrently performed tasks. The variable-priority training strategy explicitly targets this skill. Thus, although additional research is clearly needed to further examine the situations in which the age gap in performance can be reduced, one potentially fruitful area of inquiry concerns targeting training strategies to specific difficulties encountered by older adults.

Longitudinal Studies of Practice and Training

A central focus of longitudinal studies has been to examine the extent to which training remediates or improves elders' performance on tasks for which there is long-term data. Given the wide individual differences in timing of age-related ability decline, two questions arise: First, is training effective in remediating decline for elders who have shown loss in a specific ability? Second, can training enhance the performance of elders showing no decline in a specific ability?

Data from the Seattle Longitudinal Study provide some initial answers to these questions. In this study, elders were classified as to whether they had shown reliable decline over a 14-year interval on two fluid abilities known to show early age-related decline-inductive reasoning and spatial orientation (Schaie & Willis, 1986). These individuals then received 5 hr of training on either inductive reasoning or spatial orientation. More than two thirds of elders who received training on each ability showed reliable improvement on that ability. Of those who had declined on the ability trained, 40% showed remediation, such that their performance was at or above their level of performance 14 years prior to the training. Elders who had not declined also showed reliable improvement. Moreover, the effects of training on inductive reasoning lasted up to 7 years after training (Saczynski & Willis, 2001).

Summary

Cross-sectional training research suggests that both young and old adults profit from training, but that strategies targeted at skills known to decline with age are particularly effective in training of elders. Longitudinal studies make it possible to identify abilities that have declined for a given individual and to assess whether the individual can benefit from training targeted at his or her specific deficits. Using the longitudinal approach, researchers can examine the range of plasticity (i.e., the extent to which an individual can benefit from training) over time within the same individual, rather than comparing the magnitude of training effects for different age groups. Both types of training research support the position that even individuals of advanced age have considerable plasticity in their cognitive functioning. The training findings also support the descriptive experiential studies of cognitive decline in showing that effects are specific to the particular domain that was practiced or trained.

FITNESS AND COGNITIVE SPARING?

The relationship between fitness and mental function has been a topic of interest to researchers for the past several decades. Their research has been predicated on the assumption that improvements in aerobic fitness translate into increased brain blood flow, which in turn supports more efficient brain function, particularly in older adults for whom such function is often compromised. Indeed, research with older nonhuman animals has found that aerobic fitness promotes beneficial changes in both the structure and the function of the brain (Churchill et al., in press).

However the results from human studies that have examined the influence of aerobic fitness training on cognition have been mixed. Some studies have demonstrated fitness-related improvements for older adults, but others have failed to show such improvements. Clearly, there are a number of potential theoretical and methodological reasons for this ambiguity. For example, studies have differed in the length and the nature of the fitness interventions, the health and age of the study populations, and the aspects of cognition that have been examined.

A recent analysis statistically combining the results of fitness intervention studies that have been conducted since the late 1960s (Colcombe & Kramer, in press) lends support to the idea that fitness training can improve cognitive functioning. Perhaps the most important finding obtained in this analysis was that the effects of fitness were selective rather than general. That is, aerobic fitness training had a substantially larger positive impact on performance of tasks with large executive-control components (i.e., tasks that required planning, scheduling, working memory, resistance to distraction, or multitask processing) than on performance of tasks without such components. Interestingly, substantial age-related deficits have been reported for executive-control tasks and the brain regions that support them. Thus, it appears that executive-control processes can benefit through either training or improved fitness. An important question for future research is whether such benefits are mediated by the same underlying mechanisms.

CONCLUSIONS AND FUTURE DIRECTIONS

The research we have reviewed clearly suggests that the cognitive vitality of older adults can be enhanced through cognitive training, in the form of domain-relevant expertise or laboratory training, and improved fitness. However, it is important to note that these benefits are often quite specific and have not been observed in all published studies (Salthouse, 1990). Therefore, one important goal for future research is to determine when these benefits are and are not produced. Clearly, there are some obvious candidate factors that should be examined in more detail. These include age, health conditions, medication use, gender, education, lifestyle choices, genetic profile, and family and social support.

The nature and length of training, whether cognitive or fitness training, bears further study. It is important to note that many of the previous studies of "training" have examined unsupervised practice rather than specific training procedures that might be well suited to the capabilities of older adults, The development of new methods, such as the testing-the-limits approach[3] (Kliegl, Smith, & Baltes, 1989), will clearly also be important in future studies of training and other interventions.

At present, psychologists have little understanding of the mechanisms that subserve age-related enhancements in cognitive efficiency. Possibilities include improvements in basic cognitive abilities, the development of compensatory strategies, and automatization of selective aspects of a skill or task (Baltes, Staudinger, & Lindenberger, 1999). Thus, the nature of cognitive and brain processes that support improvements in cognitive efficiency is an important topic for future research.

Finally, we would like to emphasize the importance of theory-guided research in the study of interventions targeted to enhancing the cognitive function of older adults. Theories of life-span change, such as the theory of selective optimization with compensation[4] (Baltes et al., 1999), offer great promise in this endeavor.

Recommended Reading

Charness, N. (1999). Can acquired knowledge compensate for age-related declines in cognitive efficiency? In S.H. Qualls & N. Ables (Eds.), *Psychology and the aging revolution: How we adapt to longer life* (pp. 99–117). Washington, DC: American Psychological Association.

Morrow, D.G., Menard, W.E., Stine Morrow, E.A.L,, Teller, T., & Bryant, D. (2001). The influence of expertise and task factors on age differences in pilot communication., *Psychology and Aging, 16*, 31–46.

Salthouse, T.A. (1990). (See References)

Notes

1. Address correspondence to Arthur Kramer, Beckman Institute, University of Illinois, Urbana, IL 61801; e-mail: akramer@s.psych.uiuc.edu.

2. Working memory refers to processes needed to both store and retrieve information over brief periods, as well as processes necessary to manipulate the stored information (e.g., remembering a few weight measurements in pounds and converting them to kilograms).

3. Testing-the-limits examines the range and limits of cognitive reserve capacity as an approach to understanding age differences in cognitive processes.

4. This theory suggests that during aging, individuals maintain skill by focusing on selective aspects of broader skills, practicing these subskills often, and sometimes shifting strategies (e.g., shifting from speed to accuracy) to maintain performance.

References

Baltes, P.B., Staudinger, U.M., & Lindenberger, U. (1999). Lifespan psychology: Theory and application to intellectual functioning. *Annual Review of Psychology, 50,* 471–507.

Baron, A., & Mattila, W.R. (1989). Response slowing of older adults: Effects of time-contingencies on single and dual-task performances. *Psychology and Aging, 4,* 66–72.

Churchill, J.D., Galvez, R., Colcombe, S., Swain, R.A., Kramer, A.F., & Greenough, W.T. (in press). Exercise, experience and the aging brain. *Neurobiology of Aging.*

Colcombe, S., & Kramer, A.F. (in press). Fitness effects on the cognitive function of older adults: A meta-analytic study. *Psychological Science.*

Kliegl, R., Smith, J., & Baltes, P.B. (1989). Testing-the-limits and the study of adult age difference in cognitive plasticity of a mnemonic skill. *Developmental Psychology, 2,* 247–256.

Kramer, A.F., Larish, J., Weber, T., & Bardell, L. (1999). Training for executive control: Task coordination strategies and aging. In D. Gopher & A. Koriat (Eds.), *Attention and performance XVII* (pp. 617–652). Cambridge, MA: MIT Press.

Krampe, R.T., & Ericsson, K.A. (1996). Maintaining excellence: Deliberate practice and elite performance in young and older pianists. *Journal of Experimental Psychology: General, 125,* 331–359.

Saczynski, J., & Willis, S.L. (2001). *Cognitive training and maintenance of intervention effects in the elderly.* Manuscript submitted for publication.

Salthouse, T.A. (1984). Effects of age and skill in typing. *Journal of Experimental Psychology. General, 213,* 345–371.

Salthouse, T.A. (1990). Influence of experience on age difference in cognitive functioning. *Human Factors, 32,* 551–569.

Salthouse, T.A. (1996). Processing-speed theory of adult age differences in cognition. *Psychological Review, 103,* 403–428.

Schaie, K.W. (2000). The impact of longitudinal studies on understanding development from young adulthood to old age. *International Journal of Behavioral Development, 24,* 257–266.

Schaie, K.W., & Willis, S.L. (1986). Can decline in adult intellectual functioning be reversed? *Developmental Psychology, 22,* 223–232.

Verhaeghen, P., Kliegl, R., & Mayr, U. (1997). Sequential and coordinative complexity in time-accuracy functions for mental arithmetic. *Psychology and Aging, 12,* 555–564.

Critical Thinking Questions

1. What are possible mechanisms of age-related cognitive decline? Are these mechanisms differentially sensitive to age?

2. What is meant by the author's statement that cognitive abilities appear to be domain-specific and compensatory in nature? What would be a good example of this?

3. What individual study factors might explain the seemingly contradictory results of studies seeking to relate expertise to age-related cognitive decline?

Connecting the Many Levels and Facets of Cognitive Aging

Shu-Chen Li[1]

Center for Lifespan Psychology, Max Planck Institute for Human Development, Berlin, Germany

Abstract

Basic cognitive mechanisms, such as the abilities to briefly maintain, focus, and process information, decline with age. Related fields of cognitive aging research, have been advancing rapidly, but mostly independently, at the biological, information processing, and behavioral levels. To facilitate integration, this article reviews research on cognitive aging at the different levels, and describes a recent integrative theory postulating that aging-related deficiencies in neurotransmission cause increased noise in information processing and less distinctive cortical representation, which in turn lead to cognitive deficits. Aging-related attenuation of catecholaminergic modulation can be modeled by lowering a neural network parameter to reduce the signal-to-noise ratio of information processing. The performance of such models is consistent with benchmark phenomena observed in humans, ranging from age differences in learning rate, asymptotic performance, and interference susceptibility to intra- and interindividual variability and ability dedifferentiation. Although the details of the conjectured sequence of effects linking neuromodulation to cognitive aging deficits await further empirical validation, cross-level theorizing of the kind illustrated here could foster the coevolution of related fields through cross-level data synthesis and hypothesis testing.

Keywords

cognitive aging; catecholaminergic modulation; cortical representation; neural networks

Gradual declines in fundamental aspects of cognition pervade the aging process. Biologically, brain aging involves structural losses in neurons and the connections between them, along with deterioration in the neurochemical systems that support communication between neurons. Behaviorally, people's abilities to keep information in mind briefly (termed working memory), attend to relevant information, and process information promptly are compromised with age. Explanations for these cognitive aging deficits have been postulated at various levels. At the cognitive level, some researchers assume there is an aging-related reduction in processing resources, such as working memory, attention regulation, and processing speed. At the biological level, other researchers hypothesize there is an aging-related increase in neuronal noise (i.e., haphazard variations in neural information processing that reduce processing fidelity) or dysfunction of the prefrontal cortex, an area at the front of the cerebral cortex that is thought to be critical for working memory. Experimental designs used in neurobiological studies that involve animals are not always readily transferable to human cognitive studies, and vice versa. Therefore, until the recent advances with neuroimaging and related techniques that provide online measures of brain activity while people are performing cognitive tasks, data and theories of cognitive aging were mostly confined within their respective levels. The present article focuses on synthesizing what is known about cognitive aging in humans using a cross-level theory that postulates a sequence of events beginning at the mechanisms of neurotransmission and leading to the behavioral phenomena that have been documented.

AGING, CATECHOLAMINES, AND COGNITIVE PROCESSING RESOURCES

Although progressive neuroanatomical degeneration is characteristic of pathological aging such as Alzheimer's disease, there is now evidence suggesting that milder cognitive problems occurring during normal aging are mostly due to neurochemical shifts in still-intact neural circuitry (Morrison & Hof, 1997). In particular, the neurotransmitters referred to as catecholamines, including dopamine and norepinephrine, appear to play an important role in aging-related cognitive impairments.

There is consensus that catecholaminergic function in various regions of the brain, such as the prefrontal cortex and basal ganglia (a group of diverse structures, lying beneath the cortex, that regulate motor movements and category learning), declines with advancing age. Across the adult life span, in the various regions of frontal cortex and basal ganglia, the amount of dopamine and the number of protein molecules responding to the release of dopamine (i.e., dopamine receptors) decrease by 5 to 10% each decade (see Kaasinen et al., 2000, for review).

Research over the past two decades suggests that catecholamines modulate the prefrontal cortex's utilization of briefly activated cortical representations of external stimuli to circumvent constant reliance on environmental cues and to regulate attention to focus on relevant stimuli and appropriate responses (Arnsten, 1998). In addition, there are many findings indicating functional relationships between aging-related deficits in the dopaminergic system and reduced cognitive processing resources in terms of information processing speed and working memory. For instance, reduced density of dopamine receptors in old rats' basal ganglia decreases response speed and increases variability in reaction time (MacRae, Spirduso, & Wilcox, 1988). Drugs that facilitate dopaminergic modulation alleviate working memory deficits of aged monkeys who lose 50% of the dopamine in their prefrontal cortex because of aging (Arnsten & Goldman-Rakic, 1985). In humans, aging-related attenuation of one category of dopamine receptors (i.e., the D2 receptors) is associated with declines in processing speed and word and face recognition (Bäckman et al., 2000).

MODELING AGING-RELATED DECLINE OF CATECHOLAMINERGIC MODULATION

Although there is growing evidence for the catecholamines' involvement in various aging-related cognitive impairments, the details of these functional relationships await further explication. Theoretical inquiries into general computational principles aimed at capturing how neuronal signals are processed and integrated might help unravel mechanisms underlying the associations between deficient catecholaminergic modulation of neurons' responsivity and cognitive aging deficits.

The specifics of catecholamines' roles in modulating neuronal responsivity notwithstanding, in general terms, catecholamines' effects can be conceptualized as altering the balance between the intensity of the to-be-processed neuronal signals and other random background neuronal activity in the brain (i.e., the signal-to-noise ratio), thus regulating the neurons' sensitivity to incoming signals. This effect can be modeled with artificial neural networks, computational models that consist of multiple interconnected layers of simple processing units whose responsivity can be regulated by a network parameter (Servan-Schreiber, Printz, & Cohen, 1990). Neural signal transmission in such systems is simulated by forwarding the effect of an external stimulus signal, represented by the activity profile across units at the input layer, to output units via the intermediate layer. The activity level (activation) of each of the intermediate and output units is usually defined by a mathematical equation describing the function relating input signals to output (the most commonly used equation is the S-shaped logistic function). The activation function transforms the input signal into patterns of activation at the subsequent layers. The thus-transformed activation profile across units at the intermediate layer constitutes the network's internal representation for a given external stimulus. The gain (G) parameter is a component of the activation function that determines its slope. Conceptually, the G parameter captures catecholaminergic modulation by altering the slope of the activation function, thus regulating a processing unit's sensitivity to input signals (Fig. 1a). The randomness inherent in mechanisms of neurotransmitter release can be implemented by randomly choosing the values for the G parameters of the network's processing units at each processing step. Reducing the mean of these values can then simulate aging-related decline in catecholaminergic function (Li, Lindenberger, & Frensch, 2000).

FROM DEFICIENT NEUROMODULATION TO NEURONAL NOISE AND REPRESENTATION DEDIFFERENTIATION

A classical hypothesis regarding cognitive aging is that it is due to an aging-related increase in neuronal noise; however, mechanisms leading to such an increase and its immediate consequences have not been unveiled thus far. Simulating aging-related decline of neuromodulation by attenuating the average of the G parameter hints at a possible chain of mechanisms that may be involved.

Reducing mean G reduces a unit's average responsivity to input signals (Fig. 1a). For instance, a given amount of difference between two inputs—say, an excitatory input (e.g., +1) and an inhibitory input (e.g., −1)—produces a much greater difference in activation when G equals 1.00 than when G equals 0.1. At the extreme case when G equals 0, the unit's response always remains at its baseline activation regardless of differences in inputs (see Fig. 1). Furthermore, when the values of a unit's G are randomly chosen from a set of values, the lower the average of that set, the more variable is the unit's response to a given

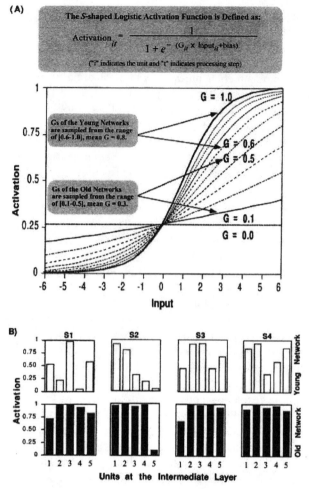

(A)

The *S*-shaped Logistic Activation Function is Defined as:

$$\text{Activation}_{it} = \frac{1}{1 + e^{-(G_{it} \times \text{Input}_{it} + \text{bias})}}$$

("i" indicates the unit and "t" indicates processing step)

B)

Fig. 1. The gain parameter: its impact on the slope of the activation function and the distinctiveness of activation patterns at the intermediate layer. The S-shaped logistic activation function is defined in (a), and graphed for different values of G. Values of G ranging from 0.6 to 1.0 were used in networks simulating young adults' performance, and values of G ranging from 0.1 to 0.5 were used in networks simulating older adults' performance. Internal activation patterns across five intermediate units of one "young" and one "old" network in response to four different stimuli (S1–S4) are shown in (b). From "Unifying Cognitive Aging: From Neuromodulation to Representation to Cognition," by S.-C. Li, U. Lindenberger, and P.A. Frensch, 2000, *Neurocomputing*, 32–33, p. 881. Copyright 2000 by Elsevier Science. Adapted with permission.

external signal. An increase in the variability of activation within the network, in turn, decreases the fidelity with which signals are transmitted. Put differently, a given amount of random variation in G, simulating random fluctuations in release of neurotransmitters, generates more haphazard activation variability during signal processing if the average of the processing units' Gs is reduced.

This sequence of effects computationally depicts a potential neurochemical mechanism for aging-related increase of neuronal noise: As aging attenuates neuromodulation, the impact of transmitter fluctuations on the overall level of neuronal noise is amplified in the aging brain.

Moreover, reduced responsivity and increased random variability in the activation within a network subsequently decrease the distinctiveness of the network's internal representations of external stimuli. Low representational distinctiveness means that the activation profiles for different external stimuli are less readily differentiable from each other at the network's intermediate layer. To illustrate, Figure 1b shows the activation levels across units at the intermediate layer of one "young" (higher average G) and one "old" (lower average G) network in response to four input signals. Clearly, the internal stimulus representations are much less distinctive in the old than in the young network. Thus, according to this simulation, as people age, at the cognitive level their mental representations of different events, such as various scenes viewed at an art exhibition, become less distinct, and therefore more confusable with each other.

A potential biological implication of this theoretical property is that as declining catecholaminergic modulation drives down cortical neurons' responsivity and increases neuronal noise in the aging brain, cortical representations (the presumed biological substrates of mental representations) elicited by different stimuli become less distinct (i.e., become dedifferentiated). Cognitive processing depends on the cortical representations created by perception and accessed by memory. Therefore, by causing less distinctive cortical representations of different events, deficient neuromodulation could have an influential impact on various aspects of cognitive functioning.

SIMULATIONS LINKING NEUROMODULATION WITH BEHAVIORAL DATA

The theoretical path from aging-related impairment of neuromodulation to increased neuronal noise in the aging brain to dedifferentiated cortical representation and on to cognitive aging deficits has been tested and supported by a series of neural network simulations.

Aging, Learning Rate, Asymptotic Performance, and Susceptibility to Interference

Behavioral memory research shows that as people get older, they take longer to learn paired associates (arbitrary word pairs, such as "computer-violin"). In agreement with these empirical findings, neural network simulations have shown that old networks also require more trials than young networks to learn paired associates (Fig. 2a). If old and young people differ only in how fast they can learn, one would expect that, given enough training, old people would eventually reach young people's performance level. Alas, ample data show that maximum (asymptotic) performance often exhibits an aging deficit as well. The lower asymptotic performance observed in people in their 60s and onward can also be accounted for by reducing average G, as old neural networks display poorer asymptotic performance than young neural networks (Fig. 2b).

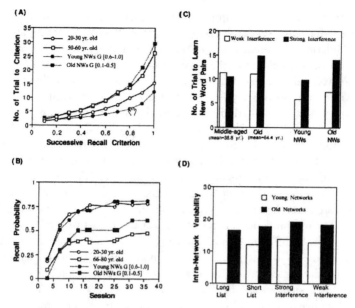

Fig. 2. Comparison of empirical data from human studies and neural network simulations of aging-related cognitive deficits. The graph in (a) shows the number of trials needed to reach increasingly stringent criteria in paired associate learning, for young and older adults and for networks (NWs) with the G parameter set to high and low values (the empirical results can be found in Monge, 1971). Asymptotic performance of young and old adults and networks in paired associate learning is illustrated in (b), which shows the number of training sessions required to reach maximum-possible recall performance (the empirical results can be found in Baltes & Kliegl, 1992). Aging- related increase in susceptibility to interference during paired associate learning is illustrated in (c), which shows performance under conditions of weak and strong interference (the empirical results can be found in Lair, Moon, & Kausler, 1969). The effect of reduction in mean G on intranetwork performance variability across different study lists in four conditions is shown in (d). Intranetwork variability is reported in units of coefficient of variance (i.e., standard deviation divided by the mean). (Reviews of aging-related increase in intraindividual variability can be found in Li & Lindenberger, 1999.) Adapted from "Unifying Cognitive Aging: From Neuromodulation to Representation to Cognition," by S.-C. Li, U. Lindenberger, and P.A. Frensch, 2000, *Neurocomputing, 32–33*, pp. 884, 886. Copyright 2000 by Elsevier Science. Adapted with permission.

Another prominent cognitive aging deficit is older people's increasing susceptibility to distraction by irrelevant or no-longer-relevant information (i.e., increased susceptibility to interference). In the context of paired associate learning, 60-year-olds are more susceptible than 40-year-olds to interference of previously learned word pairs with subsequent learning of new pairs, and they need more trials to learn new word pairs if this interference is strong. In line with this empirical evidence, the simulations have shown that the degree of interference affects the rate at which new word pairs are learned more in old than in young networks (Fig. 2c).

Aging, Performance Variability, and Covariation

The behavioral data demonstrate not only decreases in performance levels, but also aging-related increases in performance variation within a person across time (or different tasks) and aging-related increases in differences between individuals. Furthermore, aging also seems to affect the relations between different cognitive abilities: Studies conducted since the 1920s have shown that as people age, performance levels on different tasks become more correlated with each other. These phenomena can also be accounted for by reduction in mean G, suggesting that aging-related increases in intraindividual performance variability, interindividual diversity, and ability dedifferentiation might in part be associated with declining neuromodulation (Li et al., 2000). For example, Figure 2d shows the results of a simulation in which intranetwork variability was tested. Performance variability across different study lists in four conditions of paired associate learning was larger in the old than in the young networks.

COEVOLVING FIELDS VIA CROSS-LEVEL DATA SYNTHESIS AND HYPOTHESIS GENERATION

Accumulating evidence indicates that catecholaminergic neuromodulation is an influential biological underpinning of many cognitive aging deficits. However, details of the effects causing this neurobiological-behavior link remain to be unraveled. Pieces of the puzzle are emerging from the various subfields, but the field as a whole needs overarching frameworks to integrate existing data and guide concerted research efforts. The cross-level computational theory described in this article is only an initial attempt to arrive at such integrative frameworks. Indeed, the theory's main tenet—that attenuated neuromodulation leads to increased neuronal noise and less distinctive cortical representations in the aging brain, and in turn to cognitive aging deficits—awaits more direct and vigorous empirical scrutiny in the future. However, the computational simulations conducted thus far integrate evidence of aging-related decline in catecholaminergic modulation with a broad range of cognitive aging effects that have been observed in humans—an integrative task that still cannot be easily implemented in animal neurobiological or human neuroimaging studies alone.

In addition to synthesizing data, the theory generates some crosslevel hypotheses for future research. For instance, it suggests that neuromodulation might influence aging-related increases in intraindividual performance variability and interindividual diversity. Contrary to the traditional focus on average performance, this hypothesis motivates investigations of aging and intraindividual variability, an issue that is just now starting to be more broadly examined. Recent studies showed that intraindividual fluctuations in 60- to 80 year-olds' reaction times could be used to predict whether they had dementia (Hultsch, MacDonald, Hunter, Levy-Bencheton, & Strauss, 2000). In another study, fluctuations in 60- to 80-year-olds' gait and balance performance predicted verbal and spatial memory (Li, Aggen, Nesselroade, & Baltes, 2001). These results affirm that understanding aging-related performance variability and its sources may offer insight into aging-related changes in the brain-behavior link. At a different level, animal pharmacological studies could directly examine the effects of catecholarnine agonists; (drugs that facilitate the effects of catecholamines) on both intraindividual performance fluctuations and diversity of performance across individuals. Questions about how a drug affects performance levels and intraindividual fluctuations are commonly examined. However, issues relating to diversity across individuals are more rarely systematically addressed because individual differences traditionally play little role in animal research, despite the fact that such diversity is often observed in clinical settings.

Recent neuroimaging evidence suggests that many aspects of cortical information processing that involve either the left or the right hemisphere separately in young adults become less differentiated and involve activation of both hemispheres as people age. For instance, in several studies, people in their 60s and beyond showed activity in both brain hemispheres during memory retrieval and during both verbal and spatial working memory tasks. In young adults, verbal memory is processed primarily by the left hemisphere, and spatial memory is processed by the right hemisphere (see Cabeza, in press, for a comprehensive review). The fact that attenuating the average values of the G parameter causes less distinctive internal representations indicates that aging-related reduction in the extent to which the two hemispheres deal separately with different processes might, in part, be related to neurochemical changes in the aging brain. This suggests a new line of inquiry into how neuromodulation of the distinctiveness of cortical representations might affect the distribution of information processing across different neural circuitry, in addition to affecting working memory, attention regulation, and processing speed. Finally, given catecholamines' involvement in developmental attentional disorders (see Arnsten, 1998), investigations of whether normal cognitive development in children might be conceived as an increase in the efficacy of neuromodulation and cortical representations could aid the search for unifying accounts of cognitive development and aging.

Recommended Reading

Arnstert, A.F.T. (1993). Catecholamine mechanisms in age-related cognitive decline. *Neurobiology of Aging 14*, 639–641.

Craik, F.I.M., & Salthouse, T.A. (Eds.). (2000). *The handbook of aging and cognition* (2nd ed.). Mahwah, NJ: Erlbaum.

Li, S.-C., Lindenberger, U., & Sikström, S. (2001). Aging cognition: From neuromodulation to representation. *Trends in Cognitive Sciences, 5*, 479–486.

Welford, A.T. (1981). Signal, noise, performance and age. *Human Factor, 23*, 97–109.

West, R.L. (1996). An application of prefrontal cortex function theory to cognitive aging. *Psychological Bulletin, 120*, 272–292.

Acknowledgments—With this review, I would like to commemorate Alan T. Welford (1914–1995), who more than four decades ago ventured to speculate about the neuronal-noise hypothesis. I thank the Max Planck Institute and Paul Baltes for sponsoring this research.

Note

1. Address correspondence to Shu-Chen Li, Max Planck Institute for Human Development, Lentzeallee 94, D-14195 Berlin, Germany; e-mail: shuchen@mpib-berlin.mpg.de.

References

Amsten, A.F.T. (1998). Catecholamine modulation of prefrontal cortical cognitive function. *Trends in Cognitive Sciences, 2*, 436–447.

Arnsten, A.F.T., & Goldman-Rakic, P.S. (1985). Alpha 2-adrenergic mechanisms in prefrontal cortex associated with cognitive declines in aged non-human primates. *Science, 230*, 1273–1276.

Bäckman, L., Ginovart, N., Dixon, R., Wahlin, T., Wahlin, A., Halldin, C., & Farce, L. (2000). Age-related cognitive deficits mediated by changes in the striatal dopamine system. *American Journal of Psychiatry, 157*, 635–637.

Baltes, P.B., & Kliegl, R. (1992). Further testing the limits of cognitive plasticity: Negative age differences in a mnemonic skill are robust. *Developmental Psychology, 28*, 121–125.

Cabeza, R. (in press). Hemispheric asymmetry reduction in older adults: The HAROLD model. *Psychology and Aging.*

Hultsch, D.F., MacDonald, S.W.S., Hunter, M.A., Levy-Bencheton, J., & Strauss, E. (2000). Intraindividual variability in cognitive performance in older adults: Comparison of adults with mild dementia, adults with arthritis, and healthy adults. *Neuropsychology, 14*, 588–598.

Kaasinen, V., Vilkman, H., Hietala, J., Nagren, K., Helenius, H., Olsson, H., Farde, L., & Rinne, J.O. (2000). Age-related dopamine D2/D3 receptors loss in extrastriatal regions of the human brain. *Neurobiology of Aging, 21*, 683–688.

Lair, C.V., Moon, W.H., & Kausler, D.H. (1969). Associative interference in the paired-associative learning of middle-aged and old subjects. *Developmental Psychology, 5*, 548–552.

Li, S.-C., Aggen, S., Nesselroade, J.R., & Baltes, P.B. (2001). Short-term fluctuations in elderly people's sensorimotor functioning predict text and spatial memory performance. *Gerontology, 47*, 100–116.

Li, S.-C., & Lindenberger, U. (1999). Cross-level unification: A computational exploration of the link between deterioration of neurotransmitter systems and dedifferentiation of cognitive abilities in old age. In L.-G. Nilsson & M. Markowitsch (Eds.), *Cognitive neuroscience of memory* (pp. 104–146). Toronto, Ontario, Canada: Hogrefe & Huber.

Li, S.-C., Lindenberger, U., & Frensch, P.A. (2000). Unifying cognitive aging: From neuromodulation to representation to cognition. *Neurocomputing, 32–33*, 879–890.

MacRae, P.G., Spirduso, W.W., & Wilcox, R.E. (1988). Reaction time and nigrostriatal dopamine function: The effect of age and practice. *Brain Research, 451*, 139–146.

Monge, H.R. (1971). Studies of verbal learning from the college years through middle age. *Journal of Gerontology, 26*, 324–329.

Morrison, J.H., & Hof, P.R. (1997). Life and death of neurons in the aging brain. *Science, 278*, 412–429,

Servan-Schreiber, D., Printz, H., & Cohen, J.D. *(1990)*. A network model of catecholamine effects: Gain, signal-to-noise ratio, and behavior. *Science, 249*, 892–895.

Critical Thinking Questions

1. How have researchers explained cognitive aging deficits at both the biological and cognitive level?

2. How might a synthesis of what is known about cognitive aging deficits in the form of a cross-level theory contribute to a better understanding of this phenomenon?